CRITICAL INSIGHTS

Robert A. Heinlein

CRITICAL INSIGHTS

Robert A. Heinlein

Editor

Rafeeq O. McGiveron

Lansing Community College

SALEM PRESS

A Division of EBSCO Information Services, Inc.

Ipswich, Massachusetts

GREY HOUSE PUBLISHING

Publisher's Cataloging-In-Publication Data
(Prepared by The Donohue Group, Inc.)

Robert A. Heinlein / editor, Rafeeq O. McGiveron. -- [First edition].

    pages ; cm. -- (Critical insights)

    Edition statement supplied by publisher.
    Includes bibliographical references and index.
    ISBN: 978-1-61925-826-6 (hardcover)

    1. Heinlein, Robert A. (Robert Anson), 1907-1988--Criticism and interpretation. 2. Science fiction, American--20th century--History and criticism. I. McGiveron, Rafeeq O. II. Series: Critical insights.

PS3515.E288 Z75 2015
813/.54

First Printing

Contents _____

Resources

About This Volume

Rafeeq O. McGiveron

Critical Insights: Robert A. Heinlein explores the work of perhaps the most famous and influential name in modern science fiction. Writers such as Jules Verne and H.G. Wells did much, in very different ways, to shape a genre born of nineteenth-century industrialism, invention, and rapidly accelerating technological change, but for the evolution of science fiction from the mid-twentieth century onward, we must look to Robert Anson Heinlein. His career may have begun a lifetime ago—and his own lifetime ended a generation ago, in 1988, before many of his current readers were born—but still the man's works are read, pondered, hotly debated.

Heinlein's writing ranges from now-retro futures, in which hat and tie are always worn in public and cigarettes are offered at the beginning of every business meeting, to future cultures embracing unusual religions and polyamorous group marriages, and he employs settings from pulp-fiction swamp-and-jungle produced pulp-fiction settings that depict swamp-and-jungle Venus and canal-girded Mars to the twistily nested dimensions of the multiverse and the literally author-created World as Myth. This author may not have been the first to envision, say, the generation starship, the closed time-loop, or the powered military exoskeleton, but his early treatments have become the classic standards. In addition, his fiction explores not only "hard" science but also, at times, magic, spirituality, sociological systems, and methods of government. Heinlein published short stories, novellas, "juvenile" novels—which are not juvenile at all— and novels definitely, sometimes *most* definitely, for adults; he wrote essays on topics from World War III to blood donation, and his "Rhysling" poems in "The Green Hills of Earth" are very fine, too.

Heinlein has been by turns the darling of either Right or Left, and he has been both praised and criticized for almost every notion he has ever espoused, or even seemed to espouse. His so-called juveniles turned many youngsters on to space travel and even led some to careers in science, while his sometimes-shocking 1961 *Stranger in a Strange Land* became a counterculture favorite, and fans looked forward to the release of new books right up to the year of his death. The works and the man himself have been debated since the 1950s, strenuously, continuously; even his harshest critics cannot deny his stature, and still more readers, sometimes grandchildren and great-grandchildren of earlier generations of Heinlein readers, keep discovering his prodigious artistic output.

With this text, then, we examine the writings of Robert A. Heinlein and their growing legacy. This volume is divided into four main sections. In the introductory section, I will discuss Heinlein's career and certain themes of his writings in fairly broad terms, while Gary Westfahl gives a biography of the man behind the literature. The book's concluding section contains helpful resources such as a brief chronology of Heinlein's life for quick reference, a list of his works, a bibliography of critical essays and books for further study, and an index of key terms used within this text. Bracketed between the opening and closing apparatus is the "meat" of this project: a four-chapter section of critical context to help inform and set up readers' understanding of Heinlein and his art, and a ten-chapter section of critical readings exploring many various facets of the stories, novels, and occasional pieces of non-fiction.

Zahra Jannessari Ladani begins our critical context by discussing the cultural and historical milieu into which Heinlein was born and in which the writer developed. As she notes, the youthful Heinlein was a prodigious reader of pulp science fiction and fantasy—among more "serious" works as well. Ladani situates Heinlein not only in the trends of fiction but also in the scientific and philosophical notions of evolution, the nature of time, and sociology. She then examines the interplay of Heinlein's career with the Second World War, the Cold War, and the changing 1960s as well.

Donald M. Hassler helps us understand the various ways critics throughout the decades have treated the writings of Heinlein. While Heinlein remained popular with fans and also with many fellow writers, academic critics—including those particularly, well, *critical* of the author—were a consternation to the prickly Heinlein; he usually refrained from complaining in public, but the posthumous publication of his private letters revealed an author who had, or at least who affected, disdain for such academicians. From early researchers such as Alexei Panshin, through the most recent work of the twenty-first century, and of course delineating and categorizing the stances of the major scholars whom the student of Heinlein is sure to encounter, this chapter provides a very useful overview.

Robin Anne Reid then explores Heinlein's famous *The Moon Is a Harsh Mistress* (1966) with an "intersectional" perspective. Whereas some scholarship examines literature from only one perspective— political, say, or feminist, or class-based—intersectional analysis focuses on interesting overlaps and gaps between multiple perspectives; Reid here looks at the intersections of nationality and gender, plus race and gender. As she points out, Heinlein may attempt a forward-looking stance, but still odd slippages occur. Reid's final suggestion on the desirability of examining other Heinlein works from similar intersectional perspectives thus should be very well taken.

I conclude our context section by examining two works from near the endpoints of Heinlein's career: "Magic, Inc." (1940) and *Job: A Comedy of Justice* (1984). Both of these pieces—with their sometimes-befuddled first-person narrators who are swept along by events beyond their control—delve into the supernatural, and both make sure to get in a few subtle but pointed digs against racism. Both, moreover, take us in different ways to the very throne of Satan and back, and yet their differences only highlight Heinlein's valorizing of the worth and strength of the individual.

Starting our section of critical readings is Garyn G. Roberts with a useful discussion of the first ten years of Heinlein's writing, 1939 to 1949. As Roberts notes, Heinlein did not start publishing until his early 30s, but although he thus had considerably more life experience than many younger science fiction and fantasy authors, he was just as creative, just as probing, and just as technically competent—in fact, more so, if his popularity is any indication. After explaining the nature and trends of pulp magazines of the era, this chapter discusses a number of Heinlein's important SF and fantasy pieces, then concludes with a detailed list of his short fiction through 1949.

John J. Pierce follows up with an entertaining and enlightening look through perhaps my own favorite part of Heinlein's oeuvre: the so-called "juvenile" novels published with Scribner's between 1947 and 1958, which are anything but *juvenile*. Written for what we now would call the young-adult market, these books range from a four-man private first Moonshot to an interdimensional voyage to planetary judgment in the Magellanic Clouds, and nearly everything between. One constant, however—aside from the fact that they are generally rather fine stories—is their emphasis on growing up and taking one's place in the sometimes-difficult world of adult responsibilities. Never is it labored, but the attitude is unmistakable and unforgettable.

Yet what does an *author* think about the craft that entertains so many millions and which, incidentally, puts food on his table and clothes on his back? Gary Westfahl examines Heinlein's public writings on writing, along with his personal letters as well, to help us understand the attitudes of a writer who eventually needed to work only a few months each year to support himself. It is "dishonest work," Heinlein quips, for writing involves no pesky time clocks to punch, no frowning supervisors, and no calloused hands…and yet, as Westfahl notes, success indeed does require real skull-sweat and a great deal of native talent as well.

Next, Anna R. McHugh discusses proliferation of spacetimes in Heinlein's early short fiction: "Elsewhen" (1941), "They" (1941), and "The Unpleasant Profession of Jonathan Hoag" (1942). The earliest fantasists had explored other worlds in space, and the notion of other dimensions gained scientific currency from the 1870s onward, but of course it was Albert Einstein's theory of relativity that truly opened up the vistas of unified spacetime. Using the Bakhtinian lenses of *chronotope* as the literary representation of time and space and *focalizer* as the character viewpoint through which we make sense, McHugh follows Heinlein along an intriguing proliferation of realities through Einsteinian spacetime and beyond.

"By His Bootstraps" (1941), praised by editor John W. Campbell, Jr., as a novel and important treatment of time travel, is the focus of Kristine Larsen's chapter. Heinlein himself saw the story as a neat trick, but one that had no real importance—the notion of meeting oneself in a time loop, after all, seems to have awfully little to do with day-to-day reality. Larsen, however, entertainingly examines the various potential paradoxes of time travel from a scientific perspective and even draws in Heinlein's other classic tale of the twisted timeline, "'—All You Zombies—'" (1959).

Marleen S. Barr then explores *Podkayne of Mars* (1963) as a dizzying, sometimes-obfuscating, even prankish novel that plays with indeterminacies and gaps and that ultimately can point us toward our common humanity. Playful puzzles and seeming contractions abound in *Podkayne*: the narrator's age given first in Martian years rather than Terran, the way the culture of Earth is defamiliarized almost as much as those of Mars and Venus, or the competing endings in which the narrator alternately lives or dies, to name only a few. Playful herself, Barr shows how we must read with Heinlein and against him and where those attitudes can take us.

I follow this with a look at Heinlein's treatment of the emergency retreat, whether simple getaway cabin, hardened bomb shelter, or even more modern panic room, across over forty years of fiction and nonfiction. Some of it may seem a bit quaint now—the author's lovingly detailed description of the elaborate blast-resistant bunker in *Farnham's Freehold* (1964), for example—but the outlook is best understood in its historical context, a solid twenty or more years when nuclear conflict between the superpowers seemed very possible indeed. Even the most dated works, however, still entertain, and Heinlein's underlying pragmatism probably should not be abandoned so easily either.

Wolf Forrest then discusses supply-side economics in Heinlein's fiction, not just in the "usual suspect" of *The Moon Is a Harsh Mistress* (1966), but also in such disparate tales as "'—We Also Walk Dogs'" (1941), "Waldo" (1942), "Magic, Inc." (1940), and *Podkayne of Mars*. This wide-ranging chapter thus covers over two and a half decades of Heinleinian philosophy, economics, and ethics, as spelled out in different pieces of his disparate yet ever-popular entertainment. Clearly, the author's outlook shifted a fair bit since his then-unpublished *For Us, The Living* of 1938.

C. W. Sullivan III gives us a nuanced investigation of Heinlein and "empire"—with the term broadly rather than pejoratively defined. This chapter looks especially at Heinlein's Scribner-published juvenile novels, including the controversial *Starship Troopers* (1959), which originally was intended for the Scribner's young-adult series, but it also brings in the adult-oriented *The Puppet Masters* (1951) and the author's exhortatory nonfiction work, such as his 1958 campaign against a unilateral nuclear-testing freeze and his 1973 address to the US Naval Academy on "the pragmatics of patriotism." Indeed, though, Heinlein's underlying pragmatism is idealistic, for it espouses not conquest per se but instead the survival of the human species.

Ira Halpern in our final chapter gives a fresh look at the iconoclastic and enduring classic, *Stranger in a Strange Land* (1961). Whereas Heinlein always described *Stranger* as a book that asks questions rather than gives answers, Halpern suggests that, lack of Martian mental powers notwithstanding, this is rather disingenuous, at least regarding the novel's sexual mores. Indeed, Halpern not only sees the book's Church of All Worlds as something of a utopian model, but he finds the glitzy Fosterite religion, with its sanctioning of gambling, alcohol, and sex for the sanctified, to be treated with far less irony than many readers see. Despite Heinlein's attempts at satire, suggests Halpern, true utopianism shines through. After all, utopian threads of one variety or another indeed do run through much of the author's work...as, perhaps, they also must in any project examining the complex, prolific, and towering Robert A. Heinlein.

CAREER, LIFE, AND INFLUENCE

On Robert A. Heinlein and His Works_____

Rafeeq O. McGiveron

Not for nothing was Robert A. Heinlein (1907–1988) hailed as the "Dean of Science Fiction." At once deeply private and yet also larger than life, Heinlein grew from an unknown ex-naval officer—a washout from mining, graduate school, and politics, who was nerving himself to make the leap from longtime science fiction fan to submitter—to a successful and ultimately controversial literary icon, his name and works instantly recognizable. Heinlein at the height of his craft is an entertaining and exciting read, often witty and intellectually challenging as well, yet even his least successful pieces continue to be read and debated by ordinary readers and scholars alike. Such is the drawing power of the magical letters *R. A. H.*, and such is the nature of an artistic output that, in spanning nearly fifty years, helped shape science fiction and the world science fiction has made. Even over a quarter century after his death, his work still brings pleasure to so many millions. No one interested in science fiction or in space travel can avoid the towering Heinlein, and countless others have heard his pithy quotes, perhaps unknowing, on topics from sex and religion to government and gun control. We may or may not agree with all of his notions, but his deceptively effortless artistic style and the questions he raises make Heinlein's works as enjoyable and interesting now as they were in the days of our grandparents and even great-grandparents.

The Birth of the Author

Robert Anson Heinlein was born in the small town of Butler, Missouri, on 7 July 1907—closer to the end of the Civil War, it should be remembered, than to the launching of Sputnik. The third son of Rex Ivar Heinlein and Bam Lyle Heinlein, Robert was to be followed by a sister, another brother, and two more sisters. The boy's maternal grandfather was a country doctor who made house calls in a horse and buggy, while Rex, like his own father—and Rex's uncle as well—worked in hardware. At the time of Robert's birth, Rex and Bam lived in Dr. Lyle's house, and although they soon moved to Kansas City, the old doctor, who taught the boy at age four to play chess, was a formative figure for the youngster (Patterson 17–20).

The America of Heinlein's birth was a land where more than half of the population still lived in rural rather than urban areas (Census 5) and over a third of the country's workers were either farmers or farm laborers (Wyatt & Hecker 54). People in their late 50s and 60s still remembered the Civil War, and the Great War of bloody trenches, barbed-wire-strewn and machine-gun-swept no-man's lands, and blistering poison gas lay more than half a dozen years in the future, a slaughter not yet even imaginable, while the next world war and its atom bomb were merely topics of science fiction. The airplane and, really, even the automobile were in their comparative infancies; the English Channel was not crossed by a heavier-than-air vehicle until 1909, and cross-country driving in the United States was primitive at best, with the modern multilane interstate system half a century in the future. Laws requiring racial segregation in public transport, schools, and the like had been upheld at the United States Supreme Court in *Plessy vs. Ferguson* not even a dozen years previously and would not be declared unconstitutional until over forty years later in *Brown vs. Board of Education* in 1954. Even voting rights for women would not be granted until 1920.

The world was a very different place from our own, then, not just in its technological infrastructure but in its social and political aspects as well. It may not be surprising that a child born into such times would grow into a man who believed in hard work and responsibility, who was proud of his own naval service and always believed in a strong national defense, and who on a trip behind the Iron Curtain at a tense moment in the Cold War once blew up at a Soviet political officer, "out-shout[ing]" him while Mrs. Heinlein indignantly pointed out the locations of slave labor camps on the big wall map behind the official's desk and quoted figures on how many thousands upon thousands had died there ("PRAVDA" 410). This same seemingly conservative old man, however, never believed in military conscription, advocated racial equality in his novels aimed at teenagers long before the height of the Civil Rights movement, and in the 1960s with his books' exploration of free love and libertarianism even became an unwilling darling of counterculture youth. In many ways, the author was ahead of his times.

The Birth of a Career

Even as a very small child, Heinlein was captivated by the sight of Halley's Comet in 1910 (Patterson 22). As he grew older, he studied astronomy and mathematics on his own and began reading science fiction as well (Patterson 30), and after excelling in high school, he gained an appointment to the U.S. Naval Academy in 1925. In 1929 Heinlein graduated from Annapolis as an ensign and also began a year-long first marriage that, unlike his fractionally better-known 1932–1947 marriage to Leslyn MacDonald, was lost to history until the twenty-first century. In any event, after active duty at sea, Heinlein was invalided out of the Navy in 1934 due to tuberculosis, retiring at the rank of lieutenant, junior grade. After quick false starts in silver mining and then sitting in on graduate physics classes, from 1934 to 1938 Heinlein worked in California politics under the umbrella of the leftist Upton Sinclair, finally running for, and losing out on, a state Assemblyman seat for the Hollywood district…and then could begin his ultimate career in science fiction.

William H. Patterson, Jr., reminds us that Heinlein had dabbled on and off with writing what were, essentially, "desk-drawer" projects for years, including his posthumously published first novel, *For Us, the Living.* Of course it is the short story "Life-Line," however, whose submission caught the eye of John W. Campbell, Jr., influential editor of the SF magazine *Astounding Science-Fiction.* This story of a semi-crackpot scientist who creates a machine that measures the electrical signal of a body through all four dimensions to determine the date and time of an individual's future death may not exactly be Shakespeare, but for the era of magazines made of rough, cheap pulp paper that sometimes held even rougher, cheaper writing—the era of the "pulps"—it was very fine indeed, and it still is quite a decent read, considering its period. In it, moreover, we may see some character types that will recur throughout Heinlein's career:

the Man Who Knows, the Conventional Scoffers, and the Crooked Opposition—the Guiding Uncle-Figure and the Featherbrained Wife have yet to appear, but they will soon. Campbell, who ran *Astounding* from 1937 until his death in 1971, knew a good thing when he saw it, and this was $70 well spent.

"Life-Line" appeared in the August 1939 issue of *Astounding Science-Fiction*, the top-line SF pulp, and in rapid succession came more, and still more. By October 1942, scarcely three years after his debut as a professional writer, Heinlein had seen twenty-nine tales appear in print: short stories, long stories, and even novellas serialized in *Astounding* across two or three months. The best pieces usually appeared in *Astounding Science-Fiction*, but lesser ones came out in lower-tier magazines like *Super Science Stories*, *Astonishing Stories*, *Future*, and *Unknown*. Those destined to be part of his "Future History" series were printed under Heinlein's own name, solid stand-alones came out under the "Anson MacDonald" pseudonym, and more peripheral tales and even "stinkeroos" were attributed to names like "Lyle Monroe," "Caleb Saunders," and "John Riverside." The "Anson MacDonald" moniker was particularly useful in that it masked Campbell's reliance on the powerful new author and made it seem that *Astounding* was not simply Heinlein's playground. In this period, after all, Campbell published not just fourteen works under Heinlein's name, but also another seven MacDonalds, and certain issues even carried, unknown to readers, more than one story from this slippery yet oh-so readable contributor.

Heinlein's early stories are surprisingly varied. Fewer than a dozen even pertain to space travel, that seeming staple of the pulp era, while others explore such diverse topics as time travel, alternate realities, interdimensional shenanigans, even new mythos. Yes, Heinlein's fiction in the pulps occasionally asks questions like *What if a Cosmic Construction Corps were organized to "clean up" the spaceways?* ("Misfit" in *Astounding*, November 1939) or *What if the colonization of a jungle Venus brings exploitation and slavery?* ("Logic of Empire" in *Astounding*, March 1941). His imagination, however, leads off in all directions. *What if a puritanical religious dictatorship reinforced with high-tech "miracles" takes over the*

United States? ("'If This Goes On—'" in *Astounding*, February and March 1940). *What if the highway Route 66 is replaced with giant conveyor-belt "road cities"?* ("The Roads Must Roll" in *Astounding*, June 1940). *What if a wise-guy architect's tesseract house ends up poking into other dimensions?* ("'—And He Built a Crooked House—'" in *Astounding*, February 1941). *What if seeming paranoia is actually the clear-headed understanding that strange beings watch our every move in a false reality?* ("They" in *Unknown*, April 1941). *What if even stranger beings created our world as a mere art project?* ("The Unpleasant Profession of Jonathan Hoag" in *Unknown*, October 1942).

Some of these first two-dozen-odd stories are rather good in their psychological portrayals. "Blowups Happen" (*Astounding*, September 1940), for example, captures the aggrieved frustration of the lead-armored technicians working on a finicky and dangerous nuclear power plant under the surveillance of doctors watching for the signs of incipient stress-caused insanity, and "Requiem" (*Astounding*, January 1940) is beautifully poignant in its treatment of the heartbroken tycoon whose vision and commitment brought the first flight to the Moon, but who now is too old and frail to make the trip himself. Heinlein has a good ear for a snappy line, too, with casual contractions and slangy jive in all the right places in dialogue, and he is not averse to an occasional dry witticism in his own authorial voice either. Moreover, the drawing power of the Future History schema cannot be overlooked. Heinlein's stories are entertaining individually, but there is something delightful as well in seeing how the various pieces fit together in the grand sweep of the centuries-long conception from the near-future of "road cities" and the development of nuclear power and space travel, through the dark days of "Prophet" Nehemiah Scudder of "'If This Goes On—'," to the leap to the stars of "Methuselah's Children." Such a tapestry of tales, complete with a giant timeline chart showing stories, main characters' lifespans, major technological breakthroughs and trends, and pertinent social data, was new in pulp science fiction, and Campbell's reproduction of the chart in *Astounding* in mid-1941 helped captivate readers and drum up further interest.

The "Slicks" and the "Juvies"

During the Second World War, Heinlein was unable to get himself called back to active duty in the Navy, but he did work as a civilian engineer at the Naval Air Experimental Station in Philadelphia—incidentally, with fellow SF authors Isaac Asimov and L. Sprague de Camp. Here, aside from doing research on plastic canopies for aircraft and on high-altitude pressure suits, he met Lieutenant Virginia Gerstenfeld, with whom he was to begin an enduring marriage in 1948 and who, as Damon Knight reminds us, is the model for many a later "redheaded and improbably multi-skilled heroine" (11). After the war Heinlein tried his hand at "world-saving"—that is, writing articles that tried to warn the American public of the dangers of the nuclear age—but, more importantly, he got back into science fiction with a vengeance. Not only did he publish again in the pulp magazines, both science fiction and detective, but he also made the tremendous leap into those widely circulated mainstream magazines known colloquially as a category by their glossy covers and their pages of smooth, high-quality paper: the "slicks." Previously, such markets had been off-limits to SF writers working in what his snobbish editor at Scribner's soon would call "rather cheap magazine[s]" (*Grumbles* 48), but Heinlein's talent as a storyteller simply could not be denied.

Indeed, the years 1947 and 1948 saw seven new stories printed in the *Saturday Evening Post*, *Town and Country*, and *Argosy*, prestigious periodicals whose covers would not embarrass middle-class hosts when dinner guests saw them on the coffee table. Of the seven, six are further pieces of the Future History series, and all of these treat space travel as a natural and unremarkable part of the future. This movement to the slicks was a significant breakthrough, both for the author and for the genre as well. Campbell had been paying Heinlein the top-dollar rates at *Astounding* from the beginning, but the slicks, of course, paid even more. Yet aside from benefitting Heinlein's checkbook, the slicks' acceptance of his stories also brought literate science fiction to a more upscale readership, showing notions of Moon colonies and travel to Mars and Venus not as mere escapism but as seemingly possible outgrowths of the present, and something worth reading. The first of these early postwar tales, the evocative "The Green Hills of Earth," which depicts a colorful frontier of atomic-powered rocketships, Venusburg dives, and ancient Martian canals, is the perfect lead-in to the rest. Its final scene of the blind, bawdy poet of the spaceways taking a lethal dose of radiation to singlehandedly save all other lives aboard a spaceship, all the while over the intercom delivering the last lines of his haunting opus, is schmaltzy but irresistible, and the tale's disarmingly reportorial style captures the allure and the romance of the imagined future in a way that no splashy "sense of wonder" story from a 1930s pulp magazine could have.

Heinlein's writing output after moving into the slicks turned, aside from occasional essays and work in film and even television, to novels. Between 1947 and 1958 appeared one novel per year in a "juvenile" series for the publisher Scribner's. These books often were serialized first in SF magazines, but despite the misleading category label—which publishers now would call "young-adult"—they are anything but juvenile. All are stories of coming of age and joining the adult world of uncertainties and mature responsibilities, yet although they emphasize ambition and hard work, coupled with intellectual curiosity and also scientific competence, never are they mere pieces of Horatio Alger propaganda, nor is the Heinlein Hero simply a carryover of the jodhpur- and jackboot-wearing white male engineers featured prominently on so many cheap pulp magazine covers of the 1930s. In fact, the Scribner's "juvies" of the 1940s and '50s actually work subtly but repeatedly against ethnic and gender stereotypes. *Space Cadet* (1948) and *Citizen of the Galaxy* (1957), for example, both point out the multiracial compositions of their respective peacekeeping organizations, and *The Star Beast* (1954) features a highly educated and respected African bureaucrat as a major character, while just as the seeming decorative rich girl of *Starman Jones* (1953) is a better three-dimensional chess player than the male protagonist with an eidetic mathematical memory, the narrator of *Have Space Suit—Will Travel* (1958) is amusingly outclassed by an eleven-year-old girl genius. Other examples abound.[1]

The Adult Novels

Amid his work for Scribner's, Heinlein also squeezed in the occasional novel for adults in the 1950s, and although in 1963 Putnam published *Podkayne of Mars*, his last young-adult novel, Heinlein's books from the 1961 *Stranger in a Strange Land* onward otherwise are solidly aimed at the adult market. Really, the juvies did not shy away from exploring the difficult choices of adulthood—the protagonist of *Space Cadet* thinks long and hard about being on the front lines of nuclear deterrence, for example, while Kip Russell of *Have Space Suit—Will Travel* calmly evaluates the morality of drowning potential rapists and murderers at birth. Heinlein's groundbreaking first novel of the '60s, however, begins with a wry full-capital "NOTICE" indicating that this is one that the fussy "elderly lad[y]" librarians (*Grumbles* 57) who stocked the Scribner's juvies never could have taken: *"All men, gods, and planets in this story are imaginary. Any coincidence of names is regretted"* (4).

Aside from finally following through on his earlier, seemingly playful musings on the premise of "a Martian named Smith," *Stranger in a Strange Land* begins the unorthodox, sometimes shocking treatment of the formerly taboo topics of religion and sexuality, and even the very nature of reality itself, that continue through the last of Heinlein's writings. Born of parents from the lost first mission to Mars, Valentine Michael Smith was raised from infancy by Martians, so when brought to Earth a quarter-century later by the next expedition, he is the perfect "innocent" observer through which Heinlein, "taking nothing for granted and [being] free to lambaste anything from the Girl Scouts and Mother's Apple Pie to the idea of patriotism," can work at "criticiz[ing]and examin[ing] disrespectfully the two untouchables: monotheism and monogamy" (*Grumbles* 228–29). In addition to the trappings of Martian mysticism, like the binding custom of water-sharing, the notion of *grok* as total understanding, the mind-driven "disappearing" of grokked wrongness, and the underlying "Thou art God," there is commune-like living, there is ritual cannibalism, there is free love… and there are reminders that certain apparent oddities are not exactly absent, shall we say, from the scriptures of own seemingly staid Western religions either.

Group marriage, the social and sexual union among several people rather than between just two, is common in the lunar society of *The Moon Is a Harsh Mistress* (1966) and in the future of *Friday* (1982) as well. Casual nudity appears throughout *The Number of the Beast* (1980), and of course sexuality, including that between same-gender partners and occasionally even incestuous ones,[2] is a major subject of *I Will Fear No Evil* (1970), *Time Enough for Love* (1973), and *To Sail Beyond the Sunset* (1987). Ronald Sarti, writing of *Time Enough for Love*—which is almost tame compared to Heinlein's final novel in 1987—is correct to find that "the complex psychological and emotional elements that make up sexuality are ignored" (133), but the decades-long ruminations on sexuality[3] by an author born in the Bible Belt not very far after the end of the nineteenth century nevertheless are interesting and thought-provoking even when their conclusions happen to fall short.

Stranger in a Strange Land ends with a gently irreverent—or utterly blasphemous, depending on the seriousness of one's viewpoint—peek at Heaven as a prosaic organization like any big business, and the conclusion of *Job: A Comedy of Justice* makes that of *Stranger* look like a Sunday school lesson. In a way, this gets to the very nature of reality itself. From whence does existence come? If there indeed is a Creator, what motivates Him? If the afterlife is real, how much different is it from our own mundane world? The early Heinlein dabbles with the mysteries and paradoxes of creation in "By His Bootstraps," "The Unpleasant Profession of Jonathan Hoag," and "'All You Zombies—'," and the later novels return to the topic, introducing the notion as World as Myth. Some of the different dimensions investigated by the explorers of *The Number of the Beast* actually spring from works of literature—and midway through the novel, it is revealed that the protagonists come not from our own reality but from the timeline of Heinlein's own "The Man Who Sold the Moon"—while *The Cat Who Walks Through Walls* brings together the worlds of *The Moon Is a Harsh Mistress* and *Time Enough for Love*. What *is* reality, exactly? Despite a career of seeming pragmatism, this fundamental question of the final novels simply makes more explicit the hints that have appeared in many of the author's works throughout the decades.

The Legacy of Heinlein

Robert A. Heinlein may be the largest, most recognizable name in modern science fiction, from his stories in the prewar pulps and eventually the postwar slicks like the *Saturday Evening Post*, through his enduring young-adult novels published by Scribner's, to his increasingly large and sometimes-wallowing books marketed for adult audiences. Although John Campbell actually rejected the next several stories Heinlein submitted after "Life-Line," the new author quickly learned to write and write well. Readers enjoyed the tales, and fellow writers recognized his skill as well. Indeed, Alexei Panshin reminds us that Heinlein, after only two years as a professional author, already was a major and well-respected figure in SF and was invited to Denver in 1941 to speak as Guest of Honor at the Third World Science Fiction Convention. And in 1953, when L. Sprague de Camp asked "the eighteen leading writers of imaginative fiction" to name the authors who had influenced them, "[o]nly ten authors were mentioned by more than one of the eighteen, and of these ten, Robert Heinlein was the only modern writer" (Panshin 2–3). And from there, Heinlein's stature only grew greater. As Ivor Rogers puts it so well, "people, even his severest critics, like his writing, and he sells well. Most importantly, he is capable of attracting readers with a wide age difference and with widely disparate educational backgrounds" (222).

In some respects, Heinlein's writing itself is education of a kind. The author was an engineer, after all, working on developing high-altitude pressure suits, the forerunners of spacesuits, during the Second World War (Heinlein, "Science Fiction" 30), and his fiction explains such inventions as waterbeds, remote-control handling "waldoes," nuclear rocket engines, and powered military exoskeletons before they were developed in actuality. The Scribner's juvies in particular reached thousands upon thousands of youth of impressionable ages in the late '40s and 1950s, not only "shap[ing] the way that people thought about spaceflight," but also, as teenagers grew into adulthood, "inspir[ing] numerous people to enter the sciences and engineering in general—and the field of spaceflight in particular" (Kennedy 341).[4] And just as the Space Age without Heinlein's preparation would have been a different thing, the flavor of the '60s in general would have been different as well, with no *Stranger in a Strange Land* to be devoured by a restless generation of youth, no hip and ubiquitous *grok* permeating the culture, and no wry TANSTAAFL, or "There ain't no such thing as a free lunch," from *The Moon Is a Harsh Mistress*.

Heinlein's ideas continue to intrigue us as the dogged individualist throughout his career questions social and political structures in unexpected and sometimes even shocking ways, examining the interplay of duty and choice, of idealism and pragmatism. A classic piece of Heinleinian dialogue occurs in "Solution Unsatisfactory" (1940), when the creation of an unstoppable weapon of radioactive dust requires grounding all aircraft except those run by the US military; one character protests that this is "unconstitutional" and "violates civil rights," to which another replies, "Killing a man violates his civil rights, too" (126). Alexei Panshin, writing of the hard-nosed protagonist of *Farnham's Freehold* (1964), who builds a bomb shelter that enables his family, their servant, and a houseguest to ride out a nuclear war, derides the character as "a libertarian who orders people around at gunpoint" (109), but this seeming Zen-like profundity misses the obvious: when push comes to shove, something does indeed have to give. Never does Heinlein let us forget that despite all our ideals—or perhaps because of them—sometimes tough choices have to be made. Yes, contradictions abound, and yet, really, this reflects less authorial sloppiness or inconsistency than simply the messy nature of the complex psychological and social realities that humans, be they fictional or actual, must inhabit.

Surely one thing that is inarguable about Heinlein's writing is its underlying optimism, and corresponding emphasis on broad education, hands-on competence, and imagination and flexibility. The dozen "juveniles" published by Scribner's are perhaps the most obvious examples of this, but the adult novels follow suit in one way or another as well. Some protagonists have peculiar idiosyncratic talents—Zeb of *The Number of the Beast* gets a subconscious warning just before disaster strikes, for example, while his wife Deety has an innate time-telling sense—but all are clear-headed, open-eyed, and, following the adage spelled out back in the juvies that "'good luck' follows careful preparation; 'bad luck' comes from sloppiness" (*Have Space Suit* 250), they are as ready as they can be for anything. According to the aphoristic Notebooks of Lazarus Long in *Time Enough for Love*,

> A human being should be able to change a diaper, plan an invasion, butcher a hog, conn a ship, design a building, write a sonnet, balance accounts, build a wall, set a bone, comfort the dying, take orders, give orders, cooperate, act alone, solve equations, analyze a new problem, pitch manure, program a computer, cook a tasty meal, fight efficiently, die gallantly. Specialization is for insects. (248)

It is a sweeping and stirring call, but that is because Heinlein's ultimate belief in humanity, broadcast on Edward R. Murrow's radio show in 1952,[5] is sweeping and stirring, too: "I believe that this hairless embryo with the aching, oversize brain case and the opposable thumb, this animal barely up from the apes, will *endure*. Will *endure* longer than his home planet—will spread out to the stars and beyond, carrying with him his honesty and insatiable curiosity, his unlimited courage and his noble essential decency" ("This I Believe" 141). And if the past several decades are any indication, the writings of Robert A. Heinlein will help prepare generations to come for this future he helped create.

Notes

1. See, for example, Erisman, Frank, Parkin-Speer, and Rule.
2. See McGiveron, especially pages 190–96.
3. Indeed, William H. Patterson, Jr., points out that aside from having a hobby of photographing female nudes, Heinlein himself occasionally practiced nudism and had marriages with open, or "swinging," arrangements, all facts which a children's author of the 1940s and

'50s had to hide, and which even non-public figures today most likely would not noise about very widely either.

4. Moreover, an engineer whom Heinlein hired during the Second World War with the promise of working on pressure suits later became "chief engineer of life support systems" and helped develop the spacesuits that astronauts wore on the Moon (*Grumbles* 196).

5. An audio recording is available at http://www.heinleinprize.com/rah/thisibelieve.htm.

Works Cited

Erisman, Fred. "Robert Heinlein's Case for Racial Tolerance, 1954–1956." *Extrapolation* 29 (Fall 1988): 216–26.

Frank, Marietta. "Women in Heinlein's Juveniles." *Young Adult Science Fiction*. Ed. C.W. Sullivan III. Contributions to the Study of Science Fiction and Fantasy 79. Westport, CT: Greenwood, 1999. 119–30.

Heinlein, Robert A. "'All You Zombies—'." *Magazine of Fantasy and Science Fiction* Mar. 1959. *Unpleasant* 138–51.

_____."By His Bootstraps." *Astounding Science-Fiction* Oct. 1941. *The Menace from Earth*. 1959. New York: Signet, 1964. 39–88.

_____. "'—And He Built a Crooked House—.'" *Astounding Science-Fiction* Feb. 1941. *Unpleasant* 191–214.

_____. "Blowups Happen." *Astounding Science-Fiction* Sep. 1940. *Past* 73–120.

_____. *The Cat Who Walks Through Walls: A Comedy of Manners*. New York: Putnam's, 1985.

_____. *Citizen of the Galaxy*. 1957. New York: Ace, n.d.

_____. *Farnham's Freehold*. 1964. New York: Berkley, 1981.

_____. *Friday*. 1982. New York: Del Rey, 1983.

_____. "The Green Hills of Earth." *Saturday Evening Post* (8 Feb. 1947). *The Past Through Tomorrow*. 1967. New York: Berkley, 1975. 363–73.

_____. *Have Space Suit—Will Travel*. 1958. New York: Del Rey, 1978.

_____. "'If This Goes On—.'" *Astounding Science Fiction* (Feb.– Mar. 1940). *The Past Through Tomorrow*. 1967. New York: Berkley, 1975. 449–584.

_____. *I Will Fear No Evil*. 1970. New York: Berkley, 1981.

_____. *Job: A Comedy of Justice*. New York: Del Rey, 1984.

_____. "Logic of Empire." *Astounding Science-Fiction* (Mar. 1941). *The Past Through Tomorrow*. 1967. New York: Berkley, 1975. 375–421.

_____. "The Man Who Sold the Moon." 1950. *The Past Through Tomorrow*. 1967. New York: Berkley, 1975. 121–212.

_____. "Misfit." *Astounding Science-Fiction* (Nov. 1939). *The Past Through Tomorrow*. 1967. New York: Berkley, 1975. 633–653.

_____. *The Moon Is a Harsh Mistress*. 1966. New York: Berkley, 1980.

_____. *The Number of the Beast*. 1980. New York: Fawcett, 1982.

_____. *The Past Through Tomorrow*. 1967. New York: Berkley, 1975.

_____. "'PRAVDA' Means 'TRUTH'." *American Mercury* (Oct. 1960). *Expanded Universe*. 1980. New York: Ace, 1982. 405–17.

_____. "Requiem." *Astounding Science-Fiction* (Jan. 1940). *The Past Through Tomorrow*. 1967. New York: Berkley, 1975. 245–62.

_____. "The Roads Must Roll." *Astounding Science-Fiction* (June 1940). *The Past Through Tomorrow*. 1967. New York: Berkley, 1975. 35–72.

_____. *To Sail Beyond the Sunset*. 1987. New York: Ace, 1988.

_____. "Science Fictions: Its Nature, Faults and Virtues." 1957. *The Science Fiction Novel*. Ed. Basil Davenport. Chicago: Advent, 1969. 14–48.

_____. "Solution Unsatisfactory." *Astounding Science-Fiction* (May 1941). *Expanded Universe*. 1980. New York: Ace, 1982. 92–144.

_____. *Space Cadet*. 1948. New York: Del Rey, 1978.

_____. *The Star Beast*. 1954. New York: Del Rey, 1977.

_____. *Starman Jones*. 1953. New York: Del Rey, 1982.

_____. *Starship Troopers*. 1959. New York: Berkley, 1968.

_____. *Stranger in a Strange Land*. 1961. New York: Berkley, 1968.

_____. "They." *Unknown* Apr. 1941. *Unpleasant* 152-69.

_____. "This I Believe." *This I Believe*. Host Edward R. Murrow. 1 Dec. 1952. *Grumbles* 140–41.

_____. *Time Enough for Love*. 1973. New York: Berkley, 1974.

_____. "The Unpleasant Profession of Jonathan Hoag." *Unknown* (Oct. 1942). *Unpleasant* 1–121.

_____. *The Unpleasant Profession of Jonathan Hoag.* 1959. New York: Berkley, 1980.

Heinlein, Virginia, ed. *Grumbles from the Grave.* New York: Del Rey, 1989.

Kennedy, Robert G. III. "Robert A. Heinlein's Influence on Spaceflight." *Remembering the Space Age: Proceedings of the 50th Anniversary Conference.* Ed. Steven J. Dick. Washington, DC: NASA, 2008. 341–52.

Knight, Damon. "Introduction." *The Past through Tomorrow.* By Robert A. Heinlein. 1967. New York: Berkley, 1975. 9–13.

McGiveron, Rafeeq O. "'Maybe the Hardest Job of All—Particularly When You Have No Talent for It': Heinlein's Fictional Parents, 1939–1987." *Extrapolation* 44 (Summer 2003): 169–200.

Panshin, Alexei. *Heinlein in Dimension: A Critical Analysis.* Chicago: Advent, 1968.

Parkin-Speer, Diane. "Almost a Feminist: Robert A. Heinlein." *Extrapolation* 36 (Summer 1995): 112–25.

Patterson, William H., Jr. *Robert A. Heinlein: In Dialogue with His Century, Vol. 1: Learning Curve, 1907–1948.* New York: Tor, 2010.

Rogers, Ivor. "Robert Heinlein: Folklorist of Outer Space." *Robert A. Heinlein.* Ed. Joseph D. Olander & Martin Harry Greenberg. Writers of the 21st Century Series. New York: Taplinger, 1978. 222–39.

Rule, Deb Houdek. "Heinlein's Women: Strong Women Characters in the Heinlein Juveniles." *The Heinlein Society.* The Heinlein Society, 2003. Web. 22 Mar. 2015. <http://www.heinleinsociety.org/2004/02/heinleins-women/>.

Sarti, Ronald. "Variations on a Theme: Human Sexuality in the Work of Robert A. Heinlein." *Robert A. Heinlein.* Ed. Joseph D. Olander & Martin Harry Greenberg. Writers of the 21st Century Series. New York: Taplinger, 1978. 107–36.

United States Census Bureau. *Census '90: Population and Housing Unit Counts.* U.S. Census Bureau, 26 Aug. 1993. Web. 22 Mar. 2015. <https://www.census.gov/prod/cen1990/cph2/cph-2-1-1.pdf>.

Wyatt, Ian D. & Daniel E. Hecker. "Occupational Changes during the 20th Century." *Monthly Labor Review* (Mar. 2006): 35–57.

From the Ocean to the Stars: The Life of Robert A. Heinlein, 1907–1988

Gary Westfahl

While William H. Patterson, Jr.'s two-volume biography, *Robert A. Heinlein: In Dialogue with His Century* (2010, 2014), will long be valued as an authoritative account of Heinlein's life, its perspectives on Heinlein's career, heavily influenced by Heinlein himself and his third wife Virginia, can readily be challenged. The biography, for example, is governed by a questionable conceit, announced in the first volume's introduction, that Heinlein was a man "in dialogue with his century" who "spent his life—and his fortune—pushing and pulling us into our future, in a continuing contest for the human mind, in a dialogue with everything in the twentieth century that deadened the human spirit" (Patterson 15). Actually, after four years of political work during the 1930s, Heinlein thereafter only sporadically, and unsuccessfully, endeavored to influence public opinion, increasingly content to effectively ignore his century and focus on expressing his now-fixed opinions in novels that he knew would prove profitable, unconcerned about the fact that he might be alienating readers just as much as, if not more than, he was inspiring them.

Heinlein's first three decades were largely a saga of thwarted ambitions. He was born on 7 July 1907, into a family of fluctuating financial fortunes, inspiring the teenage Heinlein to take on various odd jobs while still earning high grades in school. This enabled him to enter the United States Naval Academy, though he could not achieve his original goal—to become a Navy pilot—because of weak vision. Nearing graduation, he applied to become a Rhodes Scholar to obtain the additional education he needed to qualify for another coveted position, as an astronomer at the Naval Observatory, but an ill-advised, short-lived marriage to Elinor Curry in 1929 rendered him ineligible for the scholarship. Then, after he settled into shipboard assignments as a naval engineer, a bout of tuberculosis in 1933 forced him into early retirement, and while his pension provided a modest income, he sought a new profession to better support himself and his second wife, the former Leslyn MacDonald, whom he had married in 1932. While dabbling in real estate in Los Angeles, Heinlein plunged into politics, first working for Upton Sinclair's 1934 gubernatorial campaign—EPIC, or End Poverty in California—and later seeking a seat in the California State Assembly. Only after losing the Democratic primary in June 1938—humiliatingly, to the incumbent Republican representative who had filed for both parties' nominations—did Heinlein resolve to launch a career as a professional writer.

Heinlein was unable to publish his first major project, a utopian novel entitled *For Us, the Living: A Comedy of Customs* (2004), but when he started selling stories to the science fiction magazines he had long enjoyed reading, beginning with "Life-Line" in 1939, Heinlein almost immediately became one of the field's leading writers—in large part because, unlike the moonlighting scientists and professional pulp writers who then dominated science fiction, he could draw upon his real-life experiences to provide his fiction with an aura of worldliness and sophistication that other writers could not match. And seeking to please innovative editor John W. Campbell, Jr., who published most of Heinlein's early stories and four novels in his magazines *Astounding Science-Fiction* and *Unknown*, Heinlein demonstrated an amazing ability to produce imaginative stories filled with provocative ideas; he also broke new ground by crafting a common background for many of his stories, dubbed his "Future History," which also included two early novels, "'If This Goes On—'," later published in *Revolt in 2100* (1953), and *Methuselah's Children* (1941, 1958).

Two of Heinlein's best works from this era are "The Roads Must Roll" (1940), featuring a man who prevents a strike by the workers who maintain a future America's moving roads, and "Universe" (1941), involving residents of a generation starship who forget they are living in a spaceship; both were voted by the Science Fiction Writers of America to be included in the *Science Fiction Hall of Fame* volumes devoted to outstanding short stories and novellas. Other noteworthy works include the novel *Beyond This Horizon* (1942, 1948), in part a reworked version of *For Us, the Living*; the masterful "By His Bootstraps" (1941), in which every character is the same man making multiple trips through time; and the elegiac "Requiem" (1940), about a pioneering promoter of space travel who achieves his dying wish by reaching the Moon. An uncharacteristically weak effort, the novel *Sixth Column* (1941, 1949; also published as *The Day after Tomorrow*), a tale of Americans resisting Asiatic invaders that has undeniably racist overtones, later was revealed to be based upon an unpublished novella by Campbell, who paid Heinlein to write his own version of the story.

Overall, many believe that Heinlein's variegated writings from 1939 to 1942 constitute his finest achievement. With assistance from Leslyn, who read and commented on his manuscripts, Heinlein enjoyed increasing financial success, paid off his mortgage, and relaxed by socializing with science fiction friends, occasionally visiting nudist colonies, and engaging in brief affairs tolerated by Leslyn as part of their open marriage. After the start of World War II, though, Heinlein wanted to join the war effort, and while his delicate health prevented a return to active duty, he abandoned writing to become a civilian engineer at the Naval Air Experimental Station in Philadelphia, primarily working to perfect high-altitude pressure suits—an assignment that affected his later descriptions of spacesuits.

Returning to Los Angeles after the war, Heinlein was determined, as he explained in *Expanded Universe: The New Worlds of Robert A. Heinlein* (1980), "to break out from the limitations and low rates of pulp science-fiction magazines into anything and everything" (145). Thus, among other initiatives, he began writing articles about atomic energy and space travel; stories for "slick" magazines like *The Saturday Evening Post*, beginning with the moving tale of a blind spaceman, "The Green Hills of Earth" (1947); a series of juvenile novels for Scribner's, starting with *Rocket Ship Galileo* (1947), which inspired many future scientists and science fiction writers; and screenplays for films and television, one of which became the 1950 film *Destination Moon*. Leslyn's increasing instability, complicated by chronic alcoholism, had driven him to seek a divorce in 1947, and one year later, he married the former Virginia Gerstenfeld and moved to Colorado Springs, Colorado. Virginia became an unusually effective partner in critiquing his writing, assisting with business matters, and dealing with increasing numbers of letters from enthusiastic admirers.

By the 1950s, Heinlein should have been a happy man; he had forged a solid working relationship, and friendship, with an effective agent, Lurton Blassingame, and he was earning constantly increasing sums from his juveniles, new stories and articles, foreign translations of his works, and a few novels for adults, including *Double Star* (1956), the first of his four Hugo Award-winning novels. But both Heinleins repeatedly had to deal with health problems—some relatively minor, others more serious—and Patterson's biography meticulously records a seemingly unending series of petty annoyances, including malicious, inaccurate letters sent to Heinlein's friends by the increasingly troubled Leslyn; unauthorized republications of his stories; frustrating work for television series that never materialized; a lawsuit filed against the producers of *The Brain Eaters* (1958), a film that obviously had stolen the plot of Heinlein's *The Puppet Masters* (1951) and spoiled efforts to sell the novel to Hollywood; and regular requests for revisions from Scribner's prickly editor, Alice Dalgliesh, who eventually terminated their rocky relationship by rejecting *Starship Troopers* (1959). Publication of that book as an adult novel began to alter Heinlein's relationship with the science fiction community, for while it won a Hugo Award, it was also vehemently criticized for its long passages of political commentary, foreshadowing reactions to later novels with similar contents.

The true turning point in Heinlein's career, however, came when he then returned to an unfinished manuscript, provisionally entitled *The Man from Mars*, and transformed it into the longest novel he had ever written, *Stranger in a Strange Land* (1961). Significantly edited at the insistence of editors—though the original, uncut version appeared in 1990—the controversial novel described a young man raised by Martians, Valentine Michael Smith, who returns to Earth to establish a new religion based on his telekinetic powers, a Martian reverence for water, free love, and efforts to "grok," or thoroughly understand, every person one encounters. Though it irritated many longtime fans, *Stranger in a Strange Land* won Heinlein a third Hugo Award and continued to sell numerous copies throughout the decade, as it was embraced by readers who linked its philosophy to the emerging "counterculture" of the 1960s. Heinlein followed this novel with an extravagant fantasy modeled on the works of James Branch Cabell, *Glory Road* (1963), and three more conventional novels, including his final Hugo Award winner, *The Moon Is a Harsh Mistress* (1966). As Colorado's high altitude was impacting Virginia's health, the Heinleins moved to northern California in 1966, and Heinlein began donating manuscripts and letters to the library at the nearby University of California, Santa Cruz.

During his final two decades, Heinlein was beset by increasingly grave health issues that limited his public appearances and contact with friends, though he periodically completed lengthy novels of a highly uneven quality. *Friday* (1982) was heralded as a return to Heinlein's classic mode of writing; many were impressed by the eccentric *Job: A Comedy of Justice* (1984); and if not entirely successful, *Time Enough for Love* (1973) and *The Number of the Beast* (1980) had moments that recalled his best work. However, few readers had anything kind to say about *I Will Fear No Evil* (1970), *The Cat Who Walks through Walls* (1985), or *To Sail Beyond the Sunset* (1987).

The older Heinlein also had grown considerably more conservative, a natural and untroubling development, though Patterson echoed Heinlein in shrilly insisting that Heinlein had simply remained true to the same values he had held throughout his life. Perhaps this is true to some extent, but when a man works to elect socialist Upton Sinclair in 1934 and then works to elect conservative Republican Barry Goldwater in 1964, stating that his political views had remained entirely unchanged seems disingenuous. In the 1980s, Heinlein's strong support for President Ronald Reagan's Strategic Defense Initiative, or "Star Wars" anti-missile system, led to a celebrated public argument with a former friend, British science fiction writer Arthur C. Clarke, as Heinlein maintained that a foreign citizen had no right to comment on American policies. (Clarke did concede, though, that his opposition to the project had been based on inaccurate calculations.) Still, at least one of the elderly Heinlein's crusades cannot be criticized: after his life was saved by a blood transfusion in 1970, Heinlein campaigned to encourage people to voluntarily donate blood and urged science fiction conventions to include blood drives.

After publishing *To Sail Beyond the Sunset*, Heinlein apparently never wrote again, as a recurrence of emphysema, complicated by other problems, led to months of declining health and, ultimately, his death on 8 May 1988. Virginia then edited a book of Heinlein's letters, *Grumbles from the Grave* (1989), and arranged to publish some previously unseen works: a travel book, *Tramp Royale* (1992); a political manual, *Take Back Your Government!: A Practical Manual for the Private Citizen Who Wants Democracy to Work* (1992); and the original, unedited versions of *The Puppet Masters* (1990), *Red Planet* (1990), and *Stranger in a Strange Land* (1991). After Virginia's death in 2003, Heinlein's new heir published *For Us, the Living* and launched the 46-volume Virginia Edition of Heinlein's complete works, including previously uncollected fiction and nonfiction, additional correspondence, and unproduced screenplays. Heinlein's memory also is being kept alive by occasional film adaptations, including the miniseries *Red Planet* (1994), *Robert A. Heinlein's The Puppet Masters* (1994), *Starship Troopers* (1997), which inspired several filmed and animated sequels, and *Predestination* (2014), based on "'All You Zombies—'" (1958). Anyone reading contemporary science fiction literature will regularly detect signs of his lingering influence, and most of Heinlein's own works have remained in print, still finding appreciative readers decades after they first appeared.

Works Cited

Heinlein, Robert A. *Expanded Universe: The New Worlds of Robert A. Heinlein*. New York: Ace, 1980.

Patterson, William H., Jr. *Robert A. Heinlein: In Dialogue with His Century: Volume I, 1907–1948: Learning Curve*. New York: Tor, 2010.

CRITICAL
CONTEXTS

Robert A. Heinlein in Historical and Cultural Context

Zahra Jannessari Ladani

I.

Though Robert A. Heinlein's career as a science fiction writer began at the age of thirty-two, his familiarity with this type of literature began early in life, when the pulps satisfied his thirst for adventure, but simultaneously added to his curiosity about the wonderful dimensions the cosmos possibly possessed. Since childhood, Heinlein was an avid reader of scientific and fantastic books like Roy Rockwood's Great Marvel series, including *Through Space to Mars* (1910) and *Lost on the Moon* (1911); Edgar Rice Burroughs' *A Princess of Mars* (1917), *The Gods of Mars* (1918), and *Warlord of Mars* (1919); and pulp magazines such as *Argosy* (1882–1978) and *All-Story, Electrical Experimenter* (1913–1920), *Amazing Stories* (1926–2006), and later, *Astounding Stories* (1929–).

American pulps, particularly pulp SF, a unique cultural phenomenon peculiar to the first half of the twentieth century, were sold in "forty and fifty thousand newsstands, drugstores, and tobacconists" (Bleiler and Bleiler vii). With the invention of wood pulp paper, the expansion of the railways, and cheap mail for publications, public access to inexpensive magazines became possible. This brought a new vivacity to the American publishing system, resulting in the development of genre fiction, including science fiction, which was read mostly by experimenters, inventors, and science-technology aficionados. According to pioneering SF editor Hugo Gernsback, this new genre was to take up the messianic and incredible task of displacing and offering an enlarging and emending critique of science and technology (3). Such grandiose claims kept pulp SF away from the mainstream American literature and culture, since most pulp SF was very optimistic toward technophilic progress in America, regardless of the real-life situation of the average American throughout the 1920s and 1930s, including the Great Depression, large-scale immigration, and periodic economic crisis. Despite this, science fiction had its own audience for good reasons, such as scientific and technical institutions that facilitated the training of the "lower-middle-class generation" as "scientific workers, teachers, and engineers," or the techno-scientific innovations that substantially transformed the American cultural context and saturated "everyday life experience" with "Mechanism" (Luckhurst 16–17). Thus, despite all hardships in the early twentieth century, America emerged as a nation with sprawling, large corporations to harness science and technology for the sake of progress. In this blueprint, pulp SF served the corporate system through fictional propositions and extrapolations.

Even the most unreal pulp SF stories, therefore, were the direct result of the American gigantic and sublime outlook toward science, technology, and progress. The aviation industry became an exemplary source of inspiration for many of the space operas of the 1920s and 1930s. Statistically, the number of aircraft manufacturers in America between 1914 and 1927 rose from sixteen to sixty one, producing nearly 2,000 aircraft yearly (Purcell 236). Heinlein's love for airplanes, aviation, rocketry, and spaceflight took shape during these years and turned into a serious plan for his future vocation. After Heinlein failed to qualify in his eye test for naval flight duty, flying remained an unfulfilled dream for the rest of his life, and it resurfaced in his SF works, like *Space Cadet* (1948), *Farmer in the Sky* (1950), and *Starship Troopers* (1959).

Although Heinlein joined the SF coterie relatively late, his contribution to the field was a watershed. After his career in the United States Navy was curtailed by health problems, Heinlein participated in a *Thrilling Wonder Stories* fiction contest, which offered a $50 prize. The initial outcome, *For Us, the Living: A Comedy of Customs*, served as a reservoir of ideas for many Heinlein stories in future, though it did not see publication in his lifetime. Heinlein's financial problems together with his ambition for higher magazines pushed him toward writing for John W. Campbell's *Astounding Science-Fiction*, a prestigious SF magazine with the highest pay in those days. This opened a new chapter in Heinlein's vocational life, and brought him into a long-term negotiation with Campbell, particularly between 1939 and 1943, the period roughly marked as the golden age of SF. Heinlein's first attempts, including

"Life-line" (August 1939), "Misfit" (November 1939), and "'If This Goes On—'" (1940), were mostly successful, but they encompassed sporadic subjects, not following a distinct line of thought.

After this period of trial and error, Heinlein gradually found his voice and set out his project of "Future History," which brought a revolution in SF themes and methods and instituted an essential subgenre. Heinlein's huge plan mapped out a stage-by-stage history of future events in the course of centuries. In this chart, different stories represent diverse proposed historical phases, all fitting into a more complex and coherent pattern. For example, "Methuselah's Children" (July–September 1941), with the theme of controlled breeding and longevity, starts from 1875, and "The Roads Must Roll" (June 1940) imagines rolling roads that will replace the automobile in future. On the whole, this series speculates on the diverse manifestations of inevitable change. By imparting a more mature, more philosophical, and sophisticated aspect to the field, Heinlein's Future History took the genre beyond formulaic space operas, hard SF, and gadget stories, which commonly filled the magazines of the day.

Contrary to the formulaic bulk of fiction concerned with plot rather than a plausible picture of the invented futures, Heinlein's stories stood out as pieces that worked through scientific plausibility. Of course, Heinlein owed much of this to his studies at the Naval Academy and, later, his profession as a U.S. Navy officer, which offered him the opportunity to acquire knowledge regarding military engineering and sea warfare as well as expertise in the operation of the first military computers. Heinlein also drew significantly on Charles Darwin's evolutionary theories in devising his Future History plan, since he had read *On the Origin of Species* and *The Descent of Man* in 1920 (Patterson 38). Unlike many works of mainstream literature, which portrayed a dismal capitalistic life, lamented the loss of values, and projected a hopeless future in terms of Social Darwinism and literary realism, the "forward-looking scheme" in Heinlein's Future History project seemed very optimistic (Mann 167). For instance, Heinlein's stories were nothing like Theodore Dreiser's *Sister Carrie* (1900), Frank Norris' *The Octopus* (1901), or John Dos Passos' *U.S.A.* (1930–36). Heinlein therefore became one of the most important figures of the golden age of science fiction by means of his formative attempts to shape the genre and bring it out of the ghetto in which it had been stuck during the 1920s and 1930s.

A major influence and an essential part of the American culture in the first decades of the twentieth century—that is, during Heinlein's childhood and adolescence—was the cult of the maverick, followed by the corporate system, both of which encouraged inventiveness and innovation by advocating a positivistic and pragmatic view to life. Before the great American corporations and institutions came to take control of science and technology, techno-scientific progress was advanced by individual scientists, researchers, amateurs, independents, and entrepreneurs. Examples of the maverick tradition in early twentieth-century America are Thomas Edison (1847–1931), Alexander Graham Bell (1847–1922), and Nikola Tesla (1856–1943). Mavericks became part of early American pulp SF, with Professor Van Manderpootz in Weinbaum's invention stories, Dr. John Pollard in Hamilton's "The Man Who Evolved" (1931), and Professor Martyn in Wertenbaker's "The Man from the Atom" (1926), all sharing a precedent in Hawthorne's Dr. Rappaccini.

The maverick tradition before the emergence of the corporate system was indicative of the Emersonian notion of self-reliance. The accumulative efforts of the self-reliant maverick situated in an increasingly progressive technological ideology gave rise to the corporate system, wherein more than individual work was required to satisfy a thirst for rapid progress, and a demand for organizing dispersed researchers into more economic nuclei. Of course, the transformation of the maverick tradition to the corporate system had its own backwash because not all the advocates of the maverick tradition succumbed to the new system. A case in point is Hugo Gernsback, who more than once condemned the Radio Act of 1927 as jeopardizing the vocational integrity of radio amateurs and experts.

Nonetheless, rapid progress was impossible unless diverse human sources of knowledge and expertise were amassed under the conglomerate system of technology corporations. Backed financially by research institutes and laboratories, the individual scientist and inventor could contribute to national welfare more vigorously. Moreover, systematic work under such corporations brought more efficient interdisciplinary cooperation between employed engineers. In this process, time as well as energy could be saved through human networks. Thus the principle of hope underlying the 1920s and 1930s pulp SF also associated with American pragmatism, whereby intellectuals were, in the words of Richard Rorty, put "at the service of the productive class rather than the leisure class" (30). Here, theory served "as an aid to practice," which does not imply that practice was "a degradation of theory" (Rorty 30). In a similar fashion, by putting aside the skeptical view of knowledge and instead adopting hope, American pragmatism removed many of the barriers, in the Cartesian sense of the word, in the way of human progress (Rorty 34). Consequently, the American Dream looked for the better, if not for the best, things that were useful and simultaneously liberating (Rorty 27–28).

The tendency of the SF writers of the 1920s and 1930s to create new gadgets and represent them exultingly arises from a common practice among Americans in the early twentieth century. For example,

> Washington's 1919 Independence Day parade was highlighted by an overflight of twenty planes. During the 1920s, pilots who barnstormed across the United States found eager crowds awaiting their arrival. In 1924 a crowd of 200,000 turned out at Santa Monica to greet a group of military fliers returning from the first aerial circumnavigation of the world. The excitement over aviation climaxed in the tumultuous receptions held in Paris and New York to honor Charles Lindbergh's solo hop from New York to Paris in 1927 (only a quarter-century after the Wright Brothers coaxed their machine off the ground for twelve seconds, covering a mere one hundred twenty feet). (Nye 203)

Besides such celebratory demonstrations, the American 1920s and 1930s were witness to mass participation in fairs. The 1933 Chicago Century of Progress World's Fair, for instance, opened with this motto: "Science Finds—Industry Applies—Man Conforms." The fair generally aimed at strengthening the relationship between science and the public through the rhetorical stratagem that scientific research "discovered laws of nature that were then converted into technologies that were consumed by the nation's citizens" (Pursell 230).

Such national events significantly influenced SF writers such as Heinlein. The combination of the maverick and the corporate appears throughout Heinlein's oeuvre, from "Blowups Happen" (September 1940), where engineers work in the unbearable psychological stress of an atomic power plant, to "The Man Who Sold the Moon" (1950), where entrepreneur D. D. Harriman nourishes the dream of flying to the Moon and founds the company that provides the ship for the voyage. Indeed, Heinlein himself had been directly involved in a large-scale engineering experience. William H. Patterson, Jr., discusses the details of how in 1929 the *Lexington*—the largest and most advanced American naval ship, aboard which Heinlein served—undertook the herculean task of supplying the power of Tacoma for a month after the city's power grid had collapsed (17).

But Heinlein's engineering mind steered SF from the notion of merely technological and scientific engineering toward "social engineering," and that is where the influence of the maverick and corporate system was compounded by H. G. Wells' notion of employing technical progress for the higher purpose of social progress. Wells had visualized radically altered futures and highly improved alternate societies run by the Samurai, a group of scientific elite, in works such as *A Modern Utopia* (1905) and *The Open Conspiracy* (1928). Influenced by Wells' critical attitude, Heinlein's progressivist philosophy also sprang from the American liberal heritage, whereby the field of sociology was foregrounded by thinkers like William Graham Sumner (1840–1910) and Thorstein Veblen (1857–1929). This progressivism was still forceful before the outbreak of and well into World War II (1939–1945) as a method for social reform. Along this line, Robert Heinlein's *Beyond This Horizon* (1942) deploys eugenics and genetic engineering to control and ensure the society's biological and spiritual health. Another offshoot of this inspiration, which emphasized social engineering and sociology, was the speech Heinlein made in the third World Science Fiction Convention (1941) in Denver, "The Discovery of the Future," in which Heinlein elaborated on and developed the Wellsian notion of the social effects of technological change.

Added to these broad social trends was the influence of the scientific theories of the time, such as the n-dimensional space-time concepts and the free movement of consciousness through time postulated by Irish philosopher J. W. Dunne (1875–1949) in *Experiment with Time* (1927) and Russian mathematician P. D. Ouspensky (1887–1947) in *Tertium Organum* (1912). This cross-time motif, which made it possible for consciousness to break free from its space-time matrix and move into other times and spaces, appeared in Heinlein's "Elsewhen" (September 1941). Included in this list is also German mathematical physicist Lise Meitner (1878–1968), who had published her calculations about a very compact source capable of releasing gargantuan and unrestrained energy in a flash, which for Heinlein meant the possibility of atomic power and a good motif for "Blowups Happen" (1940). Heinlein's stories up to this point fit into his large scale project of Future History, but this project was curtailed when the U.S. entered the Second World War in 1941. This changed Heinlein's line of thought and fiction for the rest of his life.

II.

World War II brought a great change in American science fiction, putting an end to its golden era and directing it into other channels. First, many SF writers and artists were drafted for war. Second, the rationing of materials during the war years resulted in the shortage of paper, so most SF magazines folded. *Astounding* was an exception, since for one thing, its economic policy of paying high rates had elevated its literary standards and kept the best stable of talented writers. For another, *Astounding* had access to numerous channels for both absorbing writers and distributing its issues. This caused the magazine to survive the Depression and WWII, but even this magazine was to lose some of its greatest writers, such as Heinlein, whose last contributions were "Goldfish Bowl" (March 1942) and "Beyond This Horizon" (April and May 1942). Indeed, Heinlein in 1942 accepted "a civil service appointment as a mechanical engineer at the Naval Aircraft Factory" in Philadelphia (Patterson 360), and he spent the war in the Philadelphia Navy Yard with L. Sprague de Camp and Isaac Asimov, who both were engineers as well as science fictionists.

On the one hand, the war had negative effects on the life of science fiction and the different circles where SF was discussed, improved, and written, such as the SF writers' club in which Heinlein was an active member. The Mañana Literary Society was a niche where famous writers such as Henry Kuttner, C. L. Moore, L. Sprague de Camp, L. Ron Hubbard, Cleve Cartmill, Arthur K. Barnes, Leigh Brackett, and Jack Williamson had met to negotiate their stories and opinions, but after the Japanese attack on the Pearl Harbor and the U.S. entry into the war, this club was debilitated. On the other hand, the war had formative effects on the SF genre. One of the longstanding and forceful SF themes was Future War, and now technology advanced with a terrifying pace and was deployed in war. Indeed, the Second World War was the war of science: helicopters, jet planes, radar, guided missiles, rockets, and the nuclear bomb (Ashley 165), all of which provided further material for the stories published in magazines thriving in wartime.

The story of the war gave new thematic directions to science fiction, too. Most earlier American SF stories had rendered a glorious picture of war and had examined new technology in military terms. With the destructive effects of the new technologies visible in the real war, however, such a positive picture gradually faded, replaced by a horrifying and disillusioning scene. A good number of stories had predicted and discussed the possibility of the atomic bomb, even before the beginning of the Manhattan Project of 1941, and science-fiction predictions came true in 1945 in Hiroshima and Nagasaki, when the bombing of these two cities forced Japan to surrender, bringing World War II to an end. Heinlein himself had considered the use of atomic power as a solution to war as early as 1940 in "Blowups Happen" and "Solution Unsatisfactory" (May 1941).

Many previously active SF writers such as Heinlein were engaged, in one way or another, in war and could not make time to write stories any longer. To remedy this, the surviving magazines brought new writers such as A. E. van Vogt, Clifford D. Simak, Kuttner, Moore, and Fritz Leiber to the field. These writers treated science fiction not in the terms of the hardcore technology and physical heroes of their precursors, but gave it a mystical, transcendental, and psychological quality. It was in the mid-1940s that van Vogt's psi powers and Hubbard's Dianetics emerged. Such trends caused a shift from pre-war techno-centric to post-war and New Wave psycho-centric concerns in SF.

During the forties, anthologies for science fiction stories began to appear. This was a step toward securing SF a better reputation and a wider scope in American culture. As a case in point, an editor named Bronner asked Heinlein for permission to publish "Life-Line" and "'—And He Built a Crooked House—'," and then Donald Wollheim's anthology, *The Pocket Book of Science Fiction* (1943), also the first paperback SF anthology in the market (Patterson 372–73), published the latter story. Three years later, Groff Conklin's *The Best of Science Fiction* (1946) included Heinlein's "Solution Unsatisfactory" and "Blowups Happen." The publication of such anthologies had two advantages. First, these anthologies were read by a wider audience, even those who did not know much about science fiction. Second, SF anthologies brought science fiction out of the pulp magazines and offered it a reputable form to adults who never purchased pulp SF for the grudge they held against low-grade pulps in general. Thus, during the time Heinlein was not active as a writer, his stories were still anthologized, and paperback anthologies and hardcover book formats appeared during and after the war, making SF classics more endurable and popular. This was mainly undertaken by old SF fans and writers who returned from the war to resume their careers and take up their interests in science fiction where they had left off, as editors, writers, or readers. Thus, from 1945 to 1950, the glory of the pulps died away, and digest magazines and books began to replace them. This change in format was further urged by the rivalry between publication and other media, like radio, movies, and television. The latter media could attract public attention, so the magazines had to catch up, with publishers beginning to pay more attention to "fine art work, interesting articles, entertainment and service" (Reynolds 232).

III.

After World War II, America became the world superpower and the agent of the military machine. At this time, America seemingly enjoyed a culture of abundance, luxury, and victory, but there was a fear of the invasion of postwar peace by enemies such as the Soviet Union. The fear sprang from the suspicion that Russia soon would come to possess the atomic bomb and would be able either to use it as a threat against the US or to start another war. This fear was dilated by Wisconsin Senator Joseph McCarthy's politics and President Eisenhower's witch-hunting, which tracked the disloyal as well as the sympathizers of communism in the hubbub of what was called the Red Scare; if Roosevelt's New Deal had encouraged hard work, controlled working conditions, and effected restrictions, McCarthyism limited governmental interference in Americans' business affairs (Gray 519–21). In the meantime, war veterans, including Heinlein's colleagues, were back home with disillusioned and shattered hopes as witnesses to and participants in global bloodshed, viewing the war as a historical crisis. The war had brought them no comfort and even left some jobless and homeless. This was very much the case with some of Heinlein's colleagues, who took shelter in his house and set out writing and working on projects until they came into better living conditions that allowed them to leave Heinlein's place. The war had similar excruciating effects on Heinlein's second wife; she lost her brother-in-law in war and had to support her sister's family out of the income she received from overworking herself in the naval aircraft factory with her husband, which eventually brought her to a psychological breakdown and divorce from Heinlein only two years after World War II.

If the atomic bombs had put an end to World War II, they also were the starters of the Cold War between America and Russia and their respective allies. The postwar era, especially the late fifties and early sixties, is dubbed the Space Age, as the first Sputnik went into orbit in 1957. The long-cherished dream in the science fiction of the first decades of the twentieth century thus now had materialized, and SF writers' predictions had turned into tangible reality. As Brian Aldiss states, "the SF ghetto walls crumbled from outside," and the "term 'science fiction' increasingly became used as a sort of okay jargon term, meaning something futuristic, unlikely, and high-powered" (288).

Although the war and its aftermath hindered Heinlein's SF career for four years, when he resumed writing, he avoided the repetition of the past formulae by channeling his power into juvenile SF novels, scientific articles, and, less frequently, SF stories. His first successful postwar story, "The Green Hills of Earth," was published in *The Saturday Evening Post* in 1947, a landmark about which some of his friends boasted to John W. Campbell, Leo Marguiles, and Mort Weisinger (qtd. in Patterson 472–73), all editors who had rejected Heinlein's stories after the war. "'It's Great to Be Back!'" was also published by the *Post* in 1947. However, the stories he wrote were mostly rejected, partly because his themes had lost their novelty when his and many other writers' fictional plans for the advancement of technology and society already had materialized and partly because the slicks invested in younger writers with new novelties and motifs, novelties that Heinlein already had brought into the field before the war and did not wish to recapitulate. Thus, the flavor of the time demanded stories of a different type, such as psi powers and cybernetics, and a new and more liberal interest in the nuclear bomb when atomic stories no longer had to be censored or banned.

If Heinlein's stories no longer fit the demands of the postwar SF magazines, he won a thriving market in the juveniles by giving them a new slant. His novels numbered sixteen during 1947–59, including *Rocket Ship Galileo* (1947) and *Have Space Suit—Will Travel* (1958). The former was widely read by both adults and the juveniles (Sands and Frank 1), which indicates the new interest that American society, particularly the youth, started to show in rocketry, atomic science, and space travel once they became possible. Heinlein's atomics shook the juveniles out of their Motor Boys and

Tom Swift traditional motifs, whereby heroes were fashioned after Thomas Edison and Henry Ford (Eggeling and Nicholls 653). The new juveniles would imagine the individual rebel revolting against oppressive political and social *status quo*, using the rocket to travel to other planets or galaxies to give himself a new alternative. This was in line with the estrangement shown by a rebel culture shaping characters of mainstream literature in novels like J.D. Salinger's *Catcher in the Rye* (1951) and Jack Kerouac's *On the Road* (1957), where the hero stands out as a member of the Beat generation capable of nourishing countercultural ideas and overthrowing the present system. In SF juveniles, this rebellious attitude became facilitated by techno-science as a source not necessarily for mass destruction, like in Japan and Vietnam, but as a promise for a better future. Falling into this category, Heinlein's *Stranger in a Strange Land* represents Valentine Michael Smith as a hero, brought up on Mars, and now back on Earth with pacifist goals. Smith is the same American "lonely hero" in a "clash with conventional society," an "exile" who desires "to merge with older, deeper forms of community" and possibly give "them a new twist" (Gray 736–37).

The Red Scare also influenced the way Heinlein shaped some of his juveniles. On the one hand, America still had to beware of enemies, whether the Russians in real life or the Nazis of *Rocket Ship Galileo*. On the other hand, Heinlein mocked the fear of and intolerance toward the alien in *The Star Beast* (1954), which on a larger scale can be viewed as a critique of resistance to the new or the strange as a general trend in American sociopolitical life. The matriarchal and pacific Venerians of *Space Cadet*, the Martian roundhead Willis in *Red Planet* (1949), the Martian flat cats in *The Rolling Stones* (1952), and the Hesperian spider puppy in *Starman Jones* (1953) are other examples of Heinlein's attempt to break social hostility toward the Other.

The postwar era created a shocking lull in which thinkers could, in one way or another, contemplate the consequences of the former colonizing spirit as well as react to it in de-colonizing terms. Having witnessed what colonization could do to other nations, some— including to various, sometimes paradoxical degrees, Heinlein—

reacted against the colonization that many SF writers of the golden age had explicitly undertaken in their fiction, such as John Campbell's colonial agents flying all over the galaxy to establish outposts on diverse planets and terraform them for their own purposes, as in *The Mightiest Machine*. But sometimes such attempts just backfired, and fictional projects, like the terraforming of other planets or the reformation of human mind planned to replace the old imperialistic agendas, yielded results no less imperialistic. Thus, paradoxically, a sort of "Cold War American neo-imperialism" expressed itself in a simultaneous critique of "territorial colonialism" by establishing its locales in "inner space as a landscape colonized by social norms and unconscious psychological urges" (Higgins 228). Heinlein's *Stranger in a Strange Land* can be categorized among these paradoxical works because although it does not try to deterritorialize the outside human world, it introduces new mechanisms for homogenizing the human race by a Martian who, in a way, renovates colonization and fascism on a psychedelic level by trying to homogenize humans even as he elevates the powers of the mind.

A similar paradoxical trend of thought weaves through the fabric of Heinlein's later novels, which include his personal reactions to and suggestions for racial problems in the context of the 1960s and 1970s Civil Rights Movement. On the one hand, *Farnham's Freehold* (1964) reverses white political and hegemonic architectonics by sketching an America where blacks rule over whites who are slaves; in this alternate world, kidnapping and raping white women, and castrating and eating white men are performed by triumphant blacks. On the other hand, American Southerners in *The Moon Is a Harsh Mistress* (1966) still punish miscegenation as a crime. Heinlein's paradoxical treatment of racial issues in different novels reflects his critique of and rebellion against the real status quo as well as his dream for a utopian society where such biases no longer exist. Thus, Heinlein's paradox depends on both realistic and idealistic motives. He lived during the time when Rosa Parks refused to give her seat to a white man on the bus. He also lived when Martin Luther King and Malcolm X were assassinated for their emancipatory and charismatic insurrections against white hegemony.

Indeed, Robert A. Heinlein's personality took shape in the socio-historical context of America in the twentieth century, when the discourse of modernism, fast-paced technological and scientific advancement, the two world wars, the Cold War, and the Civil Rights Movement all directed his talents as he evolved as a writer of science fiction stories, juvenile novels, and occasionally even criticism. Heinlein's works are still published and read because his sharp mind recorded the reality of the American life as a complete gestalt and reworked it in possible fantastic worlds that Americans needed to occupy mentally if they wished to know themselves better. Heinlein lived in a century when American literature was struggling for new literary forms and when so many literary schools abounded: realism and naturalism, formalism, confessionals, San Francisco Renaissance, New York School, Beat Generation, postmodernism, etc. In this melting pot of forms, science fiction was born and grew in the hands of writers like Heinlein and later became an established genre of American literature. Thus, if the twentieth-century American historical and social context directed Heinlein toward his destiny, Heinlein, too, shaped the history of American science fiction.

Works Cited

Aldiss, Brian W. *Trillion Year Spree: The History of Science Fiction*. London: Paladin, 1988. E-book.

Ashley, Mike. *The Time Machines: The Story of the Science-Fiction Pulp Magazines from the Beginning to 1950*. Liverpool: Liverpool U P, 2000. E-book.

Bleiler, E. Franklin & Richard Bleiler. "Preface." *Science-Fiction: The Gernsback Years*. Kent, OH: Kent State U P, 1998. vii–viii. E-book.

Eggeling, John & Peter Nicholls. "Juvenile Series." *The Encyclopedia of Science Fiction*. Ed. John Clute and Peter Nicholls. New York: St. Martin's, 1995. 653–54.

Gernsback, Hugo. "A New Sort of Magazine." Editorial. *Amazing Stories* April 1926: 3. E-book.

Gray, Richard. *The History of American Literature*. Oxford: Wiley-Blackwell, 2012. E-book.

Higgins, David M. "Psychic Decolonization in 1960s Science Fiction." *Science Fiction Studies* 40 (2013): 228–245.

Luckhurst, Roger. *Science Fiction*. London: Polity, 2005.

Mann, George. *The Mammoth Encyclopedia of Science Fiction*. London: Robinson, 2001. E-book.

Nye, David E. *American Technological Sublime*. New Baskerville: MIT P, 1994.

Patterson, William H., Jr. *Robert A. Heinlein: In Dialogue with His Century, Vol. 1: Learning Curve, 1907–1948*. New York: Tor, 2010. EPUB.

Pursell, Carroll. *The Machine in America: A Social History of Technology*. Baltimore: John Hopkins U P, 2007. E-book.

Reynolds, Quentin. *The Fiction Factory*. New York: Random, 1955.

Rorty, Richard. *Philosophy and Social Hope*. London: Penguin, 1999. E-book.

Sands, Karen & Marietta Frank. *Back in the Spaceship Again: Juvenile Science Fiction Series Since 1945*. Westport, CT: Greenwood, 1999. E-book.

Robert A. Heinlein: Critical Reception_____

Donald M. Hassler

> As for those agitators, I wish they would go the whole way
> and emasculate themselves.
> (Paul, Galatians 5:12)

> ...losing track...and wandering off into unknown places
> where he could not find his way back.
> (Heinlein, *Stranger in a Strange Land,* xv)

The reputation of a great writer and the placement of that writer in his or her proper orbit of the literary firmament are always collaborative and evolving enterprises. Further, writers themselves may be at their best as writers when they are proud, independent thinkers who resist placement. Robert A. Heinlein manifests these characteristics. He seemed to despise the categorization and even commentary of critics and members of the literary establishment. His work changed over a long writing career. He is, in fact, a wonderful prototype for and representative of the writer who "doth protest too much," the writer in spite of himself. Also, his most successful and memorable characters and situations seem, to most of us, to be transparent images of himself. So he needs the sort of analysis and work that the scholar, the critic, and the careful reader is able to bring. Not only is he a writer's writer, for whom many of his fellow SF writers step out of storytelling mode in order to offer critical praise, as my narrative below will show, but he also is, in spite of himself, wonderful fodder for the academic and theory mills. Some of his work is strange, practical, nearly non-intellectual. Heinlein presents himself always as a craftsman and an individualist, generally impatient with theory and system. One of the early academic critics that Heinlein lashes out at was David Samuelson, who has done some fine commentary on his work. In a 1979 article on *Stranger in a Strange Land*, which appeared in Salem Press' *Survey of Science Fiction Literature*, Samuelson uses the label "solipsist" to explain

Heinlein's remarkable ability as a writer to identify with his point-of-view characters and to flesh them out in his imagination and for his readers (2195–200). The characters, in fact, capture most of the facets of Heinlein the Man.

The monstrously egocentric and romantic position that Heinlein takes renders him very combative and defensive about the critical and scholarly reception that he enjoyed in his lifetime and that has only continued to expand exponentially after his 1988 death. The fans loved his work at first. The key editor and shaper at *Astounding Science-Fiction*, John W. Campbell, Jr., received and accepted him just as he did with Asimov and others. He suggested ideas to Heinlein and helped the writer shape his massive scheme of Future History, just as he had done with Asimov on the Foundation stories. Later, when Alexei Panshin and the young academics Samuelson and Thomas D. Clareson began to receive his work as both fan commentators and as sophisticated academic critics, Heinlein's notorious peevishness emerged.

But he could not just make them all go away as the Man from Mars, his wonderful and solipsistic creation in *Stranger in a Strange Land*, was able to do. Despite all of its flaws as a literary biography, one would think that the new authorized two-volume biography of Heinlein by William H. Patterson, Jr., would have included analyses of the work (this essay discusses Patterson more fully below). However, it does detail the extent of Heinlein's combativeness against reception: Panshin is one of the first to take fire from the Man himself, then Clareson, then Samuelson (271ff and 369 of volume II). In fact, Heinlein is so cocksure of the writing career that he has forged for himself that he invites the rather condescending reception early on from the smart critics and scholars that allow Samuelson to use the label "solipsist." Further, his posthumous "grumbles" have not helped to soften this characterization of Heinlein, and the indignant defensiveness got encouragement from his third wife, Virginia, who edited his *Grumbles from the Grave*. But ultimately, the reception, as in any strong family romance, is to accept the Man as father figure with all of his combative orneriness. That acceptance and the mostly favorable critical reputation that Heinlein earned is the theme of this essay, not the Freudian resonance in a writer biography, although the latter always haunts the edges in what follows.

Clearly, the image of "family" figures throughout Heinlein's fiction itself from the Lazarus Long family of the early Future Histories to the end of his career, with the complex and extended family becoming particularly prominent as an image in the two great novels from the sixties, *Stranger in a Strange Land* and *The Moon Is a Harsh Mistress*. Family connections are so dominated by the strong father himself, however, that the following explicit reaction to an acceptance of the father as credited to the young Michael Moorcock must be mentioned. As Rob Latham notes in an essay on the New Wave movement, Moorcock "rejected Heinlein...because he was 'reactionary,' an evil father-figure to be arraigned and condemned" (207). But the much earlier essay by Samuelson that is mostly about the early Future History scheme that Campbell had helped Heinlein to nurture in the early stories is nicely comprehensive on the "father," and Samuelson does acknowledge that his interpretation of solipsism for the strong father/leader had been posited originally in Panshin's fannish study of the previous year. In fact, this emergence around 1975—roughly the same moment as Moorcock's New Wave—of the prolific fannish writer and critic Panshin and of Samuelson, a young professor with a Ph.D. in literature, works well in tandem both to deeply analyze Heinlein's work and to annoy him, as Patterson documents.

Solipsism and "wolfishness," Panshin's term in his book, are two very different words for the same thing: a libertarian impatience with having one's range to roam restricted in any way. No long-lived solipsist or libertarian individualist, such as the enormously resourceful Heinlein creation Lazarus Long, wants to be pigeon-holed in some academic or fan theory, and so one can see why this analysis and fannish praise—actually one would think that Heinlein as libertarian might secretly enjoy being likened to a wolf—later vindicated by the academic Samuelson would infuriate the writer himself. Nevertheless, both studies are very helpful, and both discover an effective unity across all of Heinlein's fiction, from the early Future History to the several huge and Hugo-winning novels of the sixties. Samuelson writes beautifully, "The sense of a legend in the making haunts every scene, most of them handled with wit and practical realism..." (36). Clareson originally had published the Samuelson essay in his collection *Voices of the Future,* and the text cited here is from the reprint of the essay, which appeared in the 1978 volume on Heinlein, edited by Olander and Greenberg. The Heinlein volume was part of the short-lived series, Writers of the 21st Century, of which only six volumes were published.

So not only is Heinlein himself at times "peevish" about commentary on his work, but the solid academic reception for the literature of science fiction also was hesitant to gather momentum. And even though his reception in an early and solid collection of essays was among the few published as part of the Writers of the 21st Century series—the others were Asimov, Clarke, Bradbury, Le Guin, and Dick—Heinlein often has been omitted from the most academic discussions of the genre since 1978. David Seed does mention him in his introduction to the recent prestigious collection of essays that includes Latham's piece on the New Wave: "SF's centrality [to modern thought] was echoed by Robert Heinlein...when he declared: 'It is the only fictional medium capable of interpreting the changing, head-long rush of modern life. Speculative fiction is the main stream of fiction'" (2). In a very large volume of quality academic work, however, Seed does not include one essay devoted to Heinlein. His critical reception has been upstaged, in part, by others such as Kim Stanley Robinson and Iain Banks in the Seed volume. In the Olander and Greenberg collection from a quarter century earlier, Ivor Rogers does write about Heinlein's non-fiction comments on the genre and includes the same reference to the "speculative fiction" boast that Seed uses. Rogers writes, "Heinlein has written several articles about science fiction. The most important of these writings is his 'Science Fiction: Its Nature, Faults, and Virtues'" (224). Another important nonfiction piece of his, in my opinion, is the lead review he published in *The Saturday Review of Literature* in December 1949.

Thus with all that Heinlein has to say about the genre itself in nonfiction work that he published, his omission from some highly-sophisticated genre discussions and, in particular, from the list of Pilgrim Award winners seem worth mentioning as indicative not only of maturity in the field of academic study of science fiction but also of Heinlein's own peevishness and refusal to court popularity in any way that might even seem to violate his individualism and his impatience with theory. Pilgrim winners are chosen annually by the Science Fiction Research Association, and the list to date includes not only scholars but also writers who have commented significantly in their nonfiction work, such as Samuel R. Delany and Joanna Russ. One further indication of the theoretical aspirations in the academic community as it has evolved to study science fiction during the same time period that Heinlein's writing career flourished comes from another important essay in the Seed volume, wherein Istvan Csicsery-Ronay, Jr., works to cover the overall topic of "Science Fiction Criticism": "Disciplinary boundaries were weakened by the appearance of metatheoretical schools of thought, each of which seemed to aspire to a Grand Unified Theory of human culture on its own terms" (51).

Two fictional father figures in Heinlein, both in complex family relationships, may represent this shifting nature of his reception or reputation within the separate communities or "families" of the academic world and of the fannish world. Both Jubal Harshaw, the putative father figure of the Man from Mars, and Prof in *The Moon Is a Harsh Mistress* are harsh and blunt individualists who tend to alienate their communities and family groups. Further, both have strong values with little patience for talkative prevaricators. Prof explicitly lashes out several times at advocates of garrulous theories, such as the broad aspirations voiced in the quote above by Csicsery-Ronay. He calls such easy talkers "yammerheads" (Heinlein, *Moon* 208–209, 299). At the conclusion of this essay, I will describe the attention given recently by another of our extremely theory-oriented academic critics to the work of Heinlein, and this will seem to show how his work can be received well at high levels of theory—even if that reception may include a warning against heinous philosophic ideas.

Generally and up until recently, though, Heinlein's chances for favorable reception were better with fans than with the academic critics. The fan family or community of his got a lashing now and then, also; several rather harsh letters to fans from Heinlein stand out in *Grumbles from the Grave* (see 279ff). But continually, science fiction fans embraced him as one of their own. Four of his novels won Hugo Awards, voted for by the fans: *Double Star, Starship Troopers, Stranger in a Strange Land,* and *The Moon Is a Harsh Mistress.* Many of his other works were nominated for both Hugo Awards and Nebula Awards. (The most accurate tabulations for these numerous fan awards and awards from the Science Fiction Writers of America may be found in the later editions of *Anatomy of Wonder* by Neil Barron.) Also, Heinlein was the first writer to be named a Grand Master, the highest recognition to be bestowed by the Science Fiction Writers of America. This honor came in 1974.

The fiction writers themselves, most of whom came out of fandom, were especially appreciative in their reception of his work. Frederik Pohl and James Gunn both published extensive praise of Heinlein as a pioneer who had opened new markets and new possibilities for the writing and marketing of science fiction. Samuel Delany writes in a richly-phrased "Afterword" to *Glory Road* that Heinlein's work taught him how to plot and to expand his own fiction. Incidentally, all three of these important writers, though clearly individualists in their own ways, managed to be recognized for their non-fiction commentary on the genre by the Pilgrim Award that I mention above. But Delany in the *Glory Road* piece, comments on the "writerliness" that he sees in Heinlein "the writerly concerns and patterns that…allow us to appreciate fully what is deeply serious in the dozen 'juvenile' novels, what is profoundly inventive in some of his more ephemeral earlier works, or what is patently authentic in the more recent didactic ones" (319).

So even though the high theorizing of the academics may conclude that the "didacticism" is a little thin, Heinlein's respect among his fellow writers was mostly solid. A major exception is the critical opinion of Brian W. Aldiss, also a Pilgrim Award winner, which lines up with the criticism of Michael Moorcock mentioned above. Both writers speak from England, of course, and both are part of the New Wave. But the opinion of Aldiss in his *Billion Year Spree* seems to be a particularly harsh extension of what Panshin and Samuelson had said about "wolfishness" in Heinlein. The Aldiss analysis concludes, "[I]n the complex universe of [Heinlein's] own mind, his ideas of liberty boil down to what a man can grasp for himself" (271). This may be a bias of "national literatures"—strange in our current globalism. The fascist Hitler that we know did envy the frontier open-endedness possible in America, and the deconstructive complexity that Csicsery-Ronay, Jr., highlights above may be European in its focus. His summation of "...H. Bruce Franklin's Marxist critical biography of Robert Heinlein (1980), which accused Campbellian SF of complicity with US imperialism" expresses major fatigue by the academic theorists with twentieth-century war and with "frontier" imperialism just when Heinlein's fiction was stepping up to it (51). I myself wrestle with this semi-despair and fatigue in a recent essay on war and science fiction in the long twentieth century, listed among all this good work on and by Heinlein; but the mention of Bruce Franklin here, also a Pilgrim Award winner, leads to the consideration of the several book-length studies that constitute a part of the critical reception of the great man.

Delany observes, along with his own "Afterword" remarks above, that the Franklin book is the best book-length study of Heinlein by the end of the decade of the seventies at least. Franklin's book is a comprehensive treatment of all of the fiction up until about a decade prior to Heinlein's death. It is highly ideologic and, hence theoretic, and does fault the characterization and action from the point of view of Marxist ideology—no sense of the people, no feel for real progress in history ruled by material pressures. The accusation of complicity with a reactionary politics coincides with Heinlein's own fear that his readers, and especially the intellectuals, would misread him: they are all "yammerheads" and do not understand the true nature of leadership, resourcefulness, change, and action in his view. Just prior to Franklin's highly ideologic reading, George Slusser, once again an academic Pilgrim, had published two good, short books on Heinlein. These two are called the best "philosophic" treatment of Heinlein's vision of man by Willis E. McNelly (590). Slusser images, also, the "Americanism" in Heinlein and what he calls "classic" individualism and practical resourcefulness. But of the later fictions Slusser expresses some disappointment because of Heinlein's movement away from action and toward much more of what Prof mocks as mere "talk, talk." So in these several book-length studies of the work, there is room for some vicious attack by the critics. As I have shown, Heinlein himself "grumbles" and pushes back against any negative criticism, especially he seems to feel, like Prof, that his critics are wasting time as "yammerheads." I came across just as I was into this essay a fine declaration about writers and their critics. Reviewing a collection of essays by Renata Adler, Dwight Garner evokes Saul Bellow as follows: "A man should be able to hear, and to bear…the worst that could be said of him" (C26). Apparently, Heinlein had trouble in this area.

After the two most condescending attacks above and after Aldiss, Leon Stover produced in the Twayne United States Authors series the best and most sympathetic critical book that has been written on Heinlein to date, in my opinion. It came out nearly concurrent with Heinlein's death, and so only his wife Virginia was able to react. She was favorably enough impressed with Stover to consider him for a time as the authorized biographer for her famous husband, but then finally she selected Patterson for that work. One recent reviewer of the two-volume Patterson biography, Carol McQuirk, writes on that choice that Stover "was *not fact checking with her*" enough (156; italics McQuirk's). Nevertheless, Stover's Twayne study is a fine critical reception of all of the work. His long discussion in chapter eight of Heinlein's "Calvinism" is provocative and helpful. Stover links it not only back to Calvin himself, but also to Heinlein's Missouri upbringing, with nice parallels to Mark Twain's own Calvinism. The authorized biography mentioned above that was complete in its massive two volumes just in 2014 indicates the receptive market for more and more material on Heinlein. It does not offer much literary analysis, and the McQuirk review complains severely about that intellectual thinness. Similarly, Joe Sanders has a full book-length expansion of the original enthusiasm that Thomas D. Clareson had had to write a book on the very important Heinlein as he saw him. Clareson was an early "dean" of the academic work on science fiction, and he died just as he was getting his Heinlein project underway. The Sanders completion of the book is very useful, but mostly just detailed descriptions of all the work.

I believe that much more probing literary analysis can be done on much of Heinlein's work, and my colleague Clyde Wilcox and I had the good fortune to be able to publish three solid essays in our two collections on politics and science fiction. Everett Dolman writes a fine explanation and defense of *Starship Troopers*, arguing that it is a much deeper book than mere fascist militarism. His distinctions are carefully grounded in the theory of militarism, as it relates to both fascism and history. In his long essay that links *The Moon Is a Harsh Mistress* to novels by Le Guin and by Delany, Neil Easterbrook is very good on the need any Heinlein hero has to work with a "clean deck of cards"—the odds are stacked against heroic action. Easterbrook is good also on the need for the "joke"—the Man from Mars had learned an appreciation for humor and the comic as one of the last stages in his development—and the need now and then for the Heinlein hero "to light out for the territory." Easterbrook's essay is deep, mild in its condescension toward the less theoretic Heinlein over against Le Guin and Delany, and very useful as practical criticism. Then Darko Suvin at great length returns to the Franklin argument about complicity with imperialism and the ideologic threat Heinlein poses to Marxist doctrine. As we read Suvin, we see that Heinlein's challenge in thought is presented as no simplistic gesture. Suvin is able to show, in his usual long-winded discussion, how seriously the position of what he now labels "Fordism"—I think that coinage is excellent, since Henry Ford and Heinlein share many similar American/frontier traits—can be taken even when it is by no means acceptable as a political position. Just as the writer Delany, who is a self-proclaimed if semi-Marxist, so the highly-esteemed theorist Suvin, who is a Marxist, also can admire the artistry and craft in Heinlein, even as it promotes what may seem to them wrong ideas. In addition to the critical books,

Heinlein's papers are collected by several university libraries, and a good bit of bibliographic work has been done across his long career. All this work can be found listed in the Burgess book on reference materials, and the extent of it is a further indication of the high level of Heinlein's critical reception.

Finally, Heinlein's message and his effectiveness as the creator of "legends," as Samuelson said originally at the head of this essay, continues to receive good critical comment and, often, from places that the Man himself might prefer. He did not want to speak only to the science fiction community nor only to the academic community. One of the blurbs on the dust jacket of my Tor edition of *The Moon Is a Harsh Mistress* is by the writer of thrillers and highly-marketable war novels Tom Clancy: "We proceed down a path marked by his ideas." I think it is significant that some of the newest work published on Heinlein are two books self-published by a devoted fan, Edward M. Wysocki, Jr. Both deal with the Second World War and with the resourcefulness and action of American naval technology as seen with a Heinlein involvement and from a Heinlein perspective. The graduate of Annapolis and the loyal American patriot probably would have grumbled some if he had had the opportunity to learn of this work on him, but, in my reading, I think he would have liked Wysocki's work. It announces a kind of American belief system that even his strongest detractors from Aldiss to Franklin to Suvin must admire as heroic. Heinlein with all of his Calvinist upbringing never would have wanted to have his work associated with the strong writing of Saint Paul, but amidst all the grumbling, I think there is a similar tough-mindedness. He often conveys a message that moves beyond the despair of deconstruction, and this renewed frontier optimism has inspired a healthy reception among his readers. Heinlein, in spite of himself, would be pleased.

Works Cited

Aldiss, Brian W. *Billion Year Spree*. New York: Doubleday, 1973.

Barron, Neil, ed. *Anatomy of Wonder*. 3rd ed. New York: Bowker, 1987.

Burgess, Michael. *Reference Guide to Science Fiction, Fantasy, and Horror.* Englewood, CO: Libraries Unlimited, 1992.

Clareson, Thomas D., ed. *Voices for the Future.* Bowling Green U Popular P, 1976.

_____ & Joe Sanders. *The Heritage of Heinlein: A Critical Reading of the Fiction.* Jefferson, NC: McFarland, 2014. Critical Explorations in Science Fiction and Fantasy 42.

Csicsery-Ronay, Istvan, Jr. "Science Fiction Criticism." *Companion to Science Fiction.* Ed. David Seed. London: Blackwell, 2005. 43–59.

Delany, Samuel R. "Afterword." *Glory Road.* By Robert A. Heinlein. New York: Tor, 2004. 309–19.

Dolman, Everett Carl. "Military, Democracy, and the State in Robert A. Heinlein's *Starship Troopers.*" *Political Science Fiction.* Ed. Donald M. Hassler & Clyde Wilcox. Columbia, SC: U of South Carolina P, 1997. 196–213.

Easterbrook, Neil. "State, Heterotopia: The Political Imagination in Heinlein, Le Guin, and Delany." *Political Science Fiction.* Ed. Donald M. Hassler & Clyde Wilcox. Columbia, SC: U of South Carolina P, 1997. 43–75.

Franklin, H. Bruce. *Robert A. Heinlein: America as Science Fiction.* New York: Oxford UP, 1980. Science-Fiction Writers Ser.

Garner, Dwight. "Writing with Intent." *New York Times* 24 Apr. 2015: C 21, 26.

Gunn, James. "Introduction." *Stranger in a Strange Land.* By Robert A. Heinlein. Norwalk, CT: Easton, 1989. 1–6.

Hassler, Donald M. "The Tangled Bank of Science Fiction and War in the Long Twentieth Century." *The New York Review of Science Fiction* Jun. 2014: 27–31.

Heinlein, Robert A. *The Moon Is a Harsh Mistress.* New York: Putnam, 1966.

_____. "Baedecker of the Solar System." *The Saturday Review of Literature* 24 Dec. 1949.

Heinlein, Virginia, ed. *Grumbles from the Grave.* New York: Del Rey, 1990.

Latham, Rob. "The New Wave." *A Companion to Science Fiction.* Ed. David Seed. London: Blackwell, 2005. 202–16.

McNelly, Willis E. "*Double Star* by Robert A. Heinlein." *Survey of Science Fiction Literature*, Vol. 2. Ed. Frank Magill. Englewood Cliffs, NJ: Salem, 1979. 587–90.

McGuirk, Carol. "God in a Yellow Bathrobe." *Science Fiction Studies 42* (Mar. 2015): 151–157.

Panshin, Alexei. *Heinlein in Dimension.* Chicago: Advent, 1968.

Patterson, William H., Jr. *Robert A. Heinlein: In Dialogue with His Century, Vol. 1: Learning Curve, 1907–1948.* New York: Tor, 2010.

_____. *Robert A. Heinlein: In Dialogue with His Century, Vol. 2: The Man Who Learned Better, 1948–1988.* New York: Tor, 2014.

Pohl, Frederik. "Foreword." *The Heritage of Heinlein: A Critical Reading of the Fiction.* By Thomas D. Clareson & Joe Sanders. Critical Explorations in Science Fiction and Fantasy 42. Jefferson, NC: McFarland, 2014. 1–10.

Rogers, Ivor A. "Robert Heinlein: Folklorist of Outer Space." *Robert A. Heinlein.* Eds. Joseph D. Olander & Martin Harry Greenberg. Writers of the 21st Century Ser. New York: Taplinger, 1978. 222–39.

Samuelson, David N. "*Stranger in a Strange Land* by Robert A. Heinlein." *Survey of Science Fiction Literature.* Vol. 5. Ed. Frank Magill. Englewood Cliffs, NJ: Salem, 1979. 2195–2200.

_____. "Frontiers of the Future: Heinlein's Future History Stories." *Robert A. Heinlein.* Ed. Joseph D. Olander & Martin Harry Greenberg. Writers of the 21st Century Ser. New York: Taplinger, 1978. 32–63.

Seed, David. "Introduction." *A Companion to Science Fiction.* London: Blackwell, 2005. 1–7.

Slusser, George. *The Classic Years of Robert A. Heinlein.* Milford Series, Popular Writers of Today 11. San Bernardino, CA: Borgo, 1977.

_____. *Robert A. Heinlein: Stranger in His Own Land.* San Bernardino, CA: Borgo, 1976.

Stover, Leon. *Robert A. Heinlein.* Twayne's United States Authors Ser. 522. New York: Twayne, 1987.

Suvin, Darko. "Of *Starship Troopers* and Refusniks: War and Militarism in U.S. Science Fiction: Part I (Fordism)." *New Boundaries in Political Science Fiction.* Ed. Donald M. Hassler & Clyde Wilcox. Columbia, SC: U of South Carolina P, 2008. 115–44.

Wysocki, Edward M., Jr. *The Great Heinlein Mystery: Science Fiction, Innovation and Naval Technology.* Wysocki Publisher, CreateSpace, 2012.

_____. *An Astounding War: Science Fiction and World War II.* Wysocki Publisher, CreateSpace, 2015.

Reading the Man in the Moon: An Intersectional Analysis of Robert A. Heinlein's *The Moon Is a Harsh Mistress*

Robin Anne Reid

Intersectional theory originated in work by Kimberlé Crenshaw and other womanists and Black feminists during the 1970s and 1980s. Their work criticized racism in the American feminist movement and sexism in the Civil Rights movement of the 1960s–1970s (Crenshaw, McCall). Today, intersectionality is associated primarily with social sciences scholarship, using a variety of methodologies (Winker & Degele), but some humanities scholars are using it as well. Methodology means specific ways of framing research questions and gathering evidence, or data. Social science scholars tend to use empirical methods such as surveys or interviews, which ask people for information that is then analyzed, while humanities scholars tend towards analyzing texts. Despite different methodologies, scholars using intersectional approaches focus on the intersections, or the relationships, between those categories of identities that are grouped as race, gender, sexual orientation, nationality, and class, instead of focusing only on a single category. In this essay, I will be applying an intersectional approach to Robert A. Heinlein's 1966 novel to analyze intersections between nationality and gender and between race and gender.

H. Bruce Franklin, in *Robert A. Heinlein: America as Science Fiction* (1980), analyzes how Heinlein's fiction engages with social and political issues, including feminist and Civil Rights movements. In his fourth chapter, "A Voice of the 1960s," Franklin analyzes how the four novels published that decade engage with liberation movements: the counterculture youth, including hippie, movement (*Stranger in A Strange Land* [1961]); the Feminist movement (*Podkayne of Mars* [1963]); the anti-war and Free Speech movement (*Glory Road* [1963]); and the anti-nuclear and survivalist movements as well as white resistance to the Civil Rights movement (*Farnham's*

Freehold [1964]). Unlike some critics, Franklin does not argue that Heinlein's work takes a single, easily identified, political position, only that his novels are important because of the extent to which they engage in dialogue with the various challenges to authority, imperialism, and power by various liberation movements of the time. The last novel of the decade, *The Moon Is a Harsh Mistress* (1966), focuses on the successful revolution of a penal colony on the Moon against a unified world government, complete with allusions to historical revolutions—the American, French, and Russian—and references to Lenin (Franklin 164–65).

Differences in how political themes are presented in Heinlein's work over multiple decades is one reason for so much disagreement about the quality and meaning of Heinlein's work. The disagreement on the question of the relative quality of Heinlein's earlier or later work is analyzed by Robert James and William H. Patterson, Jr. (2006), who argue that scholarship on Heinlein's work was influenced by Alexei Panshin's *Heinlein in Dimension* (1968), the first book-length work of criticism on Heinlein. Panshin argues that Heinlein's work became worse over time, falling from his greatest artistic success of 1947–1958 to the supposedly lower-quality work published from 1959–1967. To Panshin, the later novels suppress character and story to authorial lecturing "about the morality of sex, religion, war and politics," with a change in content from scientific and technological facts to presenting Heinlein's opinions as facts (89). Other scholars, however, disagree with Panshin, arguing for the quality of Heinlein's work from the 1960s onward and against the claim that Heinlein's simplistically presents his personal views: Elizabeth Ann Hull and Robert Gorsch.

In 1979, Hull, in "Justifying the Ways of Man to God," considers the historical and cultural importance of the genre of published sermons and didactic fiction in the United States as the context for her "radical suggestion that, contrary to the most widely accepted critical theories, the Heinlein addict reads his work, *not in spite* of the sermons Heinlein crafts, but actually *for* the pleasure of the challenge of considering the moral and political questions" (38). In "The Golden Age of Heinlein" (2006), Gorsch argues that the novels of the late 1950s and 1960s, including *Moon*, are Heinlein's best, his "Golden Age." Gorsch's use of the phrase "Golden Age" is important because many science fiction critics claim that the "Golden Age" of science fiction genre was the 1950s, with Heinlein being one of the authors most identified with that period (Silverberg). Gorsch disagrees with Panshin's view of Heinlein's "lectures" and sees Heinlein as not "[forcing] options down the readers' throats... [but forcing] questions and issues into readers' minds," with the result that his novels are about ideas, specifically ideas relating to "'sex, religion, war, and politics,'—traditionally topics excluded from the Anglo-American dinner table" (50).

James and Patterson use a different approach to challenge Panshin's arguments. They analyze the first novel-length work that Heinlein wrote during the late 1930s, *For Us, The Living: A Comedy of Customs*. Discovered by Robert James, this novel was published for the first time in 2003 (Rule). By pointing to similarities between this first novel and Heinlein's later work, James and Patterson conclude that Heinlein was already "in 1938 engaged with specific pedagogical problems and a complex set of radical, social ideas," which "[came] roaring into foreground in the novels of the 1960s and onward," when it became possible to write more openly about these radical ideas (15). James and Patterson make a strong case for re-thinking earlier interpretations of Heinlein's work in the context of his first novel, arguing that the work needs to be understood as part of a "naturally dialogic process" rather than following a linear rise and fall. The process involved early attempts to gain freedom in his writing during his early days, when topics such as racism and sexism were excluded from the genre of science fiction, as well as the open engagement with the topics in later novels (James & Patterson 15–18).

One way to participate in this rethinking of how to interpret Heinlein's work is to apply a critical lens that has not been widely used in previous scholarship, a lens created by women of color who brought new perspectives and different ways of thinking about racism and sexism to political and cultural debates of the twentieth century. Part of these debates involve analyzing the extent to which popular culture, such as science fiction, draws upon the political issues and language of the period in which it was written, as Franklin does so well. My analysis will focus on aspects of the novel that I call "intersectional interstices." The term "interstices," as defined by its first entry in the *Oxford English Dictionary*, means "(1 a): An intervening space (usually, empty); *esp.* a relatively small or narrow space, between things or the parts of a body (freq. in *pl.*, the minute spaces between the ultimate parts of matter); a narrow opening, chink, or crevice." An intersectional interstice, then, means a small part of the novel—sometimes no more than a phrase, or a few lines of dialogue—that shows the intersections between two categories that exist in the novel's construction of its characters' identities. The categories of identity I focus on are nationality and gender, and race and gender.

These moments are related to ways in which the novel's language, primarily but not entirely that of Mannie, the first-person narrator, attempts but is unable to convey "intercategorical complexity" in regard to nationality, gender, and race. Intercategorical complexity is the idea that human beings' social lives and cultural identities are more complex and contradictory than the linguistic categories that exist for "gender" or "race" (McCall 1773). Since some of the linguistic conventions concerning the language of identity in the United States culture and in the genre of American science fiction were being challenged during the 1960s, I would argue that these intersectional interstices are further evidence of how Heinlein was engaging with the questions that, as Gorsch points out, were excluded from "the Anglo-American dinner table" in previous decades (50). However, I also would argue, as Diane Parkin-Speer does in "Almost a Feminist: Robert A. Heinlein" (1995), that the intersectional interstices of *Moon* show a society in which "equality and other positive aspects of women's lives are patchy and inconsistent" (119), an inconsistency which may be one reason there is still disagreement about the novel. Arguably, the extent to which readers and critics are still debating the ideas raised in Heinlein's work more than forty years after *The Moon Is a Harsh Mistress* was published is proof of the importance of his work to American literature, in part because of the extent to which it shows the complex and shifting definitions of what "American" means.

The Gendered Rhetoric of Nationality

Two categories in tension in the novel are the concept of "country" as an individual political and geographical unit with its own national sovereignty and the concept of a united world government. A good deal of the scholarship on Heinlein's work, including but not limited to discussions of *Moon*, discuss these political themes. Donna Glee Williams (1994) and Neil Easterbrook (1997) analyze similarities and differences between Heinlein's and Ursula K. Le Guin's explorations of anarchy as a possible political system in a colony established on a planet's moon. Rafeeq O. McGiveron (1999) and Jason Bourget (2008) analyze how biological determinism—the idea that there is a genetic and sex-based component to human behavior—connects to political systems in Heinlein's work, with Bourget focusing primarily on the relationship between biological determinism and libertarianism and McGiveron analyzing different ways in which Heinlein explores the idea of "transnational government" in different novels.

The concept of a transnational, or single world, government has been the subject of debate in the United States since the founding of the United Nations after World War II, and *Moon* is one of a number of science fiction novels set in a future with a world government. McGiveron characterizes the world government in Moon as one of Heinlein's negative examples of a transnational government. When the Federated Nations (F.N.) refuse to recognize the independence of the Lunar colonies, the revolutionary strategy is designed to split the global unity of the F.N. by bombing important national locations and offering to halt the bombing to any individual nation that recognizes the Loonies as a sovereign political entity, a country. Chad, the first to recognize the Lunar nation—primarily because of bribes from Stuart LaJoie—is not bombed. When the Chairman of the F.N. Committee offers Mannie the chance to become "Protector Pro Tem," one of his arguments to persuade Mannie to betray his fellow revolutionaries is that the offer is a chance to be "a practical man with your country's best interests at heart....[who would be] *a real* patriot—not some phony hero who gets himself killed in a lost cause" (269).

In the interstices of the major plotline concerning the world government's conflict with the Luna colonies are two small inconsistent aspects. The first is how the novel obscures the existence of the United States of America, and the second is how the equivalent identifier, "Loonie," is gendered. The primary economic and political institutions that control the Moon's colonies are the Lunar Authority and the Federated Nations. The F.N. consists of seven "Peace Force" nations and other minor nations. The Peace Force nations have veto powers, similar to the present United Nations' Security Council: they are the "N. A. Directorate, Great China, India, Sovunion, PanAfrica, Mitteleuropa, Brasilian Union" (Heinlein 326). One result of the formation of the single world government is that "[a]ll attack weapons were held by Peace forces but defense weapons were each nation's own pidgin and could be secret" (332).

The phrase "United States of America" does not occur in the novel, resulting in an erasure of the country on the novel's political map; it has been replaced with "North America," referring to the "North American [N.A.] Directorate" that presumably consists of the U.S. and Canada. The North American directorate is one of the most, if not the single most, powerful member of the F.N., especially because of the North American Space Defense Command in Colorado Springs. Franklin argues that the 1966 short story, "Free Men," about a revolution overtly shows the United States losing a brief war to "world government" forces (161); Franklin argues that *Moon* is a more complex exploration of the theme of an oppressive world government because Heinlein's "vision of the victimized people, ruthlessly exploited by a global monopolistic empire," is moved to Luna (162).

The question of the extent to which the United States is subsumed into the "North American Directorate" is an area of disagreement in the novel. When Mannie describes their visit to North America, he says, "North Americans are sentimental about their 'United States' even though it ceased to mean anything once their continent had been rationalized by F.N. .... They boast of being 'sovereign' (Heinlein 253). Mannie's understanding could be affected by the fact that he was trained in the area of North America that was part of the United States and has never visited Canada. In another instance, near the end of the novel, as decisions have to be made about whether or not to continue bombing, two characters disagree about the relationship between the N.A .Directorate and the F.N. in considering whether or not to keep hitting North America. One character argues that the "Americans," a group to whom he belonged before being transported, dislike the F.N. and would leave it in a moment, while the other argues that the N.A. directorate is the "roughest part of F.N." (Heinlein 352)

In a few brief phrases, the novel linguistically erases "the United States of America" while simultaneously reinscribing it by Mannie's assumption that all North Americans are "sentimental" about the United States and by other characters who use the terms interchangeably. The result reflects the conflicting meanings of the United States: a desire to praise the ideal of American freedom and the extent to which the US may be driving the global power of the FN, which parallels imperial and colonial power of the United States in the nineteenth and twentieth centuries. The connection with the idealized image of American freedom is shown by the announcement of the Loonie Declaration of Independence on July 4, 2076. Yet as Franklin argues, despite the allusions to the "socialist-Community revolution sweeping across the world as this novel was being written," and because of the connection to the eighteenth-century American Revolution, the Loonies' revolution is an attempt to "erase the modern state...and restore the small farmers and businessmen, to repeal the emerging rights to...social services and reactivate the fading rights to buy and sell everything in the marketplace" (165). In addition, I would argue that the strong emotional association connected to that revolution to achieve the goal of a sovereign nation is highly gendered.

The rhetoric of patriotism to a country, to a nation state, as the motivation for acting against an oppressive government is woven throughout the novel, but it is an inconsistently gendered rhetoric. When Mannie describes in chapters 9 and 12 how difficult it is to appeal to the "average Loonie," he is discussing apolitical and apathetic *men*. Women apparently are not Loonies—they are, instead, part of what appeals to Loonies as well as being in scarce supply: "Average Loonie was interested in beer, betting, women, and work, in that order.... Loonies had learned that there never were enough women to go around" (Heinlein 118). Later, Mannie laments again that the problem with creating a revolution lies in the fact that the average Loonie "despised Warden as matter of ritual, but was not stuff that makes revolutionists; he couldn't be bothered. Beer, betting, women and work" (169). Mannie says that the Peace Dragoons' actions were the only thing keeping the revolution going.

Two female characters in the book contradict Mannie's exclusion of women from the category of "Loonies," and from the characterization of apathy and lack of interest in patriotism, politics, and nation-building. First, of course, is Wyoming Knott, who is active enough at a high level in the first revolutionary movement to be sent from Hong Kong Luna to speak at the protest movement, where she and Mannie meet. The second is Mimi ("Mum") Davis, Mannie's senior wife. Wyoming is the major female character, and her strengths and the ways in which she moves into the background of the narrative, eventually becoming one of Mannie's wives, have been discussed by critics such as Easterbrook and Parkin-Speer. Yet despite the way in which Mannie's narrative moves away from her actions, she clearly considers herself a Loonie and is willing to engage with all the passion and patriotism that Mannie does not see in the "average Loonie." She is involved, along with the other women in the Davis family and presumably a number of other women they know and recruit, in a number of activities supporting the revolution, which includes, but is not limited to, providing food and drink at key meetings. Mannie's inability to see her as fitting his definition of a patriotic Loonie extends to other women as well.

He underestimates Wyoh's political commitment because he sees it as "personal," that is, relating to her exposure to radiation as a child transported to the Moon with her parents when the people in the ship were left outside ship during a solar storm. That exposure caused genetic damage, with her first child being born a "monster" (Heinlein 44), which led to her divorce and becoming a Free Woman who supported herself by working as a host-mother, or surrogate mother. The concept of "Free Woman" is introduced in the first chapter and never clearly defined, but given Wyoming's reluctance to let Mannie pay for their room, it seems to mean a woman who supports herself financially rather than being part of a family or sexually involved with a man.

However, as Hull argues, Heinlein's method of creating a first-person narrator who is "likable enough but not heroic or objective or omniscient...allows Heinlein to let readers draw their own conclusions" (42). Not only is it possible to understand that the lack of narrative time spent on the women's activities is not the same thing as the women, and the children, being inactive, but a reader who questions Mannie's dismissal of Wyoming's motivations for revolutionary movement could well argue that the personal experience of oppression that she—and presumably others on that ship, who included both convicts and volunteer colonists, adults and children—is in fact a valid and realistic motivation for opposing Lunar Authority. The personal experience of oppression is also not limited to women, as Mannie's own emotional response to join the riots shows. When hearing of Marie Lyons' rape and murder, he is enraged, which certainly can be described as personal, i.e., emotional as well as fitting into the Loonie cultural demand that men protect women. He acknowledges that he "[w]asn't a cold, shrewd revolutionist" and is restrained from taking immediate action by Prof and Mike (Heinlein 180).

Less narrative time is given to Mimi Davis, although she is engaged with and active in revolutionary activities from early in the narrative. She adds revolutionary activities, which she coordinates with other women and Wyoming, to all the other work she does to keep the Davis family running. While that work is never described by Mannie, any more than the revolutionary activities the women do, the women's work is invisible work of women that Mannie cannot and does not see, specifically the unpaid labor that goes into creating and maintaining families. The first night Mannie returns to his family with Wyoming in disguise, he recruits Mimi for his sub-cell. He feels the need to defend himself against the assumed reader's accusation that he was "a husband who can't keep from blurting everything to his wife," by describing her intelligence, organizational abilities, her status among the "farm families and throughout Luna City; she had been up longer than 90 percent" of Loonies, as well as the necessity of getting her help to cover up their revolutionary activities while in the house (Heinlein 114). But Mimi also has one key speech in that scene in which her sense of her self-identification as a Loonie committed to the potential of revolutionary activity is much stronger than Mannie's own, as shown by her use of the plural and inclusive pronoun *we*. She says, "I think every Loonie dreams of the day when *we* will be free" (115, emphasis added). She excludes a few "poor spineless rats" from "every Loonie," but her exclusion is based on courage and commitment, not gender, and is the opposite of Mannie's own belief.

The Gendered Construction of Race

The novel's construction of the Loonies as a multi-ethnic, multi-national, and multi-racial or racially mixed culture is acknowledged by most critics. One scene referenced for Heinlein's construction of the different understandings of race and ethnicity in the Lunar Colonies of the twenty-first century is the one in which Mannie's arrest in Kentucky is orchestrated by Stuart LaJoie and the Professor to generate sympathy for the Lunar cause. Mannie is charged with "bigamy....polygamy....open immorality and publicly inciting others to same," but learns later that it took "the range of color in Davis family [to get] judge angry enough to be foolish even beyond native talent for nonsense" (Heinlein 262, 264). When *Moon* was published, interracial marriage was still illegal in the United States: the Supreme Court decision legalizing it occurred in 1967 (Head). While the scene emphasizes the legality of polygamy for a large percentage of the Terran population, it also brings out one key difference Mannie identifies between Loonie culture and "North American culture," another small moment in which "North

American" seems to be synonymous with the United States, another example in which the categories of identity intersect.

Mannie spends little time describing himself, but when he helps Wyoming disguise herself with body paint, he notes that she "is darker than I am" (Heinlein 114). He also describes her appearance in Terran ethnic terminology: wearing the body paint, "she didn't look Afro—but not European, either. Seemed some mixed breed, and thereby more a Loonie" (39). "Afro" is a term that first was used in compound words such as *Afro-English* and *Afro-European* beginning in the nineteenth century and that later comes to be used as a stand-alone word in the twentieth century, with the earliest print reference occurring in 1938 ("Afro"). Mannie's description makes *Afro* grammatically parallel to *European*, both terms clearly meaning large continental areas containing multiple nations and language groups. Both Mimi and her senior husband, Grandpaw, use "Afro" later to describe "Wyma Beth"—Wyoh's alias—in a way that clearly signifies having some African ancestry. However, later, after Sidris helps Wyoming make her disguise more durable, Mannie describes her as looking "Tamil, a touch of Angola, German" (Heinlein 143). This list of specific Terran categories clashes with the earlier, more inclusive ones and seems out of character for Mannie, who usually speaks in the casual slang of "Loonie," with broad strokes, such as "Chinee" for all peoples transported from Asia. "Tamil" refers to an ethnic group that lives in different countries in India and East Asia. Angola, in Africa, was a Portuguese colony that became an independent nation only in 1975 after struggles by national liberation groups during the 1960s ("History"). As a result of its history, Angola has different language and ethnic groups. "German" is an ethnic group tied to a single nation-state, specifically one with strong associations with racist ideologies. Mannie criticizes "North America" for how they "care about skin color by making point of how they *don't* care. First trip I was always too light or too dark"; he refused on his earlier trip to identify "what genes I have," referencing one of his grandmothers, who "came from a part of Asia where invaders passed through as regularly as locusts, raping as they went" (Heinlein 253). He continues on his later trip to refuse to use North American national, ethnic, or racial terms for himself. His lack of identification with the North American categories makes sense for someone born on Luna. He does know the terminology relevant for his grandparents who were transported from their native lands on Earth, however. In the first chapter, he explains his grandparents' national and ethnic mixture: one grandfather from South Africa, "shipped up from Joburg for armed violence and no work permit," and another "transported for subversive activity after the Wet Firecracker war" (13). One of his grandmothers was a Tatar, a marginalized and minority ethnic group in Russia, and the other a "Peace Corps enrollee (involuntary)," with no nationality given (14). Mannie's knowledge of his ancestry differs from what he claims for "the average Loonie": "a Loonie then rarely knew who father was and, if raised in crêche, might be vague about mother" (30). But as with the casual identification of the average Loonie with men, which is contradicted by Wyoming and Mimi, so too does his sudden use of the specific Terran ethnic terminology for a woman stands out as an anomaly.

The additional extent to which his grandfathers are identified with specific political and revolutionary activities compared to the lack of information for his grandmothers implies a gendered intersection with categories of ethnicity and race as well as political and patriotic. However, the global range of his family's background is, as Franklin notes, one way in which the novel engages with the political revolutions against colonial powers during the twentieth century. The historical complexities of the twentieth-century nations that rose from those revolutions are the subject of postcolonial and neocolonial theories. Herbert G. Klein's 2010 essay, "Loonies and Others in Robert A. Heinlein's *The Moon Is a Harsh Mistress*," focuses on elements of the novel that he argues fit the criteria for postcolonial fiction, including the narrative of an oppressed colony fighting for independence, as well as including a detailed reading of Mike, the sentient computer, as an example of as "Other" in Loonie culture (147–51). In Klein's reading, the extent to which Heinlein's novel allows the chance to move beyond "national, ethnic, class and gender preoccupations to ones that concern the emancipation of all sentient beings" (153), especially given Mike's silence at the end of the narrative, opens up the possibility for a greater range of critical readings.

All of these intersectional interstices in *The Moon Is a Harsh Mistress* are moments that complicate the ways in which the novel constructs categories of identity and may well be one of the reasons why there is such disagreement about what relation the ideas in the novels play to Heinlein's own. In at least the final case of Mannie's description of Wyoming in disguise, it may be possible to argue that the use of the specific language relating to the 1960s national, ethnic, and racial categories of identity that were being challenged and changed at the time reflects Heinlein's knowledge and perspective more than those of Manuel Garcia O'Kelly, third generation Loonie and computer consultant. If so, examining Heinlein's other novels for similar intersectional interstices may contribute to the rethinking of Heinlein's science fiction called for by James and Patterson.

Works Cited

"Afro" and "Afro-." *Oxford English Dictionary*. Oxford University Press, 2015. Web. Apr. 2015. <http://www.oxforddictionaries.com/us/definition/american_english/Afro->.

Bourget, Jason. "Biological Determinism, Masculine Politics and the Failure of Libertarianism in Robert A. Heinlein's *The Moon Is a Harsh Mistress*." *Foundation: The International Review of Science Fiction* 37.104 (2008): 10–22.

Crenshaw, Kimberlé. "Demarginalizing the Intersection of Race and Sex: A Black Feminist Critique of Antidiscrimination Doctrine, Feminist Theory, and Antiracist Politics." *University of Chicago Legal Forum* (1989): 139–67.

Easterbrook, Neil. "State, Heterotopia: The Political Imagination in Heinlein, Le Guin, and Delany." *Political Science Fiction*. Ed. Donald M. Hassler & Clyde Wilcox. Columbia, SC: U of South Carolina P, 1997. 43–75.

Franklin, Bruce. *Robert A. Heinlein: America as Science Fiction*. Science-Fiction Writers Ser. Oxford: Oxford UP, 1980.

Gorsch, Robert. "The Golden Age of Heinlein." *Foundation: The International Review of Science Fiction* 35.97 (2006): 47–58.

Head, Tom. "Interracial Marriage Laws: A Short Timeline History." *About News*. About.com, 2015. Web. May 2015. <http://civilliberty.about. com/od/raceequalopportunity/tp/Interracial-Marriage-Laws-History-Timeline.htm>.

Heinlein, Robert A. *The Moon Is a Harsh Mistress*. London: Gollancz. 1966.

"History." *Embassy of Angola, Washington, DC*. The Embassy of the Republic of Angola and GlobeScope, Inc., n.d. Web. May 2015. <http://www.angola.org/index.php?page=history>.

Hull, Elizabeth Ann. "Justifying the Ways of Man to God: The Novels of Robert A. Heinlein." *Extrapolation* 20.1 (1979): 38–51.

James, Robert & William H. Patterson, Jr. "Re-Visioning Robert Heinlein's Career." *Foundation: The International Review of Science Fiction* 35.97 (2006): 11–27.

Klein, Herbert G. "Loonies and Others in Robert A. Heinlein's the *Moon Is a Harsh Mistress*." *Science Fiction, Imperialism and the Third World: Essays on Postcolonial Literature and Film*. Ed. Ericka Hoagland, Reema Sarwal, & Andy Sawyer. Jefferson, NC: McFarland, 2010. 141–55.

McCall, Leslie. "The Complexity of Intersectionality." *Signs* 30:31 (2005): 1771–1800.

McGiveron, Rafeeq O. "'Starry-Eyed internationalists' *versus* the Social Darwinists: Heinlein's Transnational Governments." *Extrapolation* 40.1 (Spring 1999): 53–70.

McGuirk, Carol. "Nowhere Man: Towards a Poetics of Post-Utopian Characterization." *Science Fiction Studies* 21.2 (1994): 141–54.

Panshin, Alexei. *Heinlein in Dimension: A Critical Analysis*. Chicago: Advent, 1968.

Parkin-Speer, Diane. "Almost a Feminist: Robert A. Heinlein." *Extrapolation* 26.2 (Summer 1995): 113–25.

Rule, Deb Houdek. "The Finding and Publishing of *For Us, the Living*." *The Heinlein Society*. The Heinlein Society, 2003. Web. May 2015. <http://www.heinleinsociety.org/newsFUTL.html>.

Silverberg, Robert. "Science Fiction in the Fifties: The Real Golden Age." *American Science Fiction: Classic Novels of the 1950s*. Library of America, 2012. Web. May 2015. <http://www.loa.org/sciencefiction/ why_silverberg.jsp>.

Williams, Donna Glee. "The Moons of Le Guin and Heinlein." *Science Fiction Studies* 21.2 (1994): 164–72.

Winker, Gabriele & Nina Degele. "Intersectional Analysis: Dealing with Social Inequality." *European Journal of Women's Studies* 18:1 (2011): 51–66.

Mr. Koshchei Makes the Law: To Hell and Back in Robert A. Heinlein's "Magic, Inc." and *Job: A Comedy of Justice*_____

Rafeeq O. McGiveron

Robert A. Heinlein may be most famous as a writer of "hard" science fiction, and yet his work occasionally also veers, either with tantalizing little asides or with mischievously iconoclastic vigor, into the paranormal or even supernatural. Indeed, the man who in his early twenties very seriously made a pact with two close friends that whoever of the three died first would communicate back "from the astral plane, or whatever lay beyond death" to give "proof of life after death" (Patterson I: 108–109) dabbles across nearly fifty years of writing with explorations into telepathy, telekinesis, magic, reincarnation, and the realms of Heaven and Hell.[1]

"Magic, Inc." (1940) and *Job: A Comedy of Justice* (1984), tales from near the beginning and end of Heinlein's career, respectively, are particularly interesting to examine together. Both are works of supernatural shenanigans, taking place in disarmingly near futures or in alternate timelines not all that different from our own, and share a similar first-person point of view, with sometimes-befuddled narrators more acted upon than acting; both works value the efforts of their comparatively "small" characters, make some subtle but very pointed digs against intolerance and racism, and ultimately take readers to the very throne of Satan and back—though near the end of his career, Heinlein has moved beyond traditional Western monotheism to ask the most probing questions of Creation. Yet despite their supernatural sweep, and their occasional differences, both tales in their own ways advocate for the doggedness and the dignity of the individual.

"Magic, Inc." actually was known for its first ten years, until it was paired with the novella "Waldo" and reprinted in book form in 1950, as "The Devil Makes the Law." The story appeared in the September 1940 issue of *Unknown*, which was edited—along with

Astounding Science-Fiction—by John W. Campbell, Jr. As James Gifford notes, Campbell changed the ironically prosaic original title to the rather more menacing "The Devil Makes the Law" because the magazine had printed another story with the word *magic* in the title just the month before, and he did not want to appear to be "in a rut" (118). While this change leans away from the actual tone of most of the piece, it does draw attention to the notions of actual evil, Hell, and even damnation, which indeed appear, powerfully albeit fleetingly, near the end of the story.

The world of "Magic, Inc." otherwise is charmingly similar to the 1940 America of Heinlein's writing. In a smallish city with telephone numbers of the "CREST 3840" variety (Heinlein, "Magic" 122), local businessmen look out for one another, store windows display "the Rotary emblem in one corner" (131), and being late to the Chamber of Commerce meeting means putting a dime in the kitty (152). Little old ladies who might "bake a cake for a grandson or sit up with a sick neighbor" serve tea "with proper ceremony" (125), and a wholesome young woman can make the narrator "think of county fairs and well water and sugar cookies" (159). An "inveterate bachelor" naturally needs a ribbing from his pals if he seems to be sweet on a girl (176), while a kind lady of experience has tolerantly polite ways to keep a potential wolf from "mak[ing] a fool of [him]self" (192). It is a town different from those "back East" (107), therefore, but even here, stereotypical Sicilians in flashy suits can move in to opine knowingly about the benefits of a protection racket, since they "like for people to be co-operative. You never can tell what bad luck you may run into not co-operating" (105).

In this world, however, magic is a given, as matter-of-fact as an ad in the Yellow Pages. Every craft has its limits, of course, and in Heinlein's fictional world, "cold iron," such as building contractor Archie Fraser often uses, is something "very few commercial sorcerers can cope with" (Heinlein, "Magic" 108), just as "[a]nybody knows that magic won't work over consecrated ground" (115). For other purposes, however, "licensed practitioners of thaumaturgy" (105) employ spells of all variety. They might "appl[y] the laws of homeopathy and contiguity" to make copies of a cut-up object from its scraps (110), use "apportation" for Cadillac "magic carpet" taxis (114), or produce "vanishing items" for restaurant menus, like liquor whose alcohol vanishes immediately upon drinking or weight-friendly desserts that similarly disappear after eating (167). The adept may tell one's future with "your palms, the stars, the sticks" (124)—not to mention tea leaves (125–126)—or may call upon the assistance of dwellers of the Half World, such as poltergeists, gnomes, fiery salamander spirits, and watery undines (106, 128–31). The unscrupulous might make mischief with "the nasty, harmful secrets hidden away in black grimoires and red grimoires," but "knowledge of the great arcane laws" generally brings "enormous boons" to society (166).

Otherwise, the world of "Magic, Inc." is homey and familiar for the reader of a more commonplace reality. It is neither a projection into a science-fictional future of technological whizz-bangery nor a harking-back to some fantasy-type past of wizards and dragons, but instead is a setting nearly contemporaneous with its time of writing. And in case it seems implausible to readers that magic ever could be accepted as reality in a world so little removed from our own, especially from the presumably more religious context of 1940, Heinlein has a character doubt that "there was any less black magic practiced between, say, 1750 and 1950 than there is now, or was before then. Take a look at Pennsylvania and the hex country.[2] Take a look at the Deep South. But since that time we have begun to have the advantages of white magic too" (166). Really, as the story's advances are all magical rather than scientific—and when we have been told that such magic has been here all along, unnoticed by mainstream society—it seems likely that the time of setting is not much beyond the referred-to 1950.

Archie Fraser, ordinary and commonsensical builder of ordinary and commonsensical structures, is the perfect first-person narrator to help make the best of both worlds in "Magic, Inc.": making the milieu seem close to that of 1940s America[3], yet also giving us something of an outsider's perspective on magic. On the one hand, Archie "wasn't born yesterday" (Heinlein, "Magic" 106); he knows his business, he understands a shakedown when he sees it, and when push comes to shove, he has no problem confronting a hood with "some magic [he] may not have heard of," the pistol the shop owner keeps under the counter (107). On the other hand, while Archie has a nodding acquaintance with the everyday magic of his society, it is only the basic familiarity of the consumer rather than the deeper understanding of the professional. As he tells us, "I've never paid much attention to the methods of magicians, feeling about them the way Thomas Edison said he did about mathematicians—when he wanted one he could hire one" (127). Archie actually is closer in outlook to readers than, say, to a magician, diviner, or witch, for to him it is simply all "a lot of cabalistic signs" and "pentacles of various shapes," plus inscrutable "writing in what [he] judge[s] to be Hebraic script" but is not (127).

Adding to Archie's almost "outsider" perspective on the workings of magic is the way he is fairly swept along by events, less the main actor of the tale, despite being its focus, than merely the trusting follower of the more experienced friends who sagely advise him. Heinlein could have set up the narrator as a "hard-boiled" type from the detective pulps, for example, a knowing wise guy who must use his own well-practiced supernatural skills to defeat evil sorcerers or demons. Instead, however, he makes Archie almost as much a neophyte in such matters as we would be. Fortunately, though, when his shop is ransacked by gnomes, burned down by a salamander, and then flooded by an undine, he brings in his friend, the "shrewd, capable" Joe Jedson, who "is considerably older than [Archie], and quite a student, without holding a degree, in all forms of witchcraft, white and black magic, necrology, demonology, spells, charms, and the more practical forms of divination" (Heinlein, "Magic" 108). Obviously, if Jedson were the narrator, the story would be a very different thing indeed, with readers likely being initiated into the workings of magic in a way Archie could never explain.[4]

Archie may be a comparative everyman, but Heinlein also uses him as a rather forward-looking exemplar of racial equality and integration.[5] This story written a full lifetime ago, almost a decade and a half before *Brown vs. Board of Education*, still may have a few clunkers that its contemporary readers might not have noticed.

Heinlein does not seem to mind some easy stereotypes about flashily dressed and superstitious Sicilian mobsters, for example, or about Zadkiel Feldstein, an agent for magicians, and apparently Jewish, of whom Archie observes, "Naturally, his religion prevented him from practicing magic himself, but, as I understand it, there was no theological objection to his turning an honest commission" (Heinlein, "Magic" 108–109). Archie, who "ha[s] had dealings with him," at least does conclude that "he was all right" (108).

Surely the most interesting character in terms of race relations, though, is Dr. Royce Worthington, the "witch-smeller" (Heinlein, "Magic" 145) referred to Archie by the kindly old Mrs. Jennings. After speaking to the man over the telephone, the impressed builder tells Jedson that "he sounds like something pretty swank in the way of an English-university don" (143–44). When their ally arrives, however, he looks rather different from expected, for this "tall, heavyset man with a face of great dignity and obvious intelligence," who is "dressed in rather conservative, expensively tailored clothes and carr[ying] gloves, stick, and a large brief case," also is "black as draftsman's ink!" (144). "There was no reason why the man should not have been a Negro," Archie tells us, exclamation point apparently already forgotten. "I simply had not been expecting it" (144). This is a bit disingenuous, though, for he admits frankly that "We white men in this country are inclined to underestimate the black man—I know I do" (147). This, he continues, is

> because we see him out of his cultural matrix. Those we know have had their culture wrenched from them some generations back and a servile pseudo culture imposed upon them by force. We forget that the black man has a culture of his own, older than ours and more solidly grounded, based on character and the power of the mind rather than the cheap, ephemeral tricks of mechanical gadgets. But it is a stern, fierce culture with no sentimental concern for the weak and the unfit, and it never quite dies out. (Heinlein, "Magic" 147)

Some of this wears rather more thinly in the twenty-first century than it would have in 1940, I think, but we nevertheless should give Heinlein his due here. On the one hand, he has made "the black man" into a mysterious Other, almost as if his very humanity were different somehow, and as if, even were he given the chance, he could not, or perhaps should not, fit in with Western culture. On the other hand, Archie's praise of Worthington's culture of origin is very strong indeed, and just as important are his initial recognition of the man's "great dignity and obvious intelligence" (Heinlein, "Magic" 144) and his later observation that Worthington's "eyes gave a conviction of wisdom beyond any comprehension" (147). It may be a little unnerving to see Worthington in a witch-smelling trance, now dressed in "a loin skin of leopard" (146), get down on all fours to sniff and whine after the traces of evil magic, including even needing to be patted on the head (188), but neither should it be forgotten that Heinlein clearly intends the watching Archie to have an open mind ready to learn from this equal, even superior, individual. Indeed, the narrator who admits that, presumably like most white readers of 1940, he habitually "underestimate[s] the black man" immediately respects and trusts Worthington, and Jedson, on first meeting, even becomes his ceremonial "brother" (146).

To stop the demon who, disguised as human, is using various magical and political chicanery to tie up all magic in the forty-eight states in a legislatively supported monopoly, Archie, Jedson, and Worthington must journey to the Half World, led by the physically frail but spiritually powerful Mrs. Jennings. Although the Half World previously has been mentioned as the source of magical power and the abode of various spirits, it has not yet been described at all. In this section of the story, Heinlein first hedges by making the place a surreal setting that humans can grasp only incompletely and sometimes confusedly, a region "where 'up' and 'down' are matters of opinion, and direction might be read as readily in days or colors as in miles" (Heinlein, "Magic" 184).

Yet soon, the Half World becomes not just surreal but instead ghastly, evoking alarm and dread:

> We were no longer alone. Life—sentient, evil undeadness—boiled round us and fogged the air and crept out of the ground. The ground itself twitched and pulsated as we walked over it. Faceless things sniffed and nibbled at our heels. We were aware of unseen presences

about us in the fog-shot gloom: beings that squeaked, grunted, and sniggered; voices that were slobbering whimpers, that sucked and retched and bleated.

They seemed vaguely disturbed by our presence—Heaven knows I was terrified by them!—for I could hear them flopping and shuffling out of our path, then closing cautiously behind, as they bleated warnings to one another. (Heinlein, "Magic" 184–85)

The term *evil* is purposeful, for this place is not just hellish—it *is* Hell, literally, and the "great throne" the travelers approach is that of "our ancient enemy" (Heinlein, "Magic" 184), none other than "Satan Mekratrig" himself, attended by familiar demons such as Beelzebub and Asmodeus and others (186). This sudden veer into the worldview of traditional Western morality is particularly surprising in what had been merely a fantasy tale of white and black magic, gnomes, salamanders, and undines. We cannot determine if all of the creatures that "terrif[y]" Archie were created in the Half World or whether some were dragged here from our own, but some unfortunate humans indeed are present, for immediately before Satan's throne, "perform[ing] for [his] amusement," Archie sees "[s]ome dozens of men and women, young and old, comely and hideous, cavort[ing] and leap[ing] in impossible acrobatic adagio" (185). Apparently it is all fun and games until someone is damned to Hell for all eternity.

Heinlein renders a scene that is ghastly, all the more so in a story that has been so areligious. After the first shock, though, he relents somewhat, giving the "evil lord" (Heinlein, "Magic" 186) a demeanor that is urbanely ironic and, ultimately, less threatening. Satan has little interest, really, in helping the interlopers find the particular demon who has been causing all the trouble in the human world, but he is bound by the "Treaty of Adam" (185) and therefore must permit an inspection—so long as Mrs. Jennings and Jedson serve as hostages, their lives forfeit if the others fail. Despite "the whole mind-twisting horror of the place and its grisly denizens" (187), the inexpert but determined Archie, assisted by Mrs. Jennings' cat and Dr. Worthington in his "witch-sniffing" dog pose, examine the "legion on legion" of devils "[d]rawn up in military order for review" (186). After "many hours, certainly so long that fatigue changed to a wooden automatism and horror died down to a dull unease" (187), the searchers eventually track down their target, and along with the unexpected, last-second help of an FBI agent disguised as a demon in his mission from "the antimonopoly division" (190) to the nab same fellow, they capture the miscreant.

Their prisoner, Satan's nephew Nebiros, "a bad lad" of whom the uncle, "clucking," is "proud," sickly declines to face the elderly Mrs. Jennings in one-on-one combat, so the little scamp is sentenced to a million years chained to a boulder—"not a stiff sentence, as such things go, I'm told," according to Archie. As he explains, obviously relaying what his more experienced protectors have told him, this is only "[a]bout equal to six months in jail in the real world," since Nebiros "had not offended their customs; he had simply been defeated by white magic" (189). Satan wishes at least to take some vengeance upon the government agent, but when he "[r]eally…must insist," the seemingly frail old woman holds her ground:

> "Satan Mekratrig," she said slowly, "do you wish to try your strength with me?"
> "With you, madame?" He looked at her carefully, as if inspecting her for the first time. "Well, it's been a trying day, hasn't it? Suppose we say no more about it. Till another time, then—"
> He was gone. (Heinlein, "Magic" 190)

Before the dangerous foray into the Half World, she and Jedson already had agreed solemnly that "[w]hite"—the type of magic, not the race—"prevails over black" (179), but it seems clear that this is true only for those who have both the gumption and the skills to stand and fight for what is right. His more knowledgeable comrades may have the skills, but even they might not have succeeded without the help of straightforward everyman Archie.

Job: A Comedy of Justice, a novel from near the very end of Heinlein's career, is an interesting one to examine in light of the magic-oriented novella from his beginnings. Like "Magic, Inc.," *Job* begins in another very near future—1994, or only ten years ahead of its publication, as cross-referenced by the narrator from the 5,998 years that have passed "from the Creation in 4004 B.C." (Heinlein, *Job* 267). Early on, the narrator wistfully remembers the now-banned lurid pulp magazines of his childhood: "Magic ships plying the ether to other stars. Strange inventions. Trips to the center of the earth. Other 'dimensions.' Flying machines. Power from burning atoms. Monsters created in secret laboratories" (14). Heinlein's joke cuts both ways, though, for whereas we may miss the flying cars the future once seemed to hold, the world of Alexander Hergensheimer lacks not only nuclear power but even heavier-than-air flight. Here the dirigible is the most advanced form of travel, since "Professor Simon Newcomb's well-known mathematical proof" showed that "flying machines were impossible" (83), while the "most brilliant light imaginable" of a rocket takeoff seen after several reality shifts makes Alex at first believe "the Rapture" has arrived (225–26). This almost-contemporaneous setting thus in a way harks back to Heinlein's use of a similarly non-science-fictional setting of "Magic, Inc."

Like Archie Frasier, Alex Hergensheimer—or Alec Graham, as he is known after the first of many dizzying shifts from one alternate reality to another—is swept along by inexplicable events he cannot fully understand, let alone fight. Like Archie, Alec is doggedly determined. "[T]oo stinkin' proud" to take charity (Heinlein, *Job* 152), not only is he willing to wash dishes endlessly to earn a living for the woman who comes to supplant the prudish wife he "would not knowingly wish…on anyone" (49), but he also searches for his love through Heaven and Hell—literally—when she is separated from him on Judgment Day. Moreover, despite the narrow-mindedness to which Heinlein repeatedly draws our attention through various amusing incidents and asides, Alec is, in some ways, a very straight arrow indeed. Even Lucifer, during a time of judgment far more important than the traditional one that ultimately disappoints and disillusions Alec so, praises the mortal creature who, "putting aside its own troubles—much too big for it!—devoted itself to a valiant (and fruitless) effort to save [a] 'soul' by the rules it had been taught. That its attempt was misguided does not matter…" (368).

At the same time, however, that Alec is a simple but determined everyman, bumbling from one unsettling change of reality to another as best he can, Heinlein uses the character as an unwitting advocate for open-mindedness and tolerance. Whereas Archie of "Magic, Inc." simply *tells* us, with Alec we must read the ironies and come to conclusions opposite of his smug ones. This deeply Protestant narrator, for example, is not certain "[w]hether Catholics were allies or enemies," but an even tougher nut to crack is "the Jewish problem—was a humane solution possible? If not, then what? Should we grasp the nettle?" (Heinlein, *Job* 129). Alec's musings about "Punishment? Surgery? Other?" for homosexuality suggest that genocide might not be out of the question for him here either (130). For "the Negro problem" he at least seems to consider only deportation to Alaska (130) rather than mass murder. In his America of 1994, after all, a black janitor is considered a "blackamoor," deferentially calling Alec "Captain" after having been addressed patronizingly as "Uncle" (252), and in a different reality, when his supervisor, who is black, has complimented his work in the kitchen, Alec tells us with some exasperation, "We are all the Lord's children, but it was the first time in my life that a blackamoor's opinion of my work had mattered" (159–60). If anything, Heinlein's message of tolerance and of worth based not on race but on deed is even harder-hitting than that of "Magic, Inc.," although his means of expressing it are artistically subtler.

This late in his career, however, what is truly hard-hitting is Heinlein's investigation of Heaven and Hell, and even Creation itself. Whereas the closest we get to Heaven in "Magic, Inc." is Archie's use of the phrase "Heaven knows," *Job* actually takes us there—and, despite Alec's initial awe at the scale and the jeweled grandeur of "the Holy City," which "covers an area more than six times as big as all of Texas" (Heinlein, *Job* 285), it is a place of petty bureaucracy and the snobbery of angels, "operat[ing] by just one rule: R.H.I.P.," or "Rank Hath Its Privileges" (290). Alec, surprising even himself, has won a sainthood, but what he truly lacks is Margrethe, his loving companion through untold harrowing reality-shifts. This modern worshiper of Odin has not been collected at the Last Trump, so Alec, after shouting to St. Peter, "You can tell the Father and His sweet-talking Son and that sneaky Ghost that they can take their gaudy Holy City and shove it!" (313), vows to search Hell.

Yet while the throne of Satan in the earlier tale lay in a region of evil and horror of the traditional Western monotheistic conception, here it is as much a comic-opera potentate as the novel's Heaven, a place ruled by "His Infernal Majesty, Satan Mekratrig, Sovereign of Hell and His Colonies beyond, First of the Fallen Thrones, Prince of Lies" (Heinlein, *Job* 331–32). Yes, there is "the famous Pit," "the caldera of an incredibly enormous volcano" complete with fire, lava, and "[t]he stench of burning brimstone" (316). "But falling in the Pit doesn't do a soul any harm…aside from scaring them silly" and sending the person "shooting out even faster than he went in" (319). In fact, the Lake of Fire is more of a tourist attraction, a scenic object to be enjoyed from one's hotel balcony, with "smoke ris[ing] and the flames throwing red lights on the smoke," while farther back are "green and sunny early summer sights, with snow-tipped mountains in the far distance" (330). Hell purports to be the "[p]rettiest planet in this galaxy. And the best kept. No snakes. No cockroaches. No chiggers. No poison ivy. No tax collectors. No rats. No cancer. No preachers. Only two lawyers" (320). The hotel facilities, by the way, with full erotic services from the "San Francisco sandwich" and "other Sodom-and-Gomorrah fanc[ies]" to "mob scene[s]" like "Persian Garden, sorority house, Turkish harem, jungle drums with obscene rites, [and] nunnery" (326–27), are top-notch as well.

Satan himself has a wry flair for the dramatic, occasionally appearing as a red-skinned "conventional Devil" twice human size, with "tail and horns and fierce eyes," plus requisite "pitchfork in lieu of scepter" and even creepy atmospheric music that is "vaguely Wagnerian" (Heinlein, *Job* 335–36), but it is mere fun and games, without any of the actual horror and dread of "Magic, Inc." Satan here is not just comical, however—he is earnest and caring and ultimately likable, and that is the real innovation.[6] He admits that he indeed was the one who "bedeviled Job" in the Bible—and Alec here—because he has "always been a sucker for a bet, any bet," yet he is "not proud" of either of these facts (345). Yahweh, he explains to Alec, is his brother, who often has "maneuver[ed]" Satan "into doing His dirty business" (345).

The notion of a God and Devil as co-equals is as old as Zoroastrianism, but Heinlein pushes it farther: here Satan actually is the sympathetic and supportive one, while Yahweh is capricious and even vengeful, feeling benevolent if only 7.1% somehow win the rigged game and get into Heaven (370). Pityingly Lucifer explains that "'justice' is not a divine concept; it is a human illusion. The very basis of the Judeo-Christian code is injustice, the scapegoat system." Decrying this notion that "runs all through the Old Testament, then reaches its height in the New Testament with the notion of the Martyred Redeemer," he wonders, "How can justice possibly be served by loading your sins on another?" (Heinlein, *Job* 352). Humans, he implicitly suggests, deserve to labor under some better system than this.

This system, moreover, is not some solemn creation that sprang from benevolence and high morality, but instead is simply a matter of art.[7] The brothers both are dabblers at art, and yet above even them are beings to whom "your lord god Jehovah is equivalent to a child building sand castles at a beach, then destroying them in childish tantrums" (Heinlein, *Job* 365)—and on and on up goes the hierarchy, for "Behind every mystery lies another mystery. Infinite recession" (346).[8] The being whom even Satan and Yahweh, along with Odin and Loki, "look up to" as a god—though he "does not demand, does not expect, and does not want, [the] sort of bootlicking" that Satan's vain brother does (365)—is called "the Chairman" or "Mr. Koshchei," and it is to Him that Satan takes the little human who, despite playing the game by Yahweh's rules, still has been deprived of the only thing that matters to him: Margrethe. "Treat Him as you would a man much older than you and one whom you respect highly," advises Satan. "*Don't* bow down or offer worship. Just stand your ground and tell the truth. If you die, die with dignity" (366).

Mr. Koshchei, wise and impartial, and godlike to gods, is the one who makes the law in this part of the universe, apparently. Tolerantly he corrects Satan's misunderstanding that a "guild rule" requires an artist to be "kind" to its "volitionals": "There is an *artistic principle*—not a rule—that volitionals should be treated consistently. But to insist on kindness would be to eliminate that degree of freedom for which volition in creatures was invented. Without the possibility of tragedy the volitionals might as well be golems" (Heinlein, *Job* 368; emphasis added). According to Mr. Koshchei, "For a creature to act out its own minor art, the rules under which it acts must be either known to it or be such that the rules can become known through trial and error—with error not always fatal. In short the creature must be able to learn and to benefit from its experience" (369).

But could Yahweh's capricious rules really be known? Or has he instead done what Satan has accused, "baited a trap and thereby lured this creature into a contest that it could not win—then declared the game over and [taken] the prize from it" (Heinlein, *Job* 369)? Satan maintains that "although this is an extreme case, a destruction test, this nevertheless is typical of his treatment of all his volitionals" (369)—yet a human, it is implied, should deserve at least a fighting chance at happiness. In the end, Mr. Koshchei is not impressed with Yahweh's shell game and, with the cooperation of Odin, gives Margrethe the choice between Valhalla and Alec, with predictable results. Yahweh protests, but Mr. Koshchei reminds him that to an artist, nothing can be higher than the art:

> "Oy! Every prophecy I fulfilled! And now He tells me consistent I am not! This is justice?"
> "No. It is Art." (Heinlein, *Job* 372)

Indeed, artfully and memorably do "Magic, Inc." and *Job: A Comedy of Justice*, tales from near the endpoints of Robert A. Heinlein's long career, both take us to Hell and back. Each work, wherein a fairly ordinary first-person narrator of a then-near future little removed from the real one is swept along by inexplicable events he cannot truly comprehend, let alone fight, plays with magic, dabbles in race relations, and tells a fine tale. By the 1980s, however, Heinlein's exploration of the notions of Heaven and Hell, and indeed the underpinnings of the cosmos itself, is significantly bolder and more iconoclastic than his earliest attempt and even more so than his sometimes-shocking *Stranger in a Strange Land* that began the 1960s. As with much Art with a capital A, it matters little whether these worlds of either biblical or playful fire and brimstone are real, or whether there truly is an "[i]nfinite regression" of Creator-Artists above us. What is clear, after all, is the way that the Creator-Artist born in Missouri in 1907 advocates powerfully for the doggedness and the dignity of the individual, who may be "ridiculous," but who nevertheless can—and should, if necessary—"suffer bravely and die gallantly for whatever it loves and believes in" (*Job* 368).

Notes

1. See, for example, variously, *Time for the Stars* (1956), "Methuselah's Children" (1941), and "Lost Legacy" (1941); "Project Nightmare" (1953) and *Stranger in a Strange Land* (1961); *Beyond This Horizon* (1942) and "The Man Who Traveled in Elephants" (1948); and even *Space Cadet* (1948) and *Red Planet* (1949).

2. Pennsylvania hex country appears again in "Waldo" (1940), wherein newly discovered scientific principles at first seem like magic.

3. Once, however, Archie notes that one magician "worked with his clothes on" (120). If this fact is worthy of comment, perhaps that world is a bit more different from the 1940 of our timeline than it first appears; Heinlein unfortunately never follows up on this tantalizing little detail.

4. Strangely, though, after Jedson uses a voodoo-type doll to squeeze some information out of a captured mobster, when Archie protests the cigarette burn, Jedson claims that he actually "didn't do anything": "Sympathetic magic isn't really magic at all, Archie. It's just an application of neuropsychology and colloidal chemistry. He did that to himself, because he believed in it. I simply correctly judged his mentality" (139–40). This science-fictional explaining-away would fit much better in a story that does not posit magic, I believe.

5. For Heinlein's "easy hospitality" in "crossing the color line" in personal life, even in the racially segregated days of 1941, see Patterson I: 279.

6. Heinlein in a 1984 letter to Isaac Asimov reminded the fellow writer that it was he, over forty years earlier, who had pointed out to

Heinlein "the fact that Jehovah had all the best press agents and that Satan wasn't getting a fair shake" (qtd. in Patterson II: 428).

7.   This notion occurs first in "The Unpleasant Profession of Jonathan Hoag" (1942).

8.   And somewhere in this hierarchy is the enigmatic "Glaroon" (367) that—or who—first appears in "They" (1941).

Works Cited

Gifford, James. *Robert A. Heinlein: A Reader's Companion*. Citrus Heights, CA: Nitrosyncretic, 2000.

Heinlein, Robert A. *Beyond This Horizon*. 1942. Revised and expanded 1948. New York: Signet, 1975.

_____. *Job: A Comedy of Justice*. New York: Del Rey, 1984.

_____. "Lost Legacy." 1941. *Assignment in Eternity*. 1953. New York: Signet, 1981. 96–170.

_____. "Magic, Inc." 1940. *Waldo and Magic, Inc.* 1950. New York: Signet, 1970. 105–92.

_____. "The Man Who Traveled in Elephants." 1948. *The Unpleasant Profession of Jonathan Hoag*. 1959. New York: Berkley, 1980. 122–137.

_____. "Methuselah's Children." 1942. Revised 1957. *The Past Through Tomorrow*. 1967. New York: Berkley, 1975. 655–830.

_____. "Project Nightmare." 1953. *The Menace from Earth*. 1959. New York: Signet, 1964. 158–78.

_____. *Red Planet*. 1949. New York: Del Rey, 1978.

_____. *Space Cadet*. 1948. New York: Del Rey, 1978.

_____. *Stranger in a Strange Land*. 1961. New York: Berkley, 1968.

_____. "They." 1941. *The Unpleasant Profession of Jonathan Hoag*. 1959. New York: Berkley, 1980. 152–69.

_____. *Time for the Stars*. New York: Ace, 1956.

_____. "The Unpleasant Profession of Jonathan Hoag." 1942. *The Unpleasant Profession of Jonathan Hoag*. 1959. New York: Berkley, 1980. 1–121.

_____. "Waldo." 1942. *Waldo and Magic, Inc.* 1950. New York: Signet, 1970. 9–104.

Patterson, William H., Jr. *Robert A. Heinlein: In Dialogue with His Century, Vol. 1: Learning Curve, 1907–1948*. New York: Tor, 2010.

_____. *Robert A. Heinlein: In Dialogue with His Century, Vol. 2: The Man Who Learned Better, 1948–1988*. New York: Tor, 2014.

CRITICAL
READINGS

Early Genius: Robert A. Heinlein's Stories from 1939 to 1949

Garyn G. Roberts

While Robert A. Heinlein published a range of fantasy works in addition to his wide-ranging science fiction and even wrote a number of nonfiction essays and editorials, it is of course for the SF that he is best remembered. By all indications, Heinlein wanted to be best known and remembered as a science fiction author, and indeed he is. In fact, he is considered one of the greatest science fiction authors of the twentieth century. While assigning the term "greatest" requires consideration of definition and parameters of historical and literary context and is, at least in part, subjective, this adjective—in regard to Robert A. Heinlein in context of the sweep of science fiction of the twentieth century—is very much appropriate. Through the years of his writing life and on through the years after his passing, the author has been assigned many superlatives as a science fiction craftsman. Among other accolades, Heinlein has been dubbed—correctly—the "Dean of Science Fiction."

We know this with certainty: Robert A. Heinlein was one of the greatest science fiction writers not just of the previous century but of all time. He was one of the most adept "pure" science fiction practitioners in terms of "hard" science fiction and political science fiction, and he numbered among the most accomplished social science fiction scribes as well. He also was one of the most varied, wide-ranging, and best-revered authors of his time.

Heinlein is the archetypal "science fiction" writer; he set the standard for the genre as we now know it. Nineteenth-century founders like Jules Verne and H. G. Wells were more heavily invested in scientific romance. While these masters' stories provided a degree of moral allegory, turn of phrase, and futuristic vision, along with clever premises, themes, and plotting, they did not provide the template, even boilerplate, for modern science fiction. Even with some fast and free applications and speculations about the uses and extensions of existing "hard" sciences—as well as "social/soft" sciences, political sciences, and so on—Verne and Wells never achieved the level of hard science that Robert A. Heinlein tackled. Prior to Heinlein, even the previous masters of science fiction never approached the SF accomplishments of, say, "The Roads Must Roll" (1940). Edward Page Mitchell (1852–1927) may have come the closest.

Heinlein was extremely effective at portraying settings, both tangible and intangible, and developing characters and character types in his stories. In his work, he often provided an invention or scientific idea upon which each story is centered. These inventions could be of great world value, but they also could be flawed and the source of great catastrophe. They often provided the complication for the storyline. With tremendous dexterity, Heinlein wrote of labor law, political theory, the military, advances in science and technology, and the human condition. Since the tales we read even three decades following the author's death were written across some fifty years of his lifetime, they went through periods of change—in terms of topic, style, and mood. Distinct phases, themes, and eras mark Heinlein's career, and just as there are masterpieces, so, too, there exist works whose worth is debated and even the occasional author-declared "stinkeroo." Yet no matter the phases and no matter the ups and downs, Heinlein stands at the forefront in his contribution to his art, a central pillar in the structure of science fiction, just as Picasso is a mainstay in the many equally important rooms in the house of popular art. To follow the career of Robert A. Heinlein is to follow not only the evolution of science fiction, but also the evolution of the twentieth century.

From 1939 to 1949, Heinlein was more than a competent pulp magazine writer. During these pre- and postwar years, he was an exquisite critic of government, the military, and big business, along with the two-dimensional, small-minded, and even paranoid people who often could be found in these organizations. What follows here is not an analysis and discussion of the detailed and complex fantastic Heinlein worldview called "Future History," nor is it a definitive chronicle of revisions, or a listing of later stories' appearances in book form. Instead, it is an introductory exploration of the science fiction and fantasy of Robert A. Heinlein from 1939 to 1949, a disparate group of tales that not only defines and serves as the basis for the author's collective works, but also serves as a defining bedrock or archetype for the larger science fiction genre.

Two cornerstone volumes of any Robert A. Heinlein library are *The Past Through Tomorrow: Future History Stories* (1967) and *Expanded Universe* (1980). These two collections are relevant to our discussion here, since each reprints *some* of those first Heinlein tales from 1939 to 1949. *The Past Through Tomorrow* collects stories of "Future History"—stories of what could be in coming days. The works of science fiction found in this collection often are allegories—moral lessons and warnings—of what could happen should humanity make technological advances with which it is incapable of dealing appropriately. *Expanded Universe* dovetails nicely with *The Past Through Tomorrow*, though it is by no means a sequel to its predecessor. *Expanded Universe* features stand-alone fiction, non-fiction, and some Future History stories in an effort to update and diversify Heinlein's paradigm of *The Past Through Tomorrow*. Just as detailed analyses of the Future History stories, or Heinlein's philosophy and worldview in *Expanded Universe*, are not the focus here, neither will we discuss the twelve-year series of juvenile novels that begins with *Rocket Ship Galileo* (1947), *Space Cadet* (1948), and *Red Planet* (1949)—a corpus that, aside from having been read and reread by countless readers across several generations, has been studied by critics elsewhere. Here, after all, the early shorter works are our focus.

Under his real name or pseudonyms, Robert A. Heinlein provided an incredible array of high-quality science fiction and fantasy even between 1939 and 1941, leaving the fan so much to explore and unearth. Major works from this very early period include numerous short stories of wide variety and also longer works, such as "'If This Goes On—'" (*Astounding*, February and March 1940), "Sixth Column" (*Astounding*, January, February, and March 1941), "Universe" (*Astounding*, May 1941), and "Methuselah's Children"

(*Astounding*, July, August, and September 1941). Some of these novellas later were expanded and then released as their own books.

Two major editors and markets account for much of Robert A. Heinlein's popular and critical reception. These were John W. Campbell, Jr., (1910–1971) and Frederik Pohl (1919–2013). John W. Campbell, Jr.'s biography is pretty common knowledge to the science fiction fan and scholar. Campbell had his early space operas published in *Amazing Stories* and similar pulp magazines in the very early 1930s. When he became editor of Street and Smith publisher's *Astounding Stories* in the mid-1930s, Campbell revolutionized the publishing of science fiction magazines. Hugo Gernsback created the first science fiction magazine in 1926 with *Amazing Stories*; Campbell, however, created the archetype for the genre when he took over editorship of *Astounding* in 1937. A "Who's Who" of science fiction authors got their professional careers jumpstarted, and some even began their careers, under the tutelage of Campbell. Isaac Asimov, Catherine L. Moore, Clifford Simak, E. E. "Doc" Smith, Theodore Sturgeon, and other legends numbered among the editor's literary stable. Robert A. Heinlein was John W. Campbell's most important author, and for more than a decade Heinlein carried *Astounding.*

Every major pulp magazine thrived especially because of certain prolific or well-loved authors. In 1920s detective fiction, for example, Joseph T. Shaw, the most important editor of *(The) Black Mask*, detective fiction's most important publication, relied on his own cadre of literary talent. Shaw had Carroll John Daly, Erle Stanley Gardner, Raymond Chandler, and others upon whom to draw for topflight private investigator stories. Shaw and *Black Mask*'s true pillar, however, was Dashiell Hammett. Robert A. Heinlein was to John W. Campbell, Jr., as Hammett was to Shaw.

Frederik Pohl was the other major science fiction magazine editor who embraced, supported, and bought Heinlein's early and later writing. There were other editors, of course, but Pohl was the editor of the pulp magazines *Super Science Stories* and *Astonishing Stories* from about 1939 to 1943—the war years—and then, in the late 1950s through the 1960s, Pohl edited science fiction digests, most notably *World of IF* and *Galaxy Science Fiction*. Pohl often bought Heinlein's work for his publications; in the postwar digest era, these stories included novellas, serials, and novels, as well as short stories.

In addition to these "traditional" science fiction markets, Heinlein in the postwar period also broke into more broadly read markets. After an early burst of creativity—with twenty-nine stories published between 1939 and 1942, under his own name and pseudonyms—the rising star's fiction output plummeted during the Second World War, when he was a civilian engineer working for the Navy and his writing then consisting solely of technical reports and memoranda. In 1947, however, following numerous unsuccessful attempts to place several nonfiction yet snappily written essays on the dangers of the then-new nuclear age, Heinlein at last began publishing new SF in upscale periodicals such as the *Saturday Evening Post*, *Town and Country*, *Argosy*, and *Blue Book*. The year 1947 also saw the first of his young-adult novels published by Scribner's, the beginning of a series whose popularity with school libraries was to spread Heinlein's name ever more widely and bring him increasing royalties.

Yet this leads away from the stories that started it all. Let us look, therefore, at some of the more notable pieces of short fiction from the 1939–1949 period.

"Life-Line"

Originally published in *Astounding Science-Fiction* (August 1939); later collected in *The Man Who Sold the Moon* (1950), *The Worlds of Robert A. Heinlein* (1966), *The Past Through Tomorrow* (1967), and *Expanded Universe* (1980).

"Life-Line" is science-based fantasy, both a political and economic tract and a morality play. In this, his *Astounding* debut, Heinlein goes big. He points out the fundamental flaw of the sociopolitical, economic model of capitalism—the doctrine, along with democracy, at the heart of United States self-definition. In the guise of story character Dr. Pinero, Heinlein writes,

"There has grown up in the minds of certain groups in this country the notion that because a man or corporation has made a profit out of the public for a number of years, the government and the courts are charged with the duty of guaranteeing such profit in the future, even in the face of changing circumstances and contrary public interest. This strange doctrine is not supported by statute or common law."

Those who wholeheartedly embrace capitalism rarely want the consequences of failure in such a system. In fact, failures in capitalism often want the safeguards of socialism and related models and doctrines to rescue them.

Heinlein was roughly thirty-two years of age at the time of the writing and then publication of "Life-Line." At this point, with some real-world experience behind him, he is not as young and immature as some other burgeoning science fiction authors. And we readers immediately note that, in this story, he already shows an advanced writing style, insightful social critique, and advanced storytelling for an author so early in his writing career.

"'Let There Be Light'"
Originally published in *Super Science Stories* (May 1940) under the penname Lyle Monroe; later collected in *The Man Who Sold the Moon* (1950).

Heinlein's story invention of the female scientist in "'Let There Be Light'" was relatively revolutionary for this story first published in 1940. Dr. M(ary) L(ou) Martin is that scientist, and like real-life science fiction and fantasy authors C(atherine) L(ucille) Moore, M(ary) E(lizabeth) Counselman, and Andre Norton, Martin uses her initials or, as in the case of Norton, pseudonyms to disguise her gender.

Dr. Martin's colleague and rival is Dr. Archibald "Archie" Douglas. There are gender and sexual tensions and banter between Archie and Mary Lou throughout the story. Martin, for example, describes Douglas as a "gangster"-type tough guy, while Douglas describes Martin as period pinup Betty Grable. Together the pair explores and provides alternate power sources for world use, and together they come up with an invention that Martin claims is the best thing since the dynamo. But there are complications in regard to social acceptance, sales, American business, and so on. Heinlein foreshadows this as he prefaces the story with the statement, "There is no room for Prometheus in American business."

"'Let There Be Light'" features scientific theory and principles from physics, and from political and economic reality. Dr. Martin asks Dr. Douglas, "Didn't you ever hear of 'Breakages Ltd.'?" This alludes to George Bernard Shaw's *Back to Methuselah* and is a sardonic way of describing the combined power of corporate industry to resist any change that might threaten their dividends. "You threaten the whole industrial set-up, son, and you're in danger where you're sitting. What do you think happened to atomic power?"

Reminiscent of Upton Sinclair's *The Jungle* (1906) and Jack London's *Iron Heel* (1908), "'Let There Be Light'" has timely, insightful implications for us seventy-five years later. It seems as if some relationships between science, government, business, and people never change. And while the scientists in the story devise a potentially great invention of energy and power, the real invention of the story is Heinlein's depiction of the inner workings and value of men and women as equal partners pursuing practical and noble causes—progressive stuff for 1940.

"Heil!"

Originally published in *Futuria Fantasia* (Summer 1940); later collected in *Futuria Fantasia* (2007) and as "Successful Operation" in *Expanded Universe* (1980).

A very early experimental writing that might have polished up well for an episode of Rod Serling's *Twilight Zone*, "Heil!" is a historical fantasy and a crafty tale of revenge. This story of Nazi Germany really captures the real-life horror of the time—it pulls no punches. Nazi leaders and concentration camps are central to this short-short story that is somewhat awkward in form and construction. Particularly awkward and abrupt are transitions between settings and scenes, and characters that are very marginally developed. Yet "Heil!" is a "neat" piece that plays off its title. It certainly gives us some insight into Heinlein's wrestle with the craft of writing. The best compliment that can be given this tale is that, as the reader, we want more.

Ray Bradbury's *Futuria Fantasia* ran only four issues. The authors who contributed to these four fanzines included Forrest Ackerman, Damon Knight, Henry Kuttner, and a thirty-two year old named Robert A. Heinlein. Heinlein, as was the case with some other *Fantasia Futuria* contributors, was leery of young Bradbury's venture, so he and other contributors used pseudonyms for bylines to protect what they hoped would one day be their own marketable names. And perhaps, given the more polished quality of Heinlein stories of the era, the author did not invest as much time and effort into "Heil!" Ultimately, though, Heinlein, thirteen years older than Bradbury, did become a good friend and mentor to the younger writer.

For all practical purposes, this is a long-lost Heinlein treasure. "Heil!" provides some important insight into Heinlein's development as a craftsman, green ink printing in *Futuria Fantasia* and all.

"The Roads Must Roll"

Originally published in *Astounding Science-Fiction* (June 1940); later collected in *The Man Who Sold the Moon* (1950) and *The Past Through Tomorrow* (1967).

"The Roads Must Roll" is quintessential Robert A. Heinlein from the early years. Featuring socio-political themes and portrayals of class structure, labor economics, and unions, the tale is reminiscent of *Metropolis*, the novel published in 1922 by Thea von Harbou and then turned into a silent film in 1927.

Directed by Fritz Lang, von Harbou's then-husband, and with a screenplay co-written by the pair, the avant-garde and surrealistic *Metropolis* was controversial for its day. Made in Germany in the era of the Weimar Republic, the motion picture still is considered a cinematic masterpiece. Heinlein's story shares not only some thematic concerns but also, in its original publication, some visual mood from the dramatic Hubert Rogers illustration that graces the cover of the June 1940 issue of *Astounding Science-Fiction*. The banner behind the bold sans-serif lettering of the magazine's cleanly modern, full-capital title that month is bright red, overlaid across the bottom with a businesslike white rectangle bearing the title of the issue's feature story, along with Heinlein's already up-and-coming byline. And below these is Rogers' painting in metallic blues and somber browns, wherein goggled, leather-jacketed men in jodhpurs and knee boots brandish pistols as their gyro-stabilized unicycles bank through a hard turn at high speed before huge industrial mechanisms looming in the background. It is the perfect visual "hook," just as Campbell's change of Heinlein's original flattish title of "Road Town" to the more driving "The Roads Must Roll" provides the perfect verbal hook.

Like "Life-Line," "The Roads Must Roll" starts with a contentious meeting—one of Heinlein's techniques for introducing social issues. The premise or invention of the story is relatively simplistic, though the practical application of science is suspect. The reader, however, grants the author literary license in terms of exact science application, for the overall idea is so fascinating. Like modern-day moving floors in airports, or even shopping mall escalators, the futuristic roads depicted in the story move millions of people around the world. With that large-scale transportation comes technological error and erratic human behavior. The "road" becomes so powerful that story characters take it for granted. Its practicality and implications go unexamined by most who blindly follow tradition. This provides the complication and storyline for Heinlein's story.

Heinlein theorizes, postulates, and predicts:

> The Age of Power blends into the Age of Transportation, almost imperceptibly, but two events stand out as landmarks in the change: the achievement of cheap sun power and the installation of the first mechanized road. The power resources of oil and coal of the United States had—save for a few sporadic outbreaks of common sense— been shamefully wasted in their development all through the first half of the twentieth century.

Seventy-five years later, these words from "The Roads Must Roll" seem not only prophetic but also profound. "The Roads Must Roll" combines scientific statistics, historical and established, with predictions of the future. What must Isaac Asimov, a real-life scientist as well as an aspiring science fiction author—whose epic Foundation series was to begin in 1942—have thought upon reading this story?

"They"

Originally published in *Unknown* (April 1941); later collected in *The Unpleasant Profession of Jonathan Hoag* (1959) and *The Fantasies of Robert A. Heinlein* (1999).

"They" predicts, in many ways, Robert A. Heinlein's 1951 novel, *The Puppet Masters*, which was serialized in *Galaxy Science Fiction* in September, October, and November of that year. Justified paranoia regarding alien invaders pervades both "They" and the later novel. This story was published in *Unknown* (*Worlds*), Campbell's fantasy companion pulp to his SF flagship, *Astounding Science-Fiction*.

The main character in "They" is held or incarcerated in a sort of asylum. In 1941, asylums were still very much part of the American landscape, and, of course, the history of these institutions is fascinating, sometimes uplifting, and often terrifying. The nameless man suspects that people and events around him, including the concerned-seeming Dr. Hayward, are not what they appear and have ulterior motives. The reader sympathizes with the character right from the start, and as the story progresses from a chess game with Dr. Hayward onward, Heinlein provides a dark, condemning critique of psychological medicine of the day. It turns out that the nameless man is right in his reasoning, and constitutes—somehow—a very real threat to his captors.

"The Green Hills of Earth"

Originally published in *Saturday Evening Post* (8 February 1947); later collected in *The Green Hills of Earth* (1951) and *The Past Through Tomorrow* (1967).

Something outside the story goes on in "The Green Hills of Earth," the first work of SF that Heinlein published after the long dry spell of the Second World War—and, moreover, the first he published in a major "mainstream" magazine rather than a genre pulp. For all the backdrop of atomic power, spaceflight, and interplanetary colonization, the story and songs of the tragic "Noisy" Rhysling, the Blind Singer of the Spaceways, evoke romance, remembrance, melancholy, and reflection more than mere "hard" science. The tale has been reprinted often in years since, and it made excellent fodder for story radio in the 1950s.

Heinlein acknowledges the influence of Catherine Lucille Moore's epic space opera "Shambleau" (*Weird Tales*, November 1933) in the writing of this story. The story is also very Bradbury-esque, and it is about this time that Ray Bradbury was writing space opera/Scientific Romances that later would be collected as his "Martian Chronicles." This type of science fiction story was not unique to Moore, Bradbury, or Heinlein during the late 1940s, but it certainly became associated with all three.

"Our Fair City"

Originally published in *Weird Tales* (January 1949); later collected in *The Unpleasant Profession of Jonathan Hoag* (1959) and *The Fantasies of Robert A. Heinlein* (1999).

An ancestor of the Urban Fantasy genre of fiction epitomized today by the works of Jim Butcher, "Our Fair City" was Robert A. Heinlein's lone publication in *Weird Tales*, with very effective interior line drawing provided by Boris Dolgov, popular *Weird Tales* illustrator in the 1940s and '50s. This piece is straight-out fantasy, as there is not one element of scientific, legal, or political theory herein. Though some veiled social issues may be involved, and some allusion to matters of class structure and city life, there really are no social theories or issues found here either. The familiar pulp magazine motif of the newspaper reporter as protagonist—Pete Perkins, in this case—is in place.

While Robert Heinlein was senior and mentor to the younger Ray Bradbury (1920–2012), "Our Fair City" is very much a Bradbury-type story. In other words, in this tale, Heinlein is the mentor imitating the mentee, Bradbury. In many ways, this Heinlein outing is a light counterpart to Bradbury's "The Wind" (*Weird Tales*, March 1943). In the earlier Bradbury weird tale, "The Wind" is the malevolent antagonist of Alan, the world-traveling central character of the story. The Wind increasingly harasses and tortures Alan, mentally, emotionally, and physically. Conversely, in Heinlein's "Our Fair City," the playful whirlwind is an obedient pet to Pappy, elderly gentleman and street person. Pappy serves as the whirlwind's master, and he lovingly names the meteorological phenomenon "Kitten."

Heinlein's "Our Fair City" just as easily could have been published in Street and Smith's *Unknown (Worlds)*, the fantasy flipside of the publisher's SF magazine archetype, *Astounding Science-Fiction*. "Our Fair City" is a fun, rewarding read that further demonstrates the dexterity and literary prowess of its author.

"The Long Watch"

Originally published in *American Legion Magazine* (December 1949); later collected in *The Green Hills of Earth* (1951) and *The Past Through Tomorrow* (1967).

"The Long Watch" is a story of heroism and sacrifice. It is also a story of what happens when a military leader becomes a megalomaniac. Lieutenant Johnny Dahlquist is the young family man under the command of Colonel Towers, stationed on the Moon, at Moon Base, as "bomb officer" to monitor volatile radioactive materials and the nuclear weaponry of deterrent with which the United Nations keeps the peace. When he realizes that Colonel Towers' notion of the desirability of having the world run by a "scientifically selected group"—the Patrol to which they belong—rather than mere politicians is no hypothetical and, indeed, that the coup is beginning now on Moon Base, the young man is faced with the ultimate self-sacrifice. The end of this story—in which Johnny, fatally radiation-poisoned from disassembling the atom bombs to keep them from Towers' use, stoically smokes and thinks of his wife and of the other American martyrs to freedom who "gathered about him in the dusky bomb room"—is one of the most poignant and heart-wrenching in all of Heinlein literature.

The place of publication—*The American Legion Magazine*—and date of publication are noteworthy, too. While Heinlein in this period was publishing stories in other "slick" magazines, such as *The Saturday Evening Post*, the placement of "The Long Watch," which is in many ways an indictment of military leadership, in *The American Legion Magazine* may have been bold. Finally, Heinlein's story references a "drone"—a robot vehicle intended for transporting radioactive material—and makes today's reader pause to consider current real-life drone deployments.

"Delilah and the Space-Rigger"

Originally published in *Blue Book* (December 1949); later collected in *The Green Hills of Earth* (1951) and *The Past Through Tomorrow* (1967).

"Delilah and the Space-Rigger" is an Old Testament tribute and reference, and the title of the story hence alerts the reader to this right from the start. The Samson character is "Tiny" Larsen, a physically large foreman-type who runs a crew in an orbiting space station. The Delilah character, the one who bests the male giant, is G(loria) B(rooks) McNye.

"Delilah and the Space-Rigger" is progressive, feminist science fiction. Gloria McNye's use of initials to mask her gender again reflects the strategies of real-life women of the day, and there are many historical references, scientific names, personalities, and terms of the era found. For example, Tiny attended Oppenheimer Tech, obviously named after the famous Manhattan Project scientist, and microwave ovens—which in real life first appeared in 1946—are mentioned.

The "golden age" of science fiction is defined by many fans and scholars as that time between 1939 and 1945, when John Campbell, Jr.'s *Astounding Science-Fiction* led other pulp magazines in imagination and creativity. Robert A. Heinlein was the science fiction genius of *Astounding* and, subsequently, of the golden age of science fiction.

There is so much to discover in the science fiction and fantasy of the first decade of Robert Heinlein's writing career. An essay of this size covers only a small selection of the master's work, so there still remains room for the student or scholar to read even more widely and pursue much more extensive analysis. One important larger work, for example, is the author's *For Us, The Living: A Comedy of Customs*. Written in 1939, but not rediscovered until long after Heinlein's death and first published in 2004, *For Us, The Living* encapsulates an overview of Robert A. Heinlein's early career—an early career that proved the foundation of fifty years of the very best in science fiction. Themes, settings, and situations from this once-unknown novel reverberate not only through Heinlein's early short fiction but also through his Scribner's juveniles and his later works clearly aimed at the adult market.

The process of discovery of the Heinlein literary genesis is complex and yet rewarding indeed, and the stories of 1939 to 1949 are a logical and enjoyable place to start. Below, therefore, are listed all of the stories of Heinlein's first decade as a professional writer, including both original magazine publications and also the later, more easily accessible books which collect them; most of the collections, of course, also have been reprinted in several editions.

Original Pulp Magazine Appearances

"Life-Line." *Astounding Science-Fiction* (August 1939)

"Misfit." *Astounding Science-Fiction* (November 1939)

"Requiem." *Astounding Science-Fiction* (January 1940)

"'If This Goes On—'." *Astounding Science-Fiction* (February and March 1940)

"'Let There Be Light'." *Super Science Stories* (May 1940), as by Lyle Monroe

"The Roads Must Roll." *Astounding Science-Fiction* (June 1940)

"Coventry." *Astounding Science-Fiction* (July 1940)

"Successful Operation." *Futuria Fantasia* (#4, Summer 1940), as "Heil" as by Lyle Monroe

"Blowups Happen." *Astounding Science-Fiction* (September 1940)

"Magic, Inc." *Unknown* (September 1940), as "The Devil Makes the Law"

"Sixth Column." *Astounding Science Fiction* (January, February and March 1941)

"'—And He Built a Crooked House—'." *Astounding Science-Fiction* (February 1941)

"Logic of Empire." *Astounding Science-Fiction* (March 1941)

"Beyond Doubt." *Astonishing Stories* (April 1941), as by Elma Wentz and Lyle Monroe

"They." *Unknown* (April 1941)

"Solution Unsatisfactory." *Astounding Science-Fiction* (May 1941), as by Anson MacDonald

"Universe." *Astounding Science-Fiction* (May 1941)

"'—We Also Walk Dogs'." *Astounding Science-Fiction* (July 1941), as by Anson MacDonald

"Methuselah's Children." *Astounding Science-Fiction* (July, August, and September 1941)

"Elsewhen." *Astounding Science-Fiction* (September 1941), as by Caleb Saunders

"By My Bootstraps." *Astounding Science-Fiction* (October 1941), as by Anson MacDonald

"Common Sense." *Astounding Science-Fiction* (October 1941)

"Lost Legacy." *Astounding Science-Fiction* (November 1941), as by Lyle Monroe

"My Object All Sublime." *Future* (February 1942), as by Lyle Monroe

"Goldfish Bowl." *Astounding Science-Fiction* (March 1942)

"Pied Piper." *Astonishing Science-Fiction* (March 1942), as by Lyle Monroe

"Beyond This Horizon." *Astounding Science-Fiction* (April and May 1942)

"Waldo." *Astounding Science-Fiction* (August 1942), as by Anson MacDonald

"The Unpleasant Profession of Jonathan Hoag." *Unknown Worlds* (October 1942), as by John Riverside

"A Bathroom of Her Own." (1946)—not previously published, but later collected in *Expanded Universe*

"Free Men" (1947)—not previously published, but later collected in *Worlds of Robert A. Heinlein* and in *Expanded Universe*

"No Bands Playing, No Flags Flying." (1947) *Vertex* #3 (1973)

"On the Slopes of Vesuvius" (1947)—not previously published, but later collected in *Expanded Universe*

"The Green Hills of Earth." *Saturday Evening Post* (8 February 1947)

"Space Jockey." *Saturday Evening Post* (26 April 1947)

"Columbus Was a Dope." *Startling Stories* (May 1947)

"They Do It with Mirrors." *Popular Detective* (May 1947), as by Simon York

"'It's Great to Be Back!'" *Saturday Evening Post* (July 26, 1947)

"Jerry Was a Man." *Thrilling Wonder Stories* (October 1947)

"The Man Who Traveled in Elephants." *Saturn* (October 1947)

"Water is for Washing." *Argosy* (November 1947)

"The Black Pits of Luna." *Saturday Evening Post* (10 January 1948)

"Gentlemen, Be Seated!" *Argosy* (May 1948)

"Ordeal in Space." *Town and Country* (May 1948)

"Our Fair City." *Weird Tales* (January 1949)

"Nothing Ever Happens on the Moon." *Boy's Life* (April and May 1949)

"Poor Daddy" *Calling All Girls* (August 1949)

"Gulf." *Astounding Science-Fiction* (November and December 1949)

"The Long Watch." *American Legion Magazine* (December 1949), as "Rebellion on the Moon"

"Delilah and the Space-Rigger." *Blue Book* (December 1949)

Book Collections that Include These Early Stories

Bradbury, Ray D. *Futuria Fantasia*. Los Angeles: Graham, 2007.

Heinlein, Robert A. *Expanded Universe: The New Worlds of Robert A. Heinlein*. New York: Ace, 1980.

_____. *For Us, The Living: A Comedy of Customs*. New York: Scribner, 2004.

_____. *The Green Hills of Earth*. Chicago: Shasta, 1951.

_____. *The Man Who Sold the Moon*. Chicago: Shasta, 1950.

_____. *The Past Through Tomorrow: Future History Stories*. New York: Putnam, 1967.

_____. *Requiem: New Collected Works by Robert A. Heinlein and Other Tributes to the Grand Master*. Ed. Yoji Kondo. New York: Tor, 1992.

_____. *Revolt in 2100*. Chicago: Shasta, 1954.

_____. *Sixth Column*. New York: Gnome, 1949.

Growing Up with Heinlein

John J. Pierce

"You had to be there."

It's one of the oldest and most tiresome clichés. It is lately even the title of a podcast comedy series. But there weren't any podcasts in 1947, when Robert A. Heinlein's *Rocket Ship Galileo* was published, nor even a hint of the kind of technology that one day would make them possible.

Young science fiction readers today know about podcasts and all sorts of other things that young SF readers of the first generation after World War II simply couldn't have imagined. Readers today also are growing up on young-adult SF works, like Suzanne Collins' Hunger Games series and their blockbuster movie adaptations. There was nothing like that in 1947.

To understand the impact of Heinlein's young adult novels, we must try to imagine how they were read by that first generation—and what those readers brought to their reading, what they knew and didn't know about science fiction, and what they took from what was then called juvenile fiction. They may or may not, for example, have been fans of the Hardy Boys or its SF counterpart, the Great Marvel (1906–1935) series, perhaps handed down by their fathers. But what they can't have known—Heinlein revealed it only in his posthumously published *Grumbles from the Grave*—was that Heinlein's working title for *Rocket Ship Galileo* was *The Young Atomic Engineers* and that it had been intended as the first of a series in the Great Marvel vein, with the same characters and double titles like *The Young Atomic Engineers in the Asteroids, or the Mystery of the Broken Planet* (47–48).

Those first-generation readers likewise couldn't have known of the running battle Heinlein had with his editor Alice Dalgliesh at Scribner's over content of the juveniles. They certainly couldn't have had any idea of the turns that Heinlein's career would take in later years, as when he put an end to his relationship with Scribner's with *Starship Troopers* (1959). They never could have imagined the Heinlein of *Stranger in a Strange Land* (1961)—and would have missed the clues in *Red Planet* (1949) that he was already thinking of elements that would go into that novel. Unless they had read *Beyond This Horizon*, which had been serialized in 1942 under the name Anson McDonald and appeared in book form from Fantasy Press under Heinlein's name only in 1948, they wouldn't have known of his mystical side—although there was a hint of that even in *Rocket Ship Galileo*.

If they had read any of the Great Marvel books, they might have recognized the resemblance of Heinlein's first juvenile to the formula and style of house author "Roy Rockwood" (Howard R. Garis, in this case):

> "Hand me that wrench, Mark," called Professor Amos Henderson to a boy who stood near some complicated machinery over which the old man was working. The lad passed the tool over.
>
> "Do you think the ship will work, Professor?" he asked.
>
> "I hope so, Mark, I hope so," muttered the scientist as he tightened some bolts on what was perhaps the strangest combination of apparatus that had ever been put together. "There is no reason why she should not, and yet—"
>
> The old man paused. Perhaps he feared that, after all, the submarine boat on which he had labored continuously for more than a year would be a failure. (1)

That's the opening of *Under the Ocean to the South Pole; Or, The Strange Cruise of the Submarine Wonder* (1907), second volume of the Great Marvel series. Henderson is the elderly inventor who had recruited Mark Sampson and Jack Darrow in the first book of the series, *Through the Air to the North Pole; Or, The Wonderful Cruise of the Electric Monarch* (1906). Later volumes would take Henderson and the boys—and a comic "colored" sidekick—to the center of the Earth, the Moon, Mars, Venus, and even Saturn. But the formula was always the same: pure action and adventure, including gunplay against savage men and animals.

Heinlein knew that formula and hewed to it closely in *Rocket Ship Galileo*. Three teenage boys—Art Mueller, Ross Jenkins, and Maurice Abrams—are busy testing a rocket when it blows up, just as Art's "atomic bomb" uncle Donald Cargraves arrives to recruit them for a trip to the Moon. Only he's been injured, and it seems at first that shrapnel from their rocket is responsible. It turns out later that Dr. Cargraves has been targeted by Nazi agents and that the Nazis even have a base on the Moon, borrowing a redoubt from a vanished lunar civilization that destroyed itself in an atomic war—not an auspicious debut, as Jo Walton and Spider Robinson have observed (Walton). And while Walton notes that the characters are diverse in their backgrounds, she complains that they are still "sketchily characterized" compared to those in later Heinlein juveniles, and that Cargraves, the adult, totally runs the show. Also lacking is the kind of literary magic that Heinlein at his best could evoke. The only real sign of it is a scene with Mueller at the controls of the *Galileo*:

> Still the black depths fascinated him. He fingered the drive control under his right hand. He had only to unlock it, twist it all the way to the right, and they would plunge ahead, nailed down by unthinkable acceleration, and speed on past the moon, too early for their date in space with her. On past the moon, away from the sun and earth behind them, on and on and out and out, until the thorium burned itself cold or until the zinc had boiled away, but not to stop even then, but to continue forever into the weary years and the bottomless depths. (Heinlein, *Four Frontiers* 86)

There are details that would have gone by most of Heinlein's readers at the time, such as the fact that Abrams is obviously Jewish: his father recalls that he had "stood up before the congregation and made your speech. 'Today I am a man—'" (*Four Frontiers* 30). That, and the whole Nazi thing, puts to bed the myth among some critics that the period's SF writers generally, and Heinlein in particular, were fascist. In a throwaway scene, we learn that Dr. Cargraves' favorite fiction includes not only Verne and Wells, but H. Rider Haggard's *When the Earth Trembled*—actually, *When the World Shook*, which has to do with a lost race and astral projection as well as a super-scientific menace—hinting at the mystical side of Heinlein that would resurface with a vengeance in later decades, but was lurking there all along.

Space Cadet (1948) marked a complete break from the formula of *Rocket Ship Galileo*: nothing about Young Atomic Engineers, and the Mystery of the Wrecked Planet is barely a footnote. Perhaps this had been Heinlein's intention all along, and he had imitated the Great Marvel model in his first juvenile just to get his foot in the door, so to speak.

This second novel follows the story of Matt Dodson and his fellow cadets William Jarman, Oscar Jensen, and Pierre Armand through their training at the Space Patrol Academy and then through the process of proving themselves on their first mission together, where they end up stranded on Venus. With their commander, Lieutenant Thurlow, comatose from the crash of their ship, they can depend only on themselves. Heinlein contrasts them with Girard Burke, a blowhard from a wealthy family who has washed out of the Academy but ended up on Venus, where he angered the natives by taking their matriarch hostage to get hold of a radioactive ore deposit. Burke was taken prisoner after they destroyed his ship, but radioed for help from the Patrol—and the Venerians naturally take the patrolmen to be hostile when they show up, taking *them* prisoner. It is Jensen, himself born on Venus, who has to win over their captors by understanding them and respecting their customs: "I guess you have to be brought up with them, like I have, to take them for granted. But everything about them is different—for instance, like the fact that you never lay eyes on anything but females" (Heinlein, *Four Frontiers* 315).

Burke is incensed that Jensen would "side up with these frog people against a *man*," even being warned that he is guilty of a crime under Terran law as well as local customs (Heinlein, *Four Frontiers* 325). Besides keeping the apparently weaker males out of sight, those customs include a taboo against eating in public, and Jensen can exploit that to shame the matriarch for having denied him and his men "the common decency of personal rooms in which to eat" (*Four Frontiers* 328).

Jensen isn't just blindly following Patrol precedent or reading a script, though—he's using his own judgment, using his *head*, and that's how he gets himself and his comrades out of a jam. In traditional boys' books, the heroes were expected to take adult authority for gospel, but in *Space Cadet* they have to think for themselves. Tellingly, in an early scene even before the cadets are sworn in, Dodson is taking an exam, and he eventually realizes something is wrong. The test doesn't make *sense*, for the purposefully confusing instructions actually preclude scoring any points:

> "Oh, come now!" the examiner answered. "Are you sure of that?"
> Matt hesitated, then answered firmly, "I'm sure of it. Want to see my proof?"
> "No. Your name is Dodson?" The examiner glanced at a timer, then wrote on a chart. "That's all."
> "But—Don't I get a chance to make a score?"
> "No questions, please! I've recorded your score. Get along—it's dinner time." (Heinlein, *Four Frontiers* 180–81)

Red Planet (1949) may have been loosely connected to *Space Cadet*: Jarman advises that "you must never mention death on Mars or to a Martian" (Heinlein, *Four Frontiers* 219), and Thurlow later mentions the Martian "double world" idea (*Four Futures* 291), apparently the life we know and the afterlife. The Martians of *Red Planet*, in any case, are the same as those in *Stranger*—even if readers couldn't have known that at the time. What they *would* have noticed was that Heinlein didn't cut any slack for stupid adults. Jim Marlowe, for example, recalls a story told by South Colony's Dr. MacRae of "this idiot" medical lieutenant who once tried to unroll a Martian who had folded himself up in protest over some sort of offense by one of his kind:

> "What happened?" Jim had demanded.
> "He disappeared."
> "The Martian?"
> "No, the medical officer." (Heinlein, *Four Frontiers* 393)

Marlowe later has to defy Mars Company authorities and even his own father when it becomes clear that the company is turning into a dictatorship:

> His father said, "Son, you can't take that attitude."
> Jim said, "Can't I? Well, I do. Why don't you find out what the score is before   you talk about giving me up?" (Heinlein, *Four Frontiers* 475)

Although the headmaster of the Mars Company boarding school—named Howe, in a pointed reference to a British general during the American Revolution, whereas Jim's full given name is James Madison—doesn't know it, he's an even worse idiot than the doctor who tried to unroll a Martian...for he has kidnapped Willis, whom Jim takes to be just a funny animal, and of whom he is very possessive, but who is actually a Martian child. The consequences thus could be dire indeed.

Quite aside from that, and the paranormal powers of Martians that anticipate *Stranger*, there are fascinating details not only about the Martians themselves, their dying cities, and their culture, including the water-sharing ceremony that raises Jim's consciousness, but also about other native life forms, from lifesaving desert cabbages to deadly water-seekers. We also learn about the everyday lives of the human colonists, the logic of their seasonal migrations, and the point of their cultural innovations, such as the fanciful designs on breathing masks that the Mars Company seeks to ban—Jim's tiger stripes may be boisterous, but they are practical, too, in aiding in identification.

Yet the Mars Company is out to ban not merely such painted designs but also firearms in private hands. Just as in *Beyond This Horizon*, gun rights are sacred to Heinlein, but although the original published version of the novel played that down at the insistence of Scribner's, Del Rey Books published an uncut version after his death, which is included in *Four Frontiers*. But even this version, in which Jim's sister Phyllis is a crack shot, retains a sexist passage that is cringeworthy today even to male readers, and it surely wouldn't have won Heinlein any female fans even in 1949: Dr. MacRae's declaration that "any girl old enough to cook and tend babies is an adult, too" (Heinlein, *Four Frontiers* 501). Contrast that with the first half of MacRae's assertion that, "any man old enough to fight is a man and must be treated as such" (*Four Frontiers* 501).

There was an intentional connection between *Space Cadet* and *Farmer in the Sky* (1950), for the Space Patrol is mentioned, and Cadet Armand had come from Ganymede. But it's a completely different kind of story than any of Heinlein's previous YA novels and not just for imagining everyday future technologies, like microwave ovens as opposed to the Big Important Things like interplanetary travel.

Well before he reaches Jupiter's moon to homestead a farm with his father, stepmother, and stepsister, young Bill Lermer gets a lesson in the meaning of heroism—and true heroism isn't only about fighting stock villains like Nazis, criminals like Burke, or would-be oppressors like the Mars Company. The torch ship *Mayflower*, on which they have shipped out, is powered by a nuclear engine "hot" enough to kill anyone who comes near it; the torch has to be shielded from the passenger and crew sections of the ship. Chief Engineer Ortega explains all this to the teens, but one wise guy keeps bugging him about what happens if he has to make a repair. Ortega brushes him off, saying that the power plant doesn't have any moving parts and that nothing can go wrong with it. Yet Bill's father George, himself an engineer, later tells him that isn't quite the truth:

> "There are certain adjustments which could conceivably have to be made in extreme emergency. In which case it would be Mr. Ortega's proud privilege to climb into a space suit, go outside and back aft, and make them."
> "You mean—"
> "I mean that the assistant chief engineer would succeed to the position of chief a few minutes later. Chief engineers are very carefully chosen, Bill, and not just for their technical knowledge." (Heinlein, *Four Frontiers* 588)

It hasn't been all sweetness and light in the Lermer family either. When George decides to marry his draftsman Molly Kenyon, Bill takes it as a personal betrayal. He reveres his late mother and can't stand Molly, whom he considers "indecent" and playing "chummy" with him just to get at his father, or her twelve-year-old "brat" of a daughter Peggy (Heinlein, *Four Frontiers* 556). "You don't love Anne any more, do you?" he bursts out (*Four Frontiers* 558), and refuses to attend the wedding. George is tempted to thrash him, but instead takes off for the wedding and a brief honeymoon, returning only the night before they're to leave for Ganymede. It's hardly an auspicious start.

But there are more serious matters to worry about aboard the *Mayflower*, and not just the torch. Bill surprises even himself, saving his bunkmates by improvising a temporary patch from a foam rubber pillow when a meteor knocks a hole in their compartment. Before long there are Boy Scout activities on the ship and even improvised schooling: "Each class consisted of about two dozen kids and some adult who knew something about something. (You'd be surprised how many adults don't know anything about anything!)" (Heinlein, *Four Frontiers* 590).

When they reach Ganymede, there isn't any cleared land waiting for them, just bare and barren rock: a wave of immigrants has overwhelmed the resources of the colony. It will take months to get a turn with a rock crusher, and even after that, making actual soil will be a matter of exhausting toil. The Lermers are tempted to throw in the towel and head home, but then they encounter a jovial homesteader named Schultz, who agrees to take them on as hands for the time being and help them get started on their own farm... whenever. Schultz has the only apple tree on the moon, and when the Lermers need compost for their newly processed land, he offers them a gift beyond price: his *garbage!*

Only there's a lot more to terraforming than that because the very ecology on Ganymede has to be created from scratch. Yet it also depends on the high technology of the heat trap, which maintains a livable temperature. When a quake knocks that out, most of the colonists—including Peggy, who has had trouble with the thin air all along—perish from the quake itself or from the bitter cold before the heat can be restored. Pioneering can be a grim business, but the Lermers decide to stick it out. Molly bears twin boys, a new generation native to their new world. Still, George wants Bill to return to Earth to complete his education. By this time, however, Bill has become a *man*, a man for whom a new world and everything that has happened there have become part of a learning experience, and who now can make his own decisions and live by them: "I am where I belong. And I'm going to stay" (Heinlein, *Four Frontiers* 709).

Two lesser works followed. *Between Planets* (1951), like *Red Planet*, is about a revolution, though in this case on Venus rather than Mars. *The Rolling Stones* (1952) is best remembered today for the flat cats, fast-breeding Martian critters that inspired David Gerrold's *Star Trek* episode "The Trouble with Tribbles" (1967).

But then came *Starman Jones* (1953), in which Heinlein threw caution to the wind in creating a flawed hero. Not only that, but he created his first interstellar young-adult novel, putting the outdated Mars and Venus behind him—even if he was to bring them back years later with *Stranger* (1961) and *Podkayne of Mars* (1963).

Max Jones comes from a broken home and breaks the law to get into space after learning that his late uncle, who had been a member of the Astrogators Guild, hadn't put him up for membership, despite having bequeathed Max his manuals. Max has grown up on a hardscrabble farm in the Ozarks; his father is dead, and his mother has just married a thug who treats her as a doormat and takes a belt to Max. No reason for him to stick around, especially since the good-for-nothing has just sold the farm.

On the way to Earthport to try to enlist in the Guild, he meets a Good Samaritan who becomes a father figure and mentor, a man who calls himself Sam Anderson. It is Sam who gets false papers for himself and Max to ship out on the *Asgard*; we eventually learn that he is a deserter from the Imperial Marines. But even before they begin their journey, we are treated to some remarkable world-building on Earth itself.

The very first scene is set next to one of the ring roads, an application of what we now would call rail gun technology to transportation. But the upshot isn't about the ring road itself, but instead about how Max later is almost killed when an unscheduled train comes through a tunnel just used as a shortcut on the way to the nearest station. In that same first scene, he was reading *Sky Beasts: A Guide to Exotic Biology*, which includes "a description of the intelligent but phlegmatic crustaceans of Epsilon Ceti IV" (Heinlein, *To the Stars* 350). Later, in Earthport, he actually spots his first alien, but he knows that, for his time period, it's no big deal: "He saw his first extra-terrestrial, an eight-foot native of Epsilon Gemini V, striding out of a shop with a package under his left arms—as casually, Max thought, as a farmer doing his week's shopping at the Corners" (*To the Stars* 371).

Aboard the *Asgard*, Max is only a steward's mate at first, but it's enough that he gets to see new worlds on the journey. He also encounters Mr. Chips, a semi-intelligent alien spider puppy, the pet of a wealthy young passenger, Ellie Coburn, who, among other things, is a champion at three-dimensional chess, and who at one point challenges his assumptions about women, of why they "sometimes prefer not to appear too bright" (Heinlein, *To the Stars* 506). Yet neither she nor Mr. Chips is there just for decoration: Ellie is the one who, having learned that Max knows astrogation, gets him a chance to apprentice as a chartsman, and her spider puppy helps save them in the harrowing climax of the novel.

A calculation error in an interstellar jump leaves the ship in unknown space, seemingly with no way back. They find a planet and start a settlement, but they are menaced by the ruling centaur-like species, which in a twist on Jonathan Swift's *Gulliver's Travels* holds a humanoid species in subjection. Unlike Swift's Houyhnhnms, though, these beings aren't noble, only brutal. Max and Ellie are captured, but manage to escape with the help of Sam, alerted by Mr. Chips. The crew and passengers beat off a siege of their colony, in which Sam dies heroically, but there is no hope of final victory. It's all up to Max now, as acting captain—the Old Man has died.

We've known from the start that Max has an eidetic memory; now he takes a chance on using it to plot a return jump and bring them back to known space. But he knows he has to face the music for his imposture, and tells all to his first officer. He ends up paying a heavy fine, but is admitted to the Guild. Only, it is that first officer who offers the real verdict:

> "Captain, no code is perfect. A man must conform with judgment and commonsense, not with blind obedience. I've broken rules; some violations I paid for, some I didn't. This mistake you made could have turned you into a moralistic prig, a 'Regulation Charlie' determined to walk the straight and narrow and to see to it that everyone else obeyed the letter of the law. Or it could have made you a permanent infant who thinks rules are for everyone but him. It doesn't seem to have had either effect; I think it has matured you." (Heinlein, *To the Stars* 530)

Heinlein admitted to his agent Lurton Blassingame that while his sympathies were with Max, he himself really didn't know whether his protagonist had been morally justified in lying his way into the space merchant service. But then, he added, "I don't much like handing kids ready-made answers in any case" (Patterson 93). Readers of *Starman Jones* were being invited to wrestle with the issue just as he had.

The Star Beast (1954) is lighter in tone, but serious in its import. The action takes place on Earth but has interstellar consequences because the creature known as Lummox isn't the mere extraterrestrial pet it seems to be. It's been in the Stuart family for generations and is now "owned" by John Thomas Stuart XI. Lummox is actually female, although the Stuarts don't know that, and she's a lot bigger than she used to be; when she gets loose one day, she wreaks destruction in the neighborhood, and a local court orders her put to death.

The case comes to the attention of Henry Gladstone Kiku, the world government's Permanent Undersecretary of Spatial Affairs, who has been approached by representatives of a previously unknown alien race that seeks the return of a lost child—or else. Kiku happens to be a black African; Heinlein had made it clear as early as *Space Cadet* that the Space Patrol was multi-racial, and condemned racism on numerous occasions, but he hadn't previously made a black man a major character. The issue was to come up again with *Tunnel in the Sky* (1955), when Alice Dalgliesh at Scribner's worried about the racial mix of his characters hurting sales in the Deep South. She doubtless would have worried a lot more had she known that Heinlein intended the lead hero to be black (Patterson 123–24).

Stuart's girlfriend Betty Sorenson, who helps him rescue Lummox from the court, is a Free Child who is studying law: "I stood up in court and divorced [my parents] and got a professional guardian who doesn't have nutty ideas" (Heinlein, *To the Stars* 660). Heinlein had allowed Dalgliesh to minimize the divorce reference, and that became a sore point between them after a reviewer for *Library Journal,* Learned T. Bulman, complained to her about it and wanted it deleted from a second edition—and she let Bulman know about her own misgivings. Bulman also had objected to Sorenson being "flippant," which led Heinlein to write Blassingame that self-appointed "guardians of youthful morals" wanted the characters in juvenile novels to be "plaster saints who never do anything naughty" and never question the shibboleths of adults: "I could write such books, of course—but the kids would not read them" (Patterson 121–23).

As for Betty Sorenson herself, she's no shrinking violet when in comes to romance. "I haven't proposed to him yet, but I will," she tells Kiku after she and John are instrumental in helping resolve an interstellar crisis (Heinlein, *To the Stars* 719). Good thing because from Lummox's point of view, it's the John Thomases who are pets, and she wants to keep raising them. As the Imperial Highness of the Hroshii, 213th of her line, there's no arguing with her, and she's the only non-human at their wedding. Only the honeymoon will have to wait, for it's off to her homeworld, where John Thomas Stuart XI will be Earth's first ambassador.

Two of the later novels, *Time for the Stars* (1956) and *Have Space Suit—Will Travel* (1958) don't bring anything new to the art of young-adult fiction, however inventive their stories. And after the latter came *Starship Troopers*, which took Heinlein in an entirely different direction. But two other juveniles remain among his finest.

In *Tunnel in the Sky* (1955), high school student Rod Walker and his classmates are taking Advanced Survival because it is a prerequisite to the college major required of men and women wishing to qualify for emigration from an overcrowded Earth to worlds opened to settlement by way of stargates. When the effects of a supernova make it impossible to reestablish a stargate doorway to bring them home on time, these teenagers on a survival exercise are marooned on a wild planet. They are entirely on their own, without adult supervision—a startling idea for the time that seems no less radical today.

Among the skills they must master for a degree in Outland Arts are "hunting, scouting, jackleg mechanics, gunsmithing, farming, first aid, group psychology, survival group tactics, law, and a dozen other things the race has found indispensable when stripped for action" (Heinlein, *Infinite Possibilities* 19). But that doesn't mean going in loaded for bear. Walker gets his best advice from his older sister, an assault captain in the Amazon Corps: don't take a gun, for example, as that can be a temptation to fatal overconfidence—better to pack just a knife, and enough rations to last until he can learn to live off the land. On his first day, he sees what she meant when he finds the body of a classmate who came through the gate armed with a high-powered energy rifle and an attack dog to boot. Walker himself isn't wary enough—he's simply lucky that whoever robs *him* of everything but one knife only knocked him out instead of killing him.

When he runs across another student finishing off and appropriating a deerlike animal that Rod had wounded and tracked, what begins as a quarrel ends in an agreement to become a team: both realize that there is safety in numbers. Something, they know, has gone terribly wrong; the deadline for recall has passed—they could be stranded for years, perhaps even for the rest of their lives. When they find yet another boy in trouble, they save him and keep a signal fire lit to alert other survivors, who straggle in a few at a time.

But forging a community takes more than just numbers, more than individual survival skills. It takes cooperation founded on trust and mutual aid. When a bunch of toughs gets the drop on them and tries to take over the camp, it's the girls—including Caroline Mshiyeni, a Zulu who becomes Walker's most trusted confidant—who save the day by ambushing the toughs. Walker emerges as the informal leader, but Grant Cowper, who has more theoretical knowledge, sweeps the election for mayor. Cowper proves to be arrogant and inept, yet it is Walker himself who squelches a motion to dump him at a later town meeting—a struggling community can't afford a factional feud. Cowper gets the message and works out his differences with Walker and his backers. Government, he later tells Rod, is "the art of getting along with people you don't like" (Heinlein, *Infinite Possibilities* 158).

Walker still argues with Cowper about building a protective wall for the community, and he is proved right when the dopy joes, seemingly harmless animals, turn vicious during a seasonal mass migration. Cowper dies heroically helping defend the camp, and Walker once again takes the reins. Only by now he has learned patience, as they all must. Art Nielsen is frustrated, for example, because until coal can be found, the best his metallurgy can produce is spongy wrought iron. True, Walker points out, but what about Cliff Pawley, who is trying to breed cereal grains from native grasses? Only their great-grandchildren will reap the rewards of Pawley's work: "But you yourself will live to build precision machinery—you know it can be done, which, as Bob Baxter says, is two thirds of the battle. Cliff can't live long enough to eat a slice of light, tasty bread. It doesn't stop him" (Heinlein, *Infinite Possibilities* 162).

He and the rest don't have to endure that, though; rescue finally comes. Yet they have to be *prepared* to. That's taking the long view, and for Heinlein, taking the long view is what being human is all about. This is what he wanted his readers to take home from the story.

In *Citizen of the Galaxy* (1957) Colonel Richard Baslim of the Hegemonic Guard has consecrated his life to the struggle against slavery, posing as a beggar in Jubbulpore, capital of the Nine Worlds, to gain intelligence on the slave trade. He buys a boy named Thorby, whom he raises as his own, teaching him languages, mathematics, galactography, and a host of other subjects.

Baslim is found out, however, and beheaded. But he has arranged for a Free Trader ship to rescue Thorby and deliver him to the Guard. Thorby's sojourn with the Free Traders—a fascinating spacefaring culture, comparable to the Merchanters in C. J. Cherryh's later Alliance-Union history—is the beginning of an odyssey that leads him to two startling revelations: that the slave trade survives in large part through the covert assistance of the Hegemony's leading starship construction concern...and that he himself is Thor Bradley Rudbek, long-missing heir to an interstellar conglomerate that controls that very firm. Already he has learned how persistent slavery is: "It starts up in every new land and it's terribly hard to root out. After a culture falls ill of it, it gets rooted in the economic system and laws, in men's habits and attitudes. You abolish it; you drive it underground—there it lurks, ready to spring up again..." (Heinlein, *Infinite Possibilities* 505–506).

Now Thorby must make the most difficult moral choice of his life. His heart's desire is to serve in the Guard and fight against slavery as Baslim did, yet the Guard itself tells him that he can make a greater contribution by asserting his authority over the family business empire. To do that, he fights a lengthy court battle to get control of it from a distant in-law, and he must learn all the subtleties of running the business so that he can root out its slave trade connections without harming its legitimate operations and the innocent people who work for them. It will be the work of a lifetime, for the struggle against evil is like the labor of Sisyphus. And yet Thorby, knowing that struggle can never end, refuses to shirk it: "A person *can't* run out on responsibility" (Heinlein, *Infinite Possibilities* 568).

This, after all, is what coming of age is all about: becoming responsible. And that is what the best of Heinlein's young adult novels are all about. From a University of Chicago symposium lecture that he gave in 1957, and subsequently adapted for book publication two years later, we know that Heinlein had a mission: "science fiction is preparing our youngsters to be mature citizens of the Galaxy...as indeed they will have to be" ("Science Fiction" 61).

Works Cited

Heinlein, Robert A. *Four Frontiers*. New York: Science Fiction Book Club, 2005. Includes *Rocket Ship Galileo* (1947), *Space Cadet* (1948) *Red Planet* (1949), and *Farmer in the Sky* (1950).

_____. *Grumbles from the Grave*. New York: Ballantine, 1991.

_____. *Infinite Possibilities*. New York: Science Fiction Book Club, 2002. Includes *Tunnel in the Sky* (1955), *Time for the Stars* (1956), and *Citizen of the Galaxy* (1957).

_____. "Science Fiction: Its Nature, Faults and Virtues." *The Science Fiction Novel*. Ed. Basil Davenport. Chicago: Advent, 1959. 17–63.

_____. *To the Stars*. New York: Science Fiction Book Club, 2004. Includes *Between Planets* (1951), *The Rolling Stones* (1952), *Starman Jones* (1953), and *The Star Beast* (1954).

Patterson, William H. *Robert A. Heinlein: In Dialogue with His Century, Vol. 2: The Man Who Learned Better, 1948–1988*. New York: Tor, 2014.

Rockwood, Roy. *Under the Ocean to the South Pole; Or, The Strange Cruise of the Wonder Submarine*. New York: Cupples and Leon, 1907. *Project Gutenberg*. 7 Nov. 2006. Web. 21 Aug. 2015. <http://www.gutenberg.org/files/19731/19731-h/19731-h.htm>.

Walton, Jo. "First Juvenile: Robert A. Heinlein's *Rocket Ship Galileo*." *Tor.com*. Macmillan, 18 Aug. 2010. Web. 21 Aug. 2015. <http://www.tor.com/blogs/2010/08/first-juvenile-robert-a-heinleins-rocket-ship-galileo>.

"Dishonest Work": Robert A. Heinlein's Attitude toward Writing

Gary Westfahl

Forty years after receiving a $70 check for "Life-Line" (1939), the first science fiction story he submitted to a science fiction magazine, Robert A. Heinlein said in *Expanded Universe: The New Worlds of Robert A. Heinlein* (1980) that "there was never a chance that I would ever again look for honest work" (4). Soon thereafter, he somewhat softened this disparaging reference to the profession of writing by defining "honest work" as

> a euphemism for underpaid bodily exertion, done standing up or on your knees, often in bad weather or other nasty circumstances, and frequently involving shovels, picks, hoes, assembly lines, tractors, and unsympathetic supervisors. It has never appealed to me. Sitting at a typewriter in a nice warm room, with no boss, cannot possibly be described as "honest work." (*Expanded* 92–93)

Earlier, in the afterword to *Revolt in 2100* (1953), "Concerning Stories Never Written: Postscript," he had conveyed the same attitude by stating that he hoped readers would "enjoy" his works because "at my age it would be very inconvenient to have to go back to working for a living" (192).

Clearly, in Heinlein's view, writing is neither physically demanding nor mentally demanding, so the "dishonesty" of writing effectively involves earning disproportionate sums of money from very little effort. Indeed, in a 31 March 1941 letter to John W. Campbell, Jr., Heinlein referred to the money he had earned from writing as his "ill-gotten gains" (*Letters I* 173), while in an 8 November 1953 letter to his father, Rex Ivar Heinlein, he described writing as "an easy racket" (*Letters II* 467), and in a 19 January 1957 letter to Damon Knight, he called it "this racket" (*Letters II* 527). Similarly, the writer in *Stranger in a Strange Land* (1961, 1990), Jubal Harshaw, characterizes his writing career as "grift" (316), or a swindle. Coming from a seemingly honest, energetic, and award-winning author, these dismissive references to his chosen profession must be regarded as surprising.

To obtain a fuller picture of Heinlein's attitudes toward writing, one can glean some insights from his 1947 article providing advice for aspiring science fiction writers, "On the Writing of Speculative Fiction" (1947); from the aforementioned "Concerning Stories Never Written"; from various comments in *Expanded Universe*; and from three works of fiction that feature writers as major characters: *The Rolling Stones* (1952), "'All You Zombies—'" (1959), and *Stranger in a Strange Land*. However, Heinlein generally chose to avoid the topic of writing in his published works, for reasons he explained in *Expanded Universe*: "Writers talking about writing are about as bad as parents boasting about their children. I have not done much of it; the few times I have been guilty, I did not instigate the project, and in almost all cases (all, I think) my arm was twisted" (378). Hence, most of Heinlein's extended discussions of writing are found in material not written for publication—his correspondence, first published selectively in *Grumbles from the Grave* (1989) and later more comprehensively in the three-volume *The Heinlein Letters* (2011), the massive compilation that constitutes the most valuable source of information on Heinlein's views. By examining his public and private comments, one can find several consistently expressed opinions, listed and explained below, about the profession of writing fiction.

1. Any intelligent person can easily become a writer.
In a 31 January 1953 letter to Richard Hoffman, Heinlein opined that "The techniques of writing are not difficult and may be picked up by anyone through observation and practice" (*Letters II* 445); he told Judith Merril in a 16 May 1957 letter that "the basic skills of writing are fairly easy to learn and do not require high intelligence" (*Letters II* 570); and in a 16 October 1963 letter to Lloyd Biggle, he commented that "the mechanics of the trade….are no great problem" (*Letters III* 226). This point is demonstrated by his own career, for

as he noted in *Expanded Universe*, he himself "had never had any literary ambitions, no training for it, no interest in it" (92).

Similarly, successful television screenwriters Roger Stone and Hazel Stone of *The Rolling Stones* previously had worked as engineers, and Hazel had the additional background of participating in the initial colonization of the Moon. Roger, however, gave up engineering because he "had let himself be trapped into a bet that he could write better stuff than was being channeled up from Earth—and had gotten himself caught in a quicksand of fat checks and options" (Heinlein, *Rolling Stones* 23); later, Hazel effortlessly assumes the task of writing the episodes. The "Unmarried Mother" of "'All You Zombies—'" first aspired, when she was a woman, to join the military as a prostitute, but after a sex change operation, he briefly worked as a "public stenographer" and happened to type a terrible story submitted to, and accepted by, the magazine *Real Life Tales*. Obviously realizing, like Roger Stone, that he could do better himself, he "bought a stack of confession magazines and studied them" (Heinlein, "Zombies" 132) and soon was selling his own stories. And Harshaw of *Stranger in a Strange Land* obtained both a medical degree and a legal degree and actively worked as a physician and a lawyer before resolving to focus on writing fiction.

2. Indeed, preparing to become a writer might even be a liability, inasmuch as training in different areas represents a better way to become an effective writer.

In a 16 May 1947 letter to his agent Lurton Blassingame, Heinlein explained why he had avoided any sort of formal training in writing:

> I'm afraid of coaching, of writers' classes, of writers' magazines, of books on how to write. They give me centipede trouble—you know the yarn about the centipede who was asked how he managed all his feet? He tried to answer, stopped to think about it, and was never able to walk another step. Articles and books on how to write have that effect on me. (*Letters II* 293)

All the help he needed, Heinlein continued, came from the valuable personal "advice" he received from Blassingame and his wife

Leslyn and from "studying other writers' stories" (*Letters II* 293). He also enjoyed, as he commented in a 25 August 1953 letter to Henry Kuttner, engaging in "shop talk" with other writers.

But Heinlein regularly condemned classes and books on writing. He asserted in his 31 January 1953 letter to Hoffman, for example, that "probably the worst way [to become a writer] is to attempt to become one by majoring in English literature and by taking courses in how to write short stories, etc." (*Letters II* 445), while he told his father in an 8 November 1953 letter that "Writing courses are almost useless and sometimes worse than useless" (*Letters II* 466). Indeed, in an 8 August 1963 letter to Marion Zimmer Bradley, he reported, "I once read a book about how to plot and it damn near ruined me, until I managed to forget it and go back to the way I taught myself" (*Letters III* 217). He later told this story in more detail in a 30 September 1976 letter to Biggle, amusingly concluding, "I threw [the book] into the trashcan, went back to my own unschooled methods—and entered the most productive period of my career" (*Letters III* 542).

Oddly, much later in his life, Heinlein reported in a 31 December 1973 letter to Walter Minton that he planned to write "a book on writing"—precisely the sort of text he had previously condemned. Yet he admitted, "I can't teach anybody *how* to write," intending instead to "teach a lot of things about what *not* to do, things I have learned by expensive mistakes over the past thirty-five years, things that really will help an aspirant if he/she will listen" (*Letters III* 510). So, although writers always must master the craft on their own, others' warnings about "mistakes" to avoid might be useful.

In contrast to unhelpful books and courses, neophyte writers should immerse themselves in diverse fields to obtain knowledge and experiences that will improve their writing. Heinlein conveyed this advice in describing the Stones' background in engineering and lunar colonization, and Harshaw's background in medicine and law. Heinlein's own background in the military and politics is instructive as well, a point he made explicitly in his 31 January 1953 letter to Hoffman: "what any writer needs (and what he will not learn in classes in writing) is a broad knowledge of people, life, science, history, business, politics, etc.—all the many activities of our race and of the tired globe" (*Letters II* 445). This is precisely the information that Heinlein had acquired prior to launching his writing career.

3. Intelligent individuals find it easy to write stories because it is largely a matter of following a few basic formulas.

This is stated most emphatically in "On the Writing of Speculative Fiction," wherein Heinlein asserted that "There are three main plots for the human interest story: boy-meets-girl, The Little Tailor, and the man-who-learned-better" (14), and explained a few specific variations on these patterns. Thus for "the man-who-learned-better" story, he provided his particular "recipe": "a man finds himself in circumstances which create a problem for him. In coping with this problem, the man is changed in some fashion inside himself" (Heinlein, "On Writing" 15–16). He then offered examples of possible stories following this pattern, including "A lonely rich man learns companionship in a hobo jungle" and "A gossip learns to hold her tongue" (16). Later, in his 25 August 1953 letter to Kuttner, he described "a dichotomy of self and environment" as "the basic structure of all stories worth telling" (*Letters II* 456). Harshaw references one of Heinlein's three categories in announcing his plan "to make an honest effort to make some commercial noises" by writing a story using "a brand-new plot, known as boy-meets-girl" (*Stranger* 462). More broadly, H. Bruce Franklin notes that as Harshaw "dictates his hack popular fiction to his trio of gorgeous secretaries, he shows us how this kind of fiction works through the magic of formulas" (131).

To be sure, "On the Writing of Speculative Fiction" also indicated that a writer requires a certain amount of intelligence in order to recognize when the standard formulas must be abandoned: "don't write to me to point out how I have violated my own rules in this story or that. I've violated all of them" (19), presumably for good reasons. Yet as if to contradict this point, *Stranger in a Strange Land*'s Harshaw "claimed that his method of literary composition was to hook his gonads in parallel with his thalamus and disconnect his cerebrum entirely; his habits lent some credibility to the theory" (107). This would suggest that sometimes, thinking while writing might actually be a liability.

4. These formulas always work because most readers are undemanding, if not outright stupid.

Tactfully, Heinlein never stated this explicitly in his articles or letters, but the point emerges in his fiction. In *The Rolling Stones*, when Roger asks Hazel how she contrived to have their series' hero, John Sterling, "get out" of a "decidedly untenable position," she explains that she shrewdly began the next episode with Sterling "jokingly disparaging his masterful escape"; before he can finish describing that escape, however, the conversation is interrupted by "action"— "so fast and so violent and so bloody" that "our unseen audience doesn't have time to think about it until the commercial. And by then they've got too much else to think about" (*Rolling Stones* 104). Clearly, she is confident that her viewers are too unintelligent or inattentive to notice that his escape was never explained. Her low opinion of her audience is immediately confirmed as she turns to the task of writing her next script and says, "I'd better get Lowell," her four-year-old grandson. "I get my best ideas from Lowell, he's just the mental age of my average audience" (105).

And while these comments might be said to pertain solely to television viewers, Heinlein's *Stranger in a Strange Land* criticizes readers as well when a stripper in the employ of the Fosterite religion, Dawn Argent, greets Harshaw and tells him, "I think your stories are simply divine.... I put one of your tapes on my player and let it lull me to sleep every night" (306). Anyone who would offer this as a compliment to an author, of course, cannot be regarded as overly bright. Later in the novel, though, when Argent reappears as a follower of the new religion founded by Michael Valentine Smith, she seems to have grown more intelligent, perhaps because her mind has been improved by exposure to his Martian philosophy.

5. Since the effective formulas are straightforward, and readers are easy to please, all that an intelligent person needs to succeed as a writer is good work habits.

In "On the Writing of Speculative Fiction," Heinlein defined those habits, his classic "group of practical, tested rules which, if followed meticulously, will prove rewarding to any writer":

1. You must *write*.
2. You must *finish* what you start.
3. You must refrain from rewriting except to editorial order.
4. You must put it on the market.
5. You must keep it on the market until sold. (19)

Heinlein himself visibly practiced these principles. As he noted in a 2 March 1940 letter to Campbell, "I never rewrite except to make a specific change that an editor has ordered. .... For me to revise, except on editorial suggestion, would make me uncertain, full of doubts, and would produce that woodenness which is to be avoided" (*Letters I* 44–45). However, after he later repeated his rules in a 7 January 1950 letter to Blassingame, the agent's apparent criticism of the third rule prompted this qualifying remark in a 15 January 1950 letter: "Re rewriting: I quite agree with your view point. The 'rule,' as stated, needs considerable elaboration. I do quite a bit of rewriting myself—but I think it is very important—essential—that a beginning writer avoid the vice of endless rewriting without advice from an editor or agent to guide him" (*Letters II* 387). Heinlein also demonstrated his fidelity to his final rule by means of his energetic efforts to find buyers for all his early stories, including those that he later characterized as "stinkers." As he explained in a 23 October 1940 letter to Frederik Pohl, "These five manuscripts are the only things I have ever written which were not immediately sold. They sit here and shame me. You will appreciate, I believe, that I would labor mightily to dispose of them" (*Letters II* 78).

6. The primary pleasure to be derived from writing is the money that one earns.

This is a recurring theme in Heinlein's writings. In a 4 February 1940 letter to his brother J. Clare Heinlein, he described a current project as "another opus-from-hunger" and reported, "I am working quite hard every day, being in need of considerable dinero this year" (*Letters II* 72, 74); in a later letter to his brother, dated 8 November 1940, he stated, "My present policy is to work when I want money for some specific purpose (*Letters II* 86). A 31 March 1941 letter to Campbell explains, "I just have an ingrained preference for all the dinero I squeeze out. Nice stuff—money. There are so many amusing things one can do with it. You and Street & Smith are largely responsible for me acquiring some champagne appetites which I had formerly inhibited, thereby chaining me to the typewriter" (*Letters I* 173). In an 18 February 1949 letter to John Arwine he complained, "I'd like to be able to take a day off without a niggling feeling that I ought to be punching the money machine" (*Letters II* 341), and he told Forrest J. Ackerman in a 25 February 1949 letter that he sometimes wrote "sheer potboilers to pay the grocery bills" (*Letters II* 349–350). In a 14 June 1949 letter to Campbell, he stated, "I am money motivated in my writing, a motive which I believe you understand and respect" (*Letters I* 574), and in "Concerning Stories Never Written," he noted that the stories in his "Future History" were "just stories, meant to amuse and written to buy groceries" (189). In a 9 October 1971 letter to Bill Busa, he claimed, "I write for money and make no bones about it" (*Letters III* 416), and in a 14 February 1947 letter to Campbell, he responded to a forwarded letter from Larry Denton by archly writing, "you might try to explain to him that writers, editors, and publishers work for money to support their families, not for glory" (*Letters I* 545). And although he seemed to contradict himself in an 11 December 1979 letter to Gene Roddenberry by conceding "it is true that an artist does not work solely for money," he immediately added that "nevertheless money is the most sincere form of applause" (*Letters III* 588).

7. Since money is the main reason for writing, writers should abandon this otherwise unrewarding labor for undiscriminating readers when they no longer need the income.

Heinlein himself reported in *Expanded Universe* that "I had always planned to quit the writing business as soon as that mortgage was paid off... [I was] always resolved to quit the silly business once I had my chart squared away" (92), and in a 14 September 1941 letter to Campbell, he asserted that he soon would be transforming himself "from full-time hack to part-time hobbyist" (*Letters I* 246). As late as 1957, in his May 15 letter to Merril, he claimed that "someday

I'm going to quite [sic] the dreary business. .... I no longer need money for any purpose, thank God [so] I'll retire again" (*Letters II* 571).

At times, Heinlein's fictional characters express similar sentiments about writing; indeed, the most striking thing about the Stones' writing career, for example, is that they repeatedly express an interest in giving it up. As noted, Roger feels compelled to keep writing because of the "fat checks and options" he receives, and when Hazel begins writing the episodes, her announced intent is to gradually kill off all of the series' characters and thus bring their writing obligations to an end. Only financial considerations prevent her from carrying out this plan: when asked "why did you let them sign us up again?" she replies, "Because they waved too much money under my nose, as you know full well. It's an aroma we Stones have hardly ever been able to resist" (*Rolling Stones* 103–104). At the end of the novel, Hazel again states that she is giving up writing, this time in order to travel to Saturn. Jubal Harshaw also suggests that he is motivated to continue writing solely to earn money when he describes himself as "a disreputable old bum who makes money writing popular trash" (*Stranger* 271).

And yet, despite repeatedly resolving to abandon writing, neither Heinlein nor the Stones ever stopped writing, and Harshaw is last observed in *Stranger in a Strange Land* beginning yet another writing project. This leads to another conclusion:

8. Writing, for some reason, is a strangely addictive profession.

In describing why he carried on with his career, Heinlein repeatedly employed the jargon of drug addiction. In a 21 September 1940 letter to Campbell, he confessed,

> Shhh—don't tell anybody, but writing has become a vice with me. I no longer need the money, having a little more income than I really need for everything I want to do, and I had planned to spend a while, at least, in doing some odd jobs which I had been putting off—but I found that I was becoming nervous, uneasy, if I stayed away from the typewriter. (*Letters I* 90)

A month later, he similarly reported in a 24 October 1940 letter to E. E. "Doc" Smith that "I no longer write from hunger. …. I fiddled around for a few days…, then realized that I was becoming very nervous. The reason was evident—I was not writing! It had become a vice" (*Letters II* 80). Decades later, in a 31 May 1970 letter he told J. Clare and Dorothy Heinlein, "I am not sure that I enjoy writing fiction… but I am hooked, the monkey is on my back" (*Letters III* 403), and in an 8 October 1978 letter to Clifford D. Simak, he stated that "I do not expect to stop writing (as you say, it's addictive)" (*Letters III* 579).

In *Expanded Universe*, Heinlein explained more fully that while he initially had disregarded the judgment of fellow writer William A. P. White, who wrote as Anthony Boucher, that "There are *no* retired writers" (92), he soon realized that

> Bill "Tony Boucher" White had been dead right. Once you get the monkey on your back there is no cure short of the grave….if I simply loaf for more than two or three days, the monkey starts niggling at me. Then nothing short of a few thousand words will soothe my nerves. And as I get older the attacks get worse; it is beginning to take 300,000 words and up to produce that feeling of warm satiation. At that I don't have it in its most virulent form; two of my colleagues are reliably reported not to have missed their daily fix in more than forty years. (94–95)

But, other than the aforementioned money, what is there about a writing career that makes it so impossible to abandon? Harshaw offers one answer in *Stranger in a Strange Land*:

9. Writing, if nothing else, provides the standard sense of satisfaction gained from performing a useful service. As Harshaw describes himself,

> I am an *honest* artist, because what I write is consciously intended to reach the customer…reach him and affect him, if possible with pity and terror…or, if not, at least to divert the tedium of his hours with a chuckle or an odd idea [….] I want the praise of the cash customer, given in cash because I've reached him. (Heinlein, *Stranger* 400)

In other words, people need chairs, and carpenters can feel fulfilled because they have built comfortable chairs for them to sit on; people need entertainment, and writers can feel fulfilled because they have provided them with some suitable diversions.

At times, Heinlein would discuss his writing career with obvious pride; for example, in a 2 November 1940 letter to Campbell, he asserted that "I know I am a profit-making commercial property" (*Letters I* 109) and elaborated on his achievements in a 24 October 1941 letter:

> It is true, I believe, that I have acquired my commercial reputation (such as it is) by breaking new trails and giving the cash customers stuff a bit different and a bit more mature and philosophical than some of the others. In so doing, I have forced (or encouraged) other writers to do the same and thereby extended the field of science-fiction. (*Letters I* 284)

And, to provide his agent Lurton Blassingame with information to impress the editors of *Cosmopolitan*, Heinlein wrote in a 15 January 1950 letter that

> In the first place I am probably the most popular and most widely read science-fiction writer living today. I have frequently been referred to as the successor to H. G. Wells and as the "modern Jules Verne." I was the first science-fiction writer to get into the *Saturday Evening Post* and am the first such writer to make a space flight motion picture. (*Letters II* 388)

Yet workers in other fields can report feelings of satisfaction from their careers and calmly proceed to retire; there must be something else, then, that makes writing such a peculiarly addictive profession. As it happens, there is one other obvious reason why authors might feel compelled to keep writing, yet Heinlein initially was reluctant to acknowledge it; in his early correspondence, there is only one remark that seemingly conveyed what was emerging as Heinlein's true motive for writing, namely:

10. Writing is enjoyable because it allows writers to convey their ideas and opinions to a large audience.

As he said in a 31 March 1941 letter to Robert Moore Williams,

> I took up writing more or less by accident, and have kept at it, aside from the pleasant usefulness of money, because this field of writing permitted me to say things that I had always wanted to say, but had been laughed at or looked at askance for saying. Even my scissorbill [stupid] friends do think that it is all right to say odd things for cash! (*Letters II* 104)

After World War II, Heinlein was more open about his desire to influence people by means of his writing, particularly in discussing his juveniles. He referred to his desire "to preach" in a 13 February 1946 letter to J. Francis McComas (*Letters II* 244) and in a 15 April 1957 letter to Lester del Rey (*Letters II* 545). He spoke of the "preaching" in his works in a 15 February 1946 letter to Cal Laning (*Letters II* 256) and in a 22 July 1961 letter to F. M. Busby (*Letters III* 46). In a 20 August 1961 letter to Pohl, he discussed his tendency to engage in "preachiness" (*Letters III* 77), and in his 25 August 1953 letter to Kuttner, he worried that his "itch to preach" might have interfered sometimes with his "obligation [...] to be entertaining" (*Letters II* 456). He even told director Fritz Lang in a 14 May 1946 letter that "my profession is propaganda, but I like to keep it impersonal" (*Letters II* 271). And while Heinlein repeatedly argued that he was seeking new markets after the war primarily in order to earn more money, he also told Campbell in a 19 November 1945 letter, "I want to be heard by more people" (*Letters I* 490). Much later, in a 19 February 1959 letter to Alice Dalgliesh, he noted that "Good literary style" primarily requires *"having something to say"* (*Letters II* 620), and very late in his career, in a 15 March 1982 letter to Robert Clifton, he stated that writing "has been remarkably rewarding financially and has almost certainly permitted me to influence more people, especially young people, than I could ever have reached had I stayed in politics" (*Letters III* 599).

Ironically, at other times, as in his 15 May 1957 letter to Merril, Heinlein criticized writers who had "an inspired yen to grab quill and instruct the world," praising himself as one of the individuals who instead "more or less drifted into [writing] as a job we could do when for reasons of circumstance most more-active jobs were not available to us" (*Letters II* 570). He told Karen Anderson in a 21 July 1961 letter, "I write for munny ($$$$$$$) and my purpose is to be entertaining enough to keep the dough rolling in" (*Letters III* 41), and he reported to Sam Moskowitz in a 15 January 1961 letter, "I always was, and still am, a money writer (I do *not* write from any need to express myself, nor to see my name in print, and never have)" (*Letters III* 17–18). Yet this contradicts some earlier statements. In a 28 September 1941 letter to Campbell, after all, he said that "I dearly love to see my name in print—I am an exhibitionist at heart" (*Letters I* 266), and in his 16 May 1957 letter to Merril, he admitted that "I enjoy seeing my name in print" (*Letters II* 571). In addition, since Heinlein also was reporting in the late 1950s, as noted, that he "no longer need[ed] money for any purpose" (*Letters II* 571), a desire to promulgate his views must have been a factor motivating his ongoing writing, however much he wished to deny it.

From all these materials, therefore, one can see how Heinlein would characterize the typical careers of successful writers. With no prior education in writing, or inclination to write, any intelligent people might stumble into a writing career and find, by mastering some simple formulas, that they are receiving large checks and garnering an appreciative audience for their works. Thrilled to discover that they can earn so much money from relatively effortless labor, they initially continue with their careers simply for the financial rewards; then, even after they no longer need the income, writers realize that they have come to enjoy the experience of expressing their thoughts and viewpoints and perhaps influencing readers, driving them to carry on with their writing careers indefinitely. This would explain why, long after he had become very wealthy, Heinlein continued to write and even picked up the pace of his work during the final decade of his life, producing five lengthy novels and a huge collection of fiction and nonfiction. And as further illustrations of the soundness of Heinlein's views, one might point to other noteworthy writers who have had similarly profitable and productive careers. The other members of science fiction's "Big Three," for example, Isaac Asimov and Arthur C. Clarke, also were intelligent men who mastered the art of writing without any training and continued writing for decades, long after they needed any additional income.

Still, even since Heinlein emerged, there also have been many other intelligent men and women who have strived to follow in his footsteps and, for the most part, have failed spectacularly to achieve the same level of success. Something else, then, must be found to explain Heinlein's astounding career, a factor that Heinlein as a matter of modesty never emphasized, a trait he consistently displayed in his correspondence. In the aforementioned passage where he described his impact on science fiction, after all, he immediately added, "Perhaps I over-rate the extent of my influence" (*Letters I* 284), and after boasting to Blassingame, he commented, "This is beginning to gag me" (*Letters II* 388). For this reason, it is necessary to complete this portrait of Heinlein's attitudes toward writing by adding one additional point that Heinlein himself was never willing to state:

11. To achieve truly remarkable writing careers, writers must in some respect be extraordinarily talented individuals—like Robert A. Heinlein.

Works Cited

Franklin H. Bruce. *Robert A. Heinlein: America as Science Fiction*. Science-Fiction Writers Series. Oxford: Oxford UP, 1980.

Heinlein, Robert A. "'All You Zombies—'." 1959. *6 x H* [*The Unpleasant Profession of Jonathan Hoag*]. New York: Pyramid, 1961. 126–37.

_____. "Concerning Stories Never Written: Postscript." *Revolt in 2100*. New York: Signet, 1953. 189–92.

_____. *Expanded Universe: The New Worlds of Robert A. Heinlein*. New York: Ace, 1980.

_____. *Grumbles from the Grave*. Ed. Virginia Heinlein. New York: Del Rey, 1989.

_____. *The Heinlein Letters: Volume I, Correspondence of John W. Campbell, Jr., and Robert A. Heinlein.* Vol. 1. Houston: Virginia Edition, 2011.

_____. *The Heinlein Letters: Volume II, General Correspondence of Robert Heinlein,* Vol. 2. Houston: Virginia Edition, 2011.

_____. *The Heinlein Letters: Volume III, General Correspondence of Robert Heinlein.* Vol. 3. Houston: Virginia Edition, 2011.

_____. "On the Writing of Speculative Fiction." *Of Worlds Beyond: The Science of Science Fiction Writing.* Ed. Lloyd Arthur Eshbach. 1947. Chicago: Advent, 1964. 13–19.

_____. *The Rolling Stones.* 1952. New York: Ace, 1969.

_____. *Stranger in a Strange Land.* 1961. Original Uncut Version. New York: Ace, 1991.

Compulsively Fruitful: Proliferation in the Short Fiction of Robert A. Heinlein, 1939–1952_____

Anna R. McHugh

Proliferation is integral to the character of both Robert A. Heinlein's writing and thought. This essay will examine how proliferations of spacetime are explored in three of Heinlein's earliest short stories: "Elsewhen," "They," and "The Unpleasant Profession of Jonathan Hoag," from *Astounding Science-Fiction* and *Unknown*. In these short stories worlds, identities, narratives-within-narratives, languages, plotlines, all multiply. I want to suggest that this proliferation of spacetimes in Heinlein's narratives plays with the idea of plenitude in both the *fabula*, or chronological order of the events of a story, and the narrative window onto these events, the *syuzhet*. But just as spacetimes multiply, so do things that have relationships with spacetime—that is, identity and narrative. The type of spacetime with which narratives deal is the chronotope, Mikhail Bakhtin's term for the space-and-time relationship against which action happens in fiction. I will examine the proliferation of chronotopes and show how they are related to—and through—the stability of the focalizer, or protagonist. Although the whole corpus of Heinlein's work is, itself, proliferative, this essay shows how his very earliest speculative fiction embraced the idea of plenitude. I hope it will provide a seed that other readers, interested in Heinlein's underlying narrative mechanics, may germinate.

I do not wish to suggest anything as explicit as a direct correlation between economic or social growth and the proliferation of chronotopes represented in Heinlein's SF. However, in the commercial, political, and scientific spheres in which Heinlein worked during the 1930s and 1940s, a persistent and organic growth was noticeable.[1] In nuclear physics, arguably the highest-profile area of scientific endeavor during the time that these stories were written, the discovery of a very specific configuration of growth—the chain reaction, proposed by Leó Szilárd in 1933—would bring about a new age and a new set of speculations. Heinlein offers equally complex proliferations within both his narrative and his narratology. Protagonists adopt one identity after another, and by keeping pace with this, an extra-diegetic narrator mediates the adventures of a highly unstable focalizer. Similarly, inset narratives appear and are either developed into whole narratives-within-a-narrative or left as potential points of proliferation, indicating Heinlein's attitude to narrative itself as a proliferant process. In fact, the proliferation with which most readers of Heinlein's work will be familiar is the growth of several short texts into entire multi-text worlds, such as the Future History series. The scope of this article is much too modest to take in the intertext produced by Heinlein's fruitful handling of the shorter fiction, but it remains substantial evidence that proliferation is integral to Heinlein's attitude to writing.

Parallel worlds, the multiverse, and extra dimensions are now respectable tropes in SF, but writing on spacetime multiplicity in the 1940s stands on the cusp of two eras: the nineteenth century's speculation about spacetime, which tended to be about either space or time—with the other gestured to, but not dealt with—and the age of popular excitement about Einstein's theory of general relativity. The concept of a plenitude of worlds had appeared intermittently in fiction, beginning with Margaret Cavendish's 1666 *The Blazing World*, a satirical study of a utopian kingdom that occupied a different place in space and time, signalled by its different stars, to which our dimension gained access through the North Pole.[2] The concept of higher dimensions was crucial to the speculations of both Simon Newcomb, the Canadian-American astronomer, who had published on the subject of four dimensions since 1877, and his associate Charles Howard Hinton, who had discussed it with the New York Mathematical Society in 1893. With the taxonomizing drive of the nineteenth century, both Newcomb and Hinton conceived of these dimensions as specifically "higher," hierarchizing them rather than merely acknowledging their proliferation.

Nineteenth-century SF already had experimented with strange geometry and narrative: Edwin A. Abbott's *Flatland: A Romance of Many Dimensions* (1884) reads like a narrative fantasia on

Riemannian geometry, and H. G. Wells, whose SF was a thin veneer for continual attempts to articulate his utopian vision, had used the popular idea of time as a fourth dimension, through which humans could move with the correct machines. *The Time Machine* (1895), *The Wonderful Visit* (1895), *A Modern Utopia* (1905), and *Men Like Gods* (1923) all rely on a four-dimensional paradigm to explain otherwise fantastical travel, but Wells does not pursue the implications of his many-worlds idea, instead using travel between the dimensions as a literary device to explore utopian concepts. Several excellent studies have shown how the stories published by *Astounding* and *Unknown* in the 1930s extrapolated certain ideas from the new physics and expressed them in narratives about social history and politics in other realities.[3] Without exception, these stories respond to the rejection of the Newtonian universe by proliferating spacetimes and, sometimes, identities.

This brings up the second important strand for narrative and narratological proliferation in Heinlein's earliest stories: the role of the percipient, the individual for whom these realities are actually multiple, and whose consciousness and sense of their own continuity through time acts as the referent against which everything else multiplies. Piotr Ouspensky, the Russian mathematician and esotericist, combined a reading of Hinton's ideas of time as a fourth dimension in space with George Gurdjieff's esoteric formulation of the self as a self-remembering entity.[4] Self-remembering was a way of conceiving of the problem of "becoming," or the "ongoing-ness" of time: what physicist and popular science writer John Dunne called "serialism." Essentially, the ongoingness or functional directionality of linear time can be realized by individuals only when they become aware of the fitting-together of new experiences with the residuum of past experience, in which consists their sense of themselves.

Around the same time that Ouspensky combined Hinton's fourth-dimension speculations with Gurdjieff's self-remembering, Dunne published the widely-read *An Experiment with Time* (1927). Dunne, an aeronautical engineer, theorized that all moments in time are concurrent, but are perceived by human consciousness as sequential because of our fixed rate of perception. Dunne's work proved highly popular with both lay and scientific audiences; physicist Arthur Eddington, whose own science writing explained Einstein's general relativity to a popular readership, not only agreed with Dunne about the importance of how time's linearity was perceived, but wrote that "the stuff of the world is mind-stuff" (276), and so conjoined the fact of general relativity (the *fabula*) with the partial and intermittent consciousness that conveyed it through the apperceptive lens (the *syuzhet*).

Just before Robert Heinlein's own entry to SF writing, Murray Leinster's story "Sidewise in Time," published in *Astounding Stories* in 1934, had involved timeline exchanges, where chunks of history assume a different, counterfactual—from our perspective—course, and become entangled with the continuum of our own space and time. But apart from Abbott's *Flatland*, narratives about other worlds had tended to focus on time rather than spacetime; the concept of time as a dimension was largely dealt with in SF set-pieces, which saw the protagonist "travelling" through time by means of a fantastic machine or convenient portal. The dimensionality of time and the role of the apperceptive focalizer are conveniently forgotten once the action has moved to a new location. The whole thrust of *The Time Machine*, for example, is that the machine remains stationary—a feature of which the 1960 film, with its Oscar-winning time-lapse photography sequences, made much. The possibility of multiple co-extensive worlds is rarely involved, and the implications of this proliferation for ideas about identity, individuality, and the decisive nature of choice are never thoroughly worked out.

The third strand in my examination of how spacetime proliferates in Heinlein's fiction involves its specifically literary nature. Ten years after Dunne published *An Experiment in Time*, the Russian semiotician Mikhail Bakhtin applied the "spacetime" terminology of relativity to the way that literature represented time and space. Drawing on the contemporary fascination with the intrinsic connectedness of temporal and spatial relationships, his 1937 essay "Forms of Time and of the Chronotope in the Novel" argued that texts' configurations of time and space, or chronotopes, were one of the integral components of genre. In the essay, he drew attention to the same pairing of features—spacetime and the focalizer—that Eddington and Dunne had, but from the opposite angle. Rather than beginning with spacetime and realizing that it was partly limited and defined by the apperception of the focalizer, Bakhtin starts with the person portrayed by the text and theorizes the narrative spacetime through which the portrayal occurs: "The chronotope as a formally constitutive category determines to a significant degree the image of man in literature as well. The image of man is always intrinsically chronotopic" (84–85). In three of Heinlein's earliest stories, "They" (1941), "Elsewhen" (1941), and "The Unpleasant Profession of Jonathan Hoag" (1942), he explores the implications of many worlds through the focalizer's struggle to deal with multiple realities. Although the proliferation of spacetime throws the protagonist into disarray, in turn triggering discourses of growth and maturity, the highly flexible, even unstable, chronotope becomes integral to the genre that Heinlein came to call speculative fiction.

"Elsewhen" (1941)

"Elsewhen," published in *Astounding Science-Fiction* in 1941, is perhaps the most orthodox of Heinlein's early stories about parallel worlds. In this story, a professor reveals to a group of graduate students that he has developed a way to travel through spacetime and insert himself into other realities. Heinlein generally followed his editor John W. Campbell, Jr.'s maxim that science fiction is at its most effective when it adheres to known scientific fact: in this case, that the existence of a two-dimensional time continuum provides for the existence of multiple realities *but* can be observed only within those realities (i.e., one at a time). Heinlein made that limitation pivotal to the plot—the professor sends his students each to different worlds, and the tension comes from their ignorance of what has become of each other. Rather heavy-handed name-dropping means that Ouspensky, Dunne, and Berkeley's work on parallel dimensions and apperceptive realities are invoked as the students try to comprehend his claims with reference to previous theories. But Heinlein engages with more than simple

---

manipulations of a fourth dimension; he describes the integrated concept of spacetime:

> Most people think of time as a track that they run on from birth to death as inexorably as a train follows its rails—they feel instinctively that time follows a straight line, the past lying behind, the future lying in front. Now I have reason to believe—to know—that time is analogous to a surface rather than a line, and a rolling hilly surface at that. Think of this track we follow over the surface of time as a winding road cut through hills. Every little way the road branches and the branches follow side canyons. At these branches the crucial decisions of your life take place. You can turn right or left into entirely different futures. Occasionally there is a switchback where one can scramble up or down a bank and skip over a few thousand or million years—if you don't have your eyes so fixed on the road that you miss the short cut.
>
> Once in a while another road crosses yours. Neither its past nor its future has any connection whatsoever with the world we know. If you happened to take that turn you might find yourself on another planet in another space-time with nothing left of you or your world but the continuity of your ego. (*Elsewhen* 94–95)

Just as Dunne and Einstein had acknowledged, in order to be communicable, alternate universes require an observer; the chronotope's instability is offset by the focalizer's constancy. As Hugh Everett would argue in the 1950s, the focalizer contributes a quantum observer effect—the Heisenberg Uncertainty Principle— partly enhancing the instability and proliferation they observe.[5] Spacetime realities seem to bifurcate at certain decision points, which refer reflexively to the focalizer, the observing individual whose linear existence generates these worlds. Each potential outcome is a world of its own. Anything, in other words, which can happen, does happen. This sounds like an indecisive author's dream, but it problematized the decisive, closure-oriented stories favored by science fiction readers of the 1930s—and, to an extent, science fiction's innate preference for charting the implications of *one* discovery, *one* course of action).[6] In fact, Heinlein added another element to literary extrapolations of Minkowski spacetime:

because each world expresses the consequences of individual action the theory assumes *either* an origin or zero-point individual, *or* that there are very many worlds for very many individuals. Heinlein combines bifurcating spacetime, the individual's deterministic role in multiplying physical realities, and the literary chronotope, and in the combination of the three, he reveals something about how reality, perception, and person are inextricably linked—in both real and fictional worlds.

"Elsewhen" does not move characters to parallel dimensions with fantastic machines. In fact, despite Heinlein's reputation as the master of "hard" SF, there are relatively few complex machines in his early work. Instead, Heinlein uses the story's nonlinear plot to model the quantum physical process. An omniscient narrator relates a narrative that begins analeptically, or in flashback, and then moves between framed narratives told homodiegetically, i.e., by the characters who experienced the events. Each inset narrative involves a different chronotope, and eventually the main narrative—the story of the protagonist or focalizer, Professor Frost—invests itself in one, then another of the alternative chronotopes.

The multiple realities with which the story plays come from a single decision by each character, just as a tree's single trunk bifurcates into many branches. Despite the unique situation the story explores, Heinlein's basic premise is as old as Aeschylus: he posits the centrality of human motivation, the mechanism that prefigures action, and from each action comes a world defined by the events that are uniquely possible in it. The mind's centrality justifies Heinlein's use of a vaguely described hypnosis as the way to move five solid adults to other dimensions and, via hypnotic suggestion, back again. Each character has another identity specific to the other chronotope: Robert is "Igor," a guerrilla fighter; Estelle is "Star-light," a priestess; Martha is a missionary and angel; and Howard is a soldier. Heinlein neatly avoids the problem of persons encountering multiples of themselves by suggesting that their consciousnesses merge when transposed to another spacetime. One character explains it thus: "I had one identity and two pasts. It was something like waking up from a clearly remembered dream, only the dream was perfectly real. I knew Monroe was real, just as I knew Igor was real" (Heinlein, *Elsewhen* 112). In this way Heinlein satisfies the conditions he has already referenced: Gurdjieff's "self-remembering" and the centrality of apperceptive consciousness from Dunne. This strategy assumes that character, identity, and physical body are all separate categories that proliferate along with, and in order to produce, chronotopes.

Yet there is a common tenor to each character's multiple identities. If, as the many-worlds theory suggests, each reality is the expression of a possible outcome from a decision in the reference world, then the actants who branch off and develop as a result of that decision will naturally be similar. For example, the character of Martha in the reference world is prone to "Bible-belt fundamentalism." This is integral to her character and, naturally, will be expressed in all the possible "Marthas" produced as a result of her decisions, and indeed, she returns posthumously in the form of an angel. Two students return physically altered and decide to go back to the war-torn world seen by one of them. One student, Estelle, does not return at all, and the professor must go and find her. Each student falls into a world which—even if frightening or confusing—seems to extrapolate an aspect of his or her character. The tough and practical woman returns to a world of guerrilla warfare as the wife of the tough and practical man. The beautiful and romantic woman goes to a kind of Byzantine harem where she has a parallel existence as a priestess/odalisque. Although the chronotope is different in each reality, Heinlein uses narrative to work through the implications of the "many worlds created by many people" theory. Each person's action results in multiple possibilities, which are worlds in themselves. But the tenor of these worlds is informed by the personality that gave rise to them. Thus the alternate realities evident to each human observer will naturally reflect variations of his or her own personality; this is why extremely rigid characters are unrewarding as focalizers— their actions tend not to produce diverse outcomes, and so do not generate multiple possible worlds.

We can chart the chronotopes experienced by each character in "Elsewhen" like this:

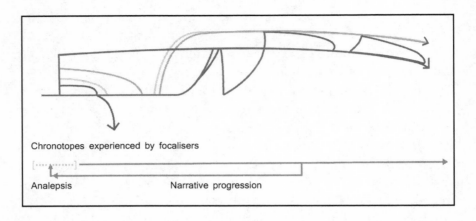

Chronotopes experienced by focalisers

Analepsis   Narrative progression

The heavy blue line shows the chronotope that commences the story, focalized through the professor. The chronotopes proliferate when the four students are transposed to different dimensions. Martha (in black) returns first, narrates her adventure, and then departs back to the alternative chronotope. Helen (in yellow) returns, remains for a while, and then returns with Robert (in green) to the chronotope he has visited. They both remain there for the rest of the narrative. Estelle (in light blue) goes to a different dimension and remains there; the professor and Howard (in gray) visit her, and Howard remains. Thereafter, the professor travels to his first dimension, but returns abruptly to his own world, where the rest of the events in the analepsis occur. He goes to Helen and Robert's dimension for a long while, then travels to Estelle and Howard's to fetch war-winning technology for them. After delivering this, he returns to Estelle and Howard and remains there.

Heinlein explored multiple realities in several other stories, but steered away from the "alternative timeline" formulation of his predecessors, in which our own universe appears with infinite variations, each comprising a universe of its own. In fact, "Life-Line" (1939), Heinlein's first published short story, revolves around the intractability of the time continuum, even for those who can determine what is going to happen. In "Life-Line," a scientist-engineer-sage called Pinero develops a machine that reads a person's "lifeline" in order to give an absolutely accurate date and time of death—frequently to Pinero's horror and in spite of his kindly attempts to avert the deaths. Although a dark coterie of insurance companies murder Pinero, dramatic irony proves the brilliance of his machine when his prediction about his own death is proved immutably correct. Thereafter, the intractability of time rarely featured in his fiction—even if a strong sense of determinism did. Heinlein also eschewed more sensational "other worlds" of gratuitously weird alien creatures. Instead, his earliest short stories use plot, chronotope, and characterization to suggest the subtle ways in which reality may proliferate. "Life-Line" proposes a single reality, but endows the focalizer Pinero with a plenitude of narratives— from data produced by the machine and interpreted by him—about others' lives. "Elsewhen" posits multiple realities, reflective of, and through, focalizers' actions. A third type of reality-proliferation is found in his stories about a dual reality—two co-existing realities, one atop the other, to which the focalizer alone is privy. These stories revolve around the focalizer's attempts to convince others of this palimpsested reality, and his discovery that they either are part of a conspiracy to conceal it, or deny the possibility of its existence.

"They" (1941) and "The Unpleasant Profession of Jonathan Hoag" (1942) demonstrate this dual-reality theory, a type of narrative precursor to Hans Moravec's simulation hypothesis.[7] The two stories propose that there is a covert reality that underlies the "ordinary world" and which, in fact, controls it. This is more than a variation of the conspiracy narrative, for rather than there being one reality with some covert and some overt actions, there are actually two realities: one can be thought of as a "synthetic" reality—usually the world we think we know, which turns out to be a giant game, or a delusion, or a fabrication—and a more ethically unattractive or foreign, but nonetheless ontologically "true," reality.

"They" (1941)

Published in the spring 1941 edition of *Unknown*, "They" relates the treatment, in a mental hospital, of an anonymous man who believes that the world is really a vast deception, created by sinister aliens as part of a conspiracy to deceive him and a few other entities considered "real" because they are not part of the deception. At the end of the story it turns out that a god-like alien character called "the Glaroon," who masquerades as the man's doctor, has indeed engineered this world-sized deception, although that knowledge is kept from the imprisoned patient.

"They" echoes Eric Frank Russell's *Sinister Barrier*, a novel about aliens who own the entire human race, which appeared in the first edition of John W. Campbell's magazine *Unknown* in 1939. Heinlein's narrative is more compressed than Russell's, and this makes it more effective—the surprise ending works because of the care with which Heinlein develops the protagonist's neurotic nature. "They" proposes one reality—that of the Glaroon—which produces a complex illusion, complete and coherent enough to qualify as a second reality, extant in the minds of millions. Many of these sentient beings have a second identity as alien creatures, who, as in Jack Finney's *The Body Snatchers*, have assumed human form and consciousness in order to pass off the mass deception. The trope of multiple identities that correlate with proliferant realities is common to "Elsewhen," "They," and "The Unpleasant Profession of Jonathan Hoag" and shows a strongly-rooted association in Heinlein's fiction between individual identity and the chronotope, which is unstable in the speculative fiction genre. A third similarity between these early short stories is the proliferation of narratives: "Life-Line" consists of multiple narrative "stubs" of all the people who come to Pinero to discover the time and date of their death, and "Elsewhen," as we have seen, contains a series of inset narratives from the dimension-travelling students, which construct and convey the alternative chronotopes. Narratives also proliferate in "They," as the unnamed protagonist hunts for a text-type—from chess games, dream-narratives, music, logic problems, and *apologia*, among others—which will accurately convey his suspicions about a dual reality. In "The Unpleasant Profession," Jonathan Hoag, who suffers from a recurrent amnesia, pays a pair of private detectives to uncover what he actually does all day. They must narrate a terrifying story back to him, which he takes up himself when he sheds his human identity and returns to his "real" identity of a higher life-form that creates and critiques the world we know.

In "They," Heinlein suggests that a subjectively-conceived universe is as legitimate a reality as an objectively-measured one. This focus on subjectivity is a logical outcome of the many-worlds interpretation. What the story does not explain is why the vast delusion perpetrated by the Glaroon's people would be done simply to fool the unnamed protagonist. Why is he so special? Why must he believe in a unified reality, instead of being admitted into the synthetic duality that really obtains? Perhaps he is special *because* he has the capacity to understand the duality; in a similar vein, characters like Potiphar Breen, hero of "The Year of the Jackpot" (1952), can distance themselves from the events surrounding them and discern the pattern—often expressed as a proliferation of some element, such as madness or aggression—which enslaves everyone else. He expresses this understanding of the meta-processes that underlie cognition: "Self-awareness is not relational; it is absolute, and cannot be reached to be destroyed, or created. Memory, however, being a relational aspect of consciousness, may be tampered with and possibly destroyed" ("They" 91).

Memory, the story suggests, connects the proliferant worlds. The protagonist remembers his "true" identity when his human body is asleep, and in the state of languor between sleep and wakefulness, he recalls the reason for the attempt to deceive him—his true self had the power to end the cycle of domination by the creature called the Glaroon. When his human body is fully awake, the identity that accompanies it takes over and supresses his underlying 'true' consciousness, or memory:

> He felt himself slipping, falling, wrenched from reality back into the fraud world in which they had kept him. It was gone, gone completely, with no single association around him to which to anchor memory.

There was nothing left but the sense of heartbreaking loss and the acute ache of unsatisfied catharsis. ("They" 93)

The duality is synthetic—there really is only one spacetime, which constructs another within it, like a nested simulacrum,[8] the narrative demonstrating this via the focalizer's subjectivity. In other words, like "Elsewhen," "They" also posits the primacy of consciousness in constructing and conveying alternative spacetimes. But "They" goes rather further than "Elsewhen." It posits that, essentially, worlds are made as we make sense of experiences caught in spacetime. It is not only consciousness that predicates worlds, but cognition.[9] This complex process requires proliferative *qualia*, or raw sense-data, in order to produce a sensible world, and the nameless protagonist has drawn attention to himself by recognizing this. The extent to which a paradigm-altering delusion could be perpetrated on millions of individual consciousnesses must have been fairly evident to observers of Europe in the early 1940s, and in retrospect Heinlein's story can be read as a figurative treatment of how complete the illusion was and how significant the danger to those who pointed it out.

"The Unpleasant Profession of Jonathan Hoag"

The third story in the trio under scrutiny was published in 1942 in *Unknown Worlds* under the pseudonym "John Riverside." Like "They," this story posits at least three realities: our world; a second, higher reality from whence comes a Creator who has created our world as a kind of student art project; and a mirror-world inhabited by the "Sons of the Bird," who are an early artistic mistake by the Creator, but who nonetheless retain power over our own, created world. Jonathan Hoag comes from this higher reality, but has assumed the human form of a jeweller from Chicago in order to judge the Creator's work—he is a Critic. He asks Ted and Cynthia Randall, private detectives, to follow him in order to find out what he does during the day, since he seems to succumb to daily amnesia. The Sons of the Bird are very anxious that Ted and Cynthia do not find out that Hoag is, in fact, their nemesis, who wants to expunge them from the Creator's second, more perfect work. The Sons haul the couple through mirrors, which function as portals to their dimension, and threaten them, until eventually the couple escape. Shortly before the end, Jonathan Hoag explains the truth about the three worlds—the Creator's world, the Sons of the Bird's "mirror world," and their own world—and then sets it all to rights before disappearing. The couple live with no reflective surfaces around them, so that the Sons, if they still exist, have no portal to their dimension.

"The Unpleasant Profession" is a genuinely frightening story, and its closure by no means reassures the reader that the threats have been neutralized. Many metaphysical elements from "They" have been expanded and endowed with intentionality; the treatment of our dimension as a "pantheistic solipsism"—which Heinlein would explore in *The Number of the Beast* (1980)—or creation by a higher reality is made more complex and terrifying by the idea that it is done as a mere pastime. In "They," the Glaroon maintains his dominance by fooling his rivals with a vast deception; there is no such survivalist motive in "The Unpleasant Profession." Unlike "Elsewhen," which shows movement between dimensions by hypnosis-cum-metempsychosis only, "The Unpleasant Profession" uses the old trope of mirrors as dimensional portals. Uniquely, it also proposes intermediate worlds between one dimension and its efficient cause/creator and ranks these created worlds by their aesthetic value. The Sons of the Bird inhabit a world that preceded ours, according to the temporal sequence of the reference world, and is less perfect but more powerful, since it can interfere at will with ours.

Nested realities in 'They'

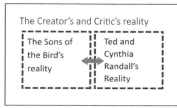
Nested realities in 'The Unpleasant Profession of Jonathan Hoag'

"Elsewhen," "They," and "The Unpleasant Profession of Jonathan Hoag" all show a proliferation of spacetimes, but they also demonstrate the common-sense point that multiple realities are only "real" relative to each other; we categorize something as a spacetime only when something else, specifically another spacetime, makes us objectify it. This does not mean that there are no other realities, just that we do not posit them—bring them into focus, if you like— until a conflict, either physical or cognitive, makes us question their singularity. When these two states come into contact through the experience of a focalizer, they spring into sharp focus relative to each other. The ontological duality can be conveyed only by a consciousness: the narrative focalizer. But because chronotope largely produces character, the focalizer will be different—either subtly, as in "Elsewhen" and "The Unpleasant Profession," or dramatically, as in "They"—in each chronotope they perceive. Proliferation, in a way, cannot be limited: if worlds proliferate, so does everything else—character, identity, even narrative. The proliferation of worlds in Heinlein's fiction evokes that unique configuration of spacetime and plenitude which fascinated his era: the chain-reaction. Only the necessity of narrative closure required by the genre ends the endless proliferation, but by evoking the chain-reaction structure, Heinlein reminds the reader of the weirder, more astounding properties in reality to which the text gestures—and this is the task of speculative fiction.

Notes

1. See, for example, H. Bruce Franklin on "America as Science Fiction, 1939."

2. Cavendish's work was published twice, both times accompanied by *Observations Upon Experimental Philosophy*.

3. See particularly Stanislaw Lem, Albert I. Berger, and George Slusser and Daniele Chatelain.

4. Shortly before his death in 1947, Ouspensky published a short novel exploring this idea, called *The Strange Life of Ivan Osokin*.

5. Werner Heisenberg, "Über den anschaulichen Inhalt der quantentheoretischen Kinematik und Mechanik," *Zeitschrift für Physik* 43.3–4 (1927): 172–198.

6. In fact, Jorge Luis Borges' short story "El jardin de senderos que se bifurcan," translated in 1948 as *The Garden of Forking Paths*, remains the earliest working-out in narrative, of which I am aware, of the outcomes-as-worlds theory. Borges published this story, which was the first of his works to be translated into English for *Ellery Queen's Mystery Magazine*, 1941.

7. See Hans Moravec, "Simulation, Consciousness, Existence."

8. See Phil Torres, "Why Running Simulations May Mean the End is Near."

9. Descartes recognized the role of cognition in his "evil genius" concept, described in his 1641 *Meditations on First Philosophy*. Descartes, however, also used this as one of his strategies of scepticism; see Alan E. Musgrave, *Common Sense, Science and Scepticism* (202).

Works Cited

Abbott, Edwin. *Flatland: A Romance of Many Dimensions*. Princeton: Princeton UP, 2015.

Bakhtin, Mikhail M. "Forms of Time and of the Chronotope in the Novel: Notes Toward a Historical Poetics." *The Dialogic Imagination*. Trans. Caryl Emerson & Michael Holquist. Austin: U of Texas P, 1981. 84–258.

Berger, Albert I. "Theories of History and Social Order in 'Astounding Science Fiction' 1933–55." *Science Fiction Studies* 15.1 (1988): 12–35.

Cavendish, Margaret. *The Blazing World, and Other Writings*. Ed. Kate Lilley. London: Penguin, 1994.

Dunne, J. W. *An Experiment with Time*. London: Faber, 1939.

Eddington, Arthur. *The Nature of the Physical World*. Oxford: MacMillan, 1928.

H. Bruce Franklin. "America as Science Fiction: 1939 (*L'Amerique comme Science-Fiction: 1939*)." *Science Fiction Studies* 9.1 (1982): 38–50.

Heinlein, Robert A. "Elsewhen." *Assignment in Eternity*. Riversdale NY: Baen, 1987. 91–134.

_____."Life-Line." *Astounding Science-Fiction* Aug. 1939. 83-95. Baen Books, n.d. Web. 22 Aug. 2015. <http://www.baenebooks.com/chapters/0743471598/0743471598___2.htm>.

_____. "They." *Unknown* (Apr. 1941): 84–95.

_____. "The Unpleasant Profession of Jonathan Hoag." *Unknown* (Oct. 1942): 9–58.

Leinster, Murray. "Sideways in Time." *Astounding Stories*. June 1934. *Scribd*. 22 Aug. 2015. <http://www.scribd.com/doc/199920368/Murray-Leinster-Sidewise-in-Time#scribd>.

Lem, Stanislaw. "The Time Travel Story and Related Matters of SF Structuring," *Science Fiction Studies* 1.3 (1974): 143–54.

Moravec, Hans. "Simulation, Consciousness, Existence." 1998. *Field Robotics Center at the Carnegie Mellon Robotics Institute*. CMU, 2015. Web. 22 Feb. 2015. <https://www.frc.ri.cmu.edu/~hpm/project.archive/general.articles/1998/SimConEx.98.html>.

Musgrave, Alan E. *Common Sense, Science and Scepticism: A Historical Introduction to the Theory of Knowledge*. Cambridge, UK: Cambridge UP, 1993.

Russell, Eric Frank. *Sinister Barrier*. 1939. Del Rey, 1985.

Slusser, George & Daniele Chatelain. "Spacetime Geometries: Time Travel and the Modern Geometrical Narrative." *Science Fiction Studies* 22.2 (1995): 161–86.

Torres, Phil. "Why Running Simulations May Mean the End Is Near." *Institute for Ethics and Emerging Technologies*. IEET, 31 Dec. 2014. Web. 22 Feb. 2015. <http://ieet.org/index.php/IEET/more/torres20141231>.

Wells, H. G. *The Time Machine: An Invention: A Critical Text of the 1985 London First Edition*. Jefferson, NC: McFarland, 1996.

_____. *The Wonderful Visit*. Auckland, NZ: The Floating Press, 2012.

_____. *A Modern Utopia*. Lincoln, NE: University of Nebraska Press, 1967.

_____. *Men Like Gods*. New York: Macmillan, 1923.

"Who Wrote the Notebook?" Physics, Fiction, and the Bootstrap Paradox___

Kristine Larsen

Heinlein and the Allure of Time Travel

The possibility of time travel into the past has long tantalized philosophers, scientists, and writers and their corresponding audiences. A plausible explanation for our fascination is the possibility for a "do-over" in our lives and, with it, a chance to benefit from the greater wisdom that comes with so-called "Monday morning quarterbacking." It seems logical to yearn for the chance to return to the past in order to right wrongs, both personal and societal. An oft-cited example is returning to the past and killing Hitler before he rises to power. But who is to say that killing Hitler as a young man would not, instead, have paved the way for the rise of an even more horrific dictator? Perhaps Hitler's rise to power, while certainly devastating and fraught with atrocities, actually stopped the rise to power of another dictator who would have succeeded in procuring the atomic bomb and brought about a nuclear war that would have killed billions. Such philosophical questions are central to the genre of literature referred to as "speculative fiction." But what about the purely scientific aspects of time travel? Does science fiction remain true to the physics? Is it possible to write a self-consistent tale about time travel that can simultaneously captivate its audience?

Jeff Jensen's review of physically-plausible time travel science fiction leads off with "two of the most influential pieces of science fiction ever written, both of them by the revered Robert Heinlein: 'By His Bootstraps' (1941) and 'All You Zombies—' (1959)." He credits these two works with helping to "create the storytelling grammar and philosophical terms for countless time-travel stories since." ("'Star Trek' vs. 'Lost'"). Both of these tales also are widely cited by physicists when attempting to explain time travel paradoxes to a nontechnical audience. For example, despite its origin as a work of fiction, Heinlein's tale of Bob Wilson, a man caught in a causal loop, has become synonymous with a paradox of time travel now often referred to as the "bootstrap paradox." The physics community is notoriously merciless in its derision of "bad" science fiction; its enthusiastic embrace of Heinlein's tale therefore speaks volumes both to the quality of the science contained within the work and to the clarity with which the author explains the convoluted causal network. In exploring the science of the Bootstrap paradox, as well as the so-called "sexual paradoxes" that form the central theme of Heinlein's brilliant short story "'All You Zombies—'," we come to understand why Heinlein's tales not only have become so inextricably linked to our understanding of time travel but simultaneously illustrate the power of science fiction to motivate, elucidate, and educate as well as entertain.

Time Travel and the Laws of Physics

In his now-century-old General Theory of Relativity, physicist Albert Einstein revolutionized our understanding of gravity by postulating that it represents the warping of the four-dimensional fabric of reality called *spacetime* by mass and energy. For example, the Earth orbits the Sun as it does because the Sun warps spacetime in its vicinity in a specific way. If the presence of matter—and energy—can warp spacetime, is it possible to warp it in such a way as to permit information or a material object to travel in time? A number of solutions to Einstein's equations that allow for time travel to the past and future have been found, involving, among other scenarios, rotating universes, cosmic strings, wormholes, and circulating laser beams. Such solutions contain *closed timelike curves* (CTCs) in which a particle or observer returns to its starting point in time over and over again. These are, therefore, loops in time, or time loops, and they make travel back and forth in time at least hypothetically possible.

As physicists, philosophers, and science fiction writers—who always seem more than willing to adapt any speculative physics to their cause—begin to look more closely at the possibility of time travel into the past, a number of paradoxes rear their ugly heads. Take, for example, the so-called Grandfather paradox. Rosie the time traveler theoretically can travel back in time and kill her paternal grandfather, say, when Grandpa Joe is a mere seven years old. This means that Rosie's father will never be born and therefore that Rosie herself will never be born. But how, then, can Rosie be there to kill her grandfather in the first place? Clearly this is impossible. Therefore, there must be some restriction in the laws of physics that prevents a time traveler from committing an act that would create such a paradoxical situation. In their seminal work *The Large Scale Structure of Space-time*, physicists Stephen Hawking and George Ellis address the paradox as follows:

> Of course, there is a contradiction only if one assumes a simple notion of free will; but this is not something which can be dropped lightly since the whole of our philosophy of science is based on the assumption that one is free to perform an experiment. It might be possible to form a theory in which there were closed timelike curves and in which the concept of free will was modified, but one would be much more ready to believe that space-time satisfies what we shall call the *chronology condition*: namely, that there are no closed timelike curves. (189)

Stephen Hawking further postulates the Chronology Protection Conjecture, stating that "the laws of physics do not allow the appearance of closed timelike curves." He adds the humorous remark that "It seems there is a chronology protection agency, which prevents the appearance of closed timelike curves and so makes the universe safe for historians" (Hawking 603).

Hawking's opinion notwithstanding, time travel to the past is possible *if* it obeys the laws of physics. This places important constraints on the circumstances under which past-directed time travel might occur. In his guide for science fiction authors, engineer and popular science writer Paul J. Nahin succinctly describes the two most fundamental rules of time travel:

> (1) if your story has a single time track or line, the events around a closed loop in time must be consistent; e.g., you can't have a time traveler changing the past (although he or she can *affect* the past, and you'll see that there is a difference), and (2) if your story does depend

on changing the past, you must also introduce multiple time tracks, as with splitting universes. (*Time Travel* 4)

The latter refers to an alternative to the standard Copenhagen interpretation of quantum mechanics, called the Many Worlds Interpretation, or MWI. In this model, every time an experiment with several possible outcomes is conducted, the universe branches into parallel realities, one for each of the possible outcomes. The entirety of all realities is termed the Multiverse. The MWI does allow for a time traveler to change the past in a different timeline, but only if the laws of physics allow these realities to interact with each other, a possibility that is still debated by physicists (Toomey 251–64). If so, Rosie hypothetically can go back into the past of a different timeline and kill her young grandfather. There is no paradox because in the universe from which Rosie originates, her grandfather survives and reproduces, and Rosie eventually is born. What Rosie actually does is prevent her birth in this particular alternate timeline, but no paradox arises. It is obvious why the MWI has been useful to writers of literature and screenplays who wish to indulge in speculative alternative timelines. Examples include the television series *Sliders* and *Terra Nova.* Heinlein's novel *The Number of the Beast* (1980) employs a variation of the MWI in which there are also clearly fictional timelines, such as the Land of Oz.

Time Travel and Causal Loops

Ignoring the possibility of multiple timelines severely limits what a time traveler can do in the past, but, importantly, it does not actually prevent such travel out of hand. As early as 1979, physicist Igor Novikov argued that "the close of time curves does not necessarily imply a violation of causation, since the events along such a closed line may be all 'self-adjusted'—they all affect one another through the closed cycle and follow one another in a self-consistent way" (169). In plain English, a time traveler can journey to the past, do only what is allowed, and then return to a present that has not been changed from what he or she remembers. Any actions that the time traveler takes in the past are exactly what they were "supposed" to do—what they have, in a sense, already done. So Rosie can time travel into the past only if she has already done so and can do only precisely what she has already done. This paradoxical seeming chain of events with no beginning or end is termed a causal loop. One cannot kill a young Hitler, using our previous example, but a time traveler might unwittingly become the reason *why* Hitler rises to power in the first place—perhaps by mistakenly killing one of Hitler's rivals.

But wouldn't a time traveler know if he or she has done that and refuse to travel back into the past in order to prevent him or herself from setting that chain of events into motion in the first place? The key here is to remember that there is only a single path or trajectory of the time traveler in our four-dimensional spacetime. An illustrative example might help. Let us assume that the time machine works nearly instantaneously. You walk into it and immediately are whisked away to another time and place, as with the Time Gate in Heinlein's "By His Bootstraps." Wallace travels from 10:00 AM GMT on 1 April 2000 CE to 3:00 PM GMT on 15 May 1975 CE and decides to take a week-long vacation in Paris. He returns to 10:01 AM GMT on 1 April 2000 CE; although he has been gone only a minute by his kitchen clock, in reality he is a week older and a lot more relaxed for having taken the vacation. When he leaves at 10:00 GMT, he honestly does not know if his trip to the past or his return to the future will work until he tries them because he has no memory of either happening—they have not happened for *him* yet. After returning, Wallace remembers the entire event: leaving, vacationing, coming home. This is because he, and the adventure, occur on a single loop in time, or on a single world line, to use physics jargon. Nahin uses the following dialogue from Heinlein's novel *Farnham's Freehold* as a succinct (and scientifically correct) explanation:

> "The way I see it, there are no paradoxes in time travel, there can't be. If we are going to make this time jump, then we already did; that's what happened. And if it doesn't work, then it's because it didn't happen.... We don't know whether it has already happened or not. If it did, it will. If it didn't, it won't." (qtd. in *Time Travel* 122)

Such causal loops certainly are counterintuitive and dizzying, but they do not violate the laws of physics. They are apparently, however uncomfortable, a necessary condition for the possibility of time travel between the past and present, or the present and future, since the present is merely the past of the future.

The previous sentence may appear incorrect. After all, in our experience, the past has already occurred, the present is unfolding, and the future is completely open—it is only a potential that has not yet been realized. However, if causal loops are possible, this seems to suggest that reality is in the form of what is termed a "block universe," in which the past, present, and future have a simultaneous reality and are fixed (Nahin, *Time Machines* 150). This certainly has dire consequences for free will if the future as well as the past is written in stone. It is as Heinlein explains in "'All You Zombies—'": "A thing either is, or it isn't, now and forever amen" (413).

Information Paradoxes, or "Bootstrapping"

The Grandfather paradox is an example of a "consistency paradox," in which an event "both happens and doesn't happen, which is logically inconsistent" (Everett & Roman 136). This stands in contrast to a so-called "information paradox," in which "information (or even objects) can exist without an origin, apparently popping out of nowhere" (Everett and Roman 136). This, too, seems impossible, but it does not violate the laws of physics outright. The problem is that we are using the term "paradox" in two different contexts. The Grandfather paradox is an example of something that is clearly impossible. On the other hand, we have things that are scientifically and logically possible, just disconcerting and confusing. The causal loop and any accompanying information paradoxes are included in the latter and form the backbone of Heinlein's "By His Bootstraps." Heinlein's tale is rather intricate—although by far not his most intricate time travel tale—so perhaps a simpler example should be first offered as an introduction.

It is 2005, and Rosie travels back to 15 June 1981 to try to convince her younger self to buy a different prom dress. But she can only do it if she has already done so, and she would remember meeting her older self, right? If she thinks carefully, she suddenly recalls that an older woman who did, in some ways, remind her of her mother, actually did try to talk her out of buying that dress, so isn't it worth a try? Perhaps she can be more persuasive this time! Into the time machine she goes, but she returns to her present disappointed that she is unable to prevent the purchase of that hideous dress. She can't change the past, but she does affect it.

Young Rosie buys the dress in 1981, but the encounter with the mysterious stranger causes her to run a few minutes late; when she arrives at the shoe store she is disappointed because they have just sold the last pair of size eight sequined platform shoes that were made exclusively for that store. As a result of her encounter with her future self, young Rosie will (thankfully) not be able to wear the shoes she had hoped to wear. Instead, she stops in a local thrift store and spies a pair of brand new shoes, in a style and material that she has never seen before. Another stranger, a woman who looks somewhat like her grandmother, points them out, saying they are perfect for dancing the night away. Rosie buys the shoes and does, indeed, dance the night away at her prom in those wonderful shoes.

Fast-forward to 2040, and an elderly Rosie is cleaning out an old steamer trunk. Suddenly she comes across a very well-worn, faded pair of dress shoes—her old prom shoes. As she reminisces, she wonders how they got to that thrift shop in the first place. Rosie realizes that her future self must have brought them there! But how could these old shoes be the brand new ones her younger self had been convinced to purchase? She programs her 3-D printer to the correct material, scans the old shoes, tweaks a few settings, and voilà! A brand new pair of the shoes is created, identical to the pair she had bought in 1981. Off into the time machine Rosie goes, surreptitiously placing the shoes on the thrift store rack at just the right moment, and when she sees her younger self pondering the selections, she offers, "This pair would be perfect, young lady. Classy enough for the prom, but as comfy as a pair of Tevas." As the younger version of her smiles and tries on the shoes, Old Rosie is stunned—she suddenly remember being confused at that grandmotherly-like stranger in the thrift store saying something about divas. Of course, she couldn't have understood the reference to *Tevas* because they hadn't been invented yet! Without meaning to, Old Rosie says exactly what she now remembers herself saying in the past. But of course she does because she *has* to! There is another problem—how many pairs of shoes *are* there? Seemingly paradoxically, there is only one, the one that Rosie makes with the 3-D printer in the future and brings back into the past. But she makes that new pair as a perfect copy of the shoes young Rosie buys in the past. How can they be their own template? How can she copy something that is its own copy? Welcome to the information paradox. It is not coincidental that shoes were used in this example, as the information paradox is also commonly referred to as the "bootstrap paradox," named for Heinlein's famous tale (Everett & Roman 136).

The Best Bootstraps of Them All

M. Keith Booker and Anne-Marie Thomas claim that "By His Bootstraps" "brought time-travel narrative into science fiction's Golden Age" (18). Initially published in *Astounding Science-Fiction* in October 1941 under the pseudonym Anson MacDonald, "By His Bootstraps" has become what is termed the "Trope Codifier" for causal loop/bootstrap paradox stories. It is not the first work to use this trope; indeed, Wittenberg explains that such stories had become "standard fodder" in pulp fiction magazines by the early 1940s (31). Instead, "By His Bootstraps" is, without a doubt, the most famous example of its type, the archetype and "the template that all later uses of this trope follow" ("Trope Codifier").

The brilliance of this story was recognized immediately, seemingly by everyone except Heinlein himself. In a 1 October 1941 letter to Heinlein, the editor of *Astounding Science-Fiction*, John W. Campbell, Jr., describes it as "the first all-out, frank attack on the circle-of-time story. It's a magnificent idea, and it's been worked out beautifully. You've taken a minute, but highly intriguing point in the whole theory of time-travel, and built it up to the proportions it deserved" (Heinlein, *Grumbles* 21–22). In response, Heinlein writes back that the tale "is still hack—a neat trick, sure, but no more than a neat trick. Cotton candy" (*Grumbles* 22). Physicists Allen Everett and Thomas Roman refer to the tale as, in their opinion, "one of the best time travel stories ever written" (144), while famed cultural historian H. Bruce Franklin calls Heinlein's novella "one of his masterpieces" and "rigorous in its logic" (55).

The causal loop in the story involves a young man named Bob Wilson, who, while writing a thesis about time travel, is interrupted by several time travelers, all of whom turn out to be his future self, some from only a few hours into the future, while one—named Diktor—is many years older. Diktor is the literal dictator of a future world populated by relatively savage human beings, and his prized possession is a dog-eared notebook in which he has written down the language of the primitives he rules. As Bob begins slowly to understand how his future selves are interacting with his original self, he tries to exert his free will by attempting to change the past, but he discovers, like Rosie in our previous example, that he cannot do so. For example, without meaning to, he says and does exactly what he has seen his then future selves doing. Bob eventually finds himself alone in the building on the other side of the Time Gate, with Diktor nowhere in sight.

Over the years, Diktor's old notebook becomes more fragile, so Bob begins to carefully copy from the old book to a new book. Bob eventually realizes that Diktor is never returning because he *is* Diktor, and the dog-eared notebook is exactly the one he has copied, like Rosie's shoes. Bob observes,

> *there never had been two notebooks.* The one he had now would become, after being taken through the Gate to a point ten years in the past, the notebook from which he had copied it. They were simply different segments of the same physical process, manipulated by means of the Gate to run concurrently, side by side, for a certain length of time…. His older self had taught his younger self a language which the older self knew because the younger self, after being taught, grew up to be the older self and was, therefore, capable of teaching. But where had it started?…. Who wrote the notebook? Who started the chain? (Heinlein, "Bootstraps" 113).

The book, and Bob, have been pulled up by their own bootstraps, referring to an American slang expression dating back to at least a 1834 article in the *Workingman's Advocate* (Freeman 2009). The phrase has either a negative connotation, in reference to something that is clearly impossible, because one can't literally lift oneself up by the tag on the back of one's boot, or a more positive one, referring to someone who is self-motivated and fends for him- or herself: a self-starter. Bob Wilson clearly fits this second definition, as someone who goes back in time to his younger self and sets into motion the very chain of events that ultimately leads to his future self as Diktor.

There are good reasons for critics—and physicists—to laud "By His Bootstraps" for its "realistic" portrayal of time travel, if one can say such a thing. Firstly, as Nahin notes, Heinlein's tale is not one of those that falls into the trap of representing a causal loop as a multiplication table that duplicates the traveler with each encounter with him or herself (*Time Machines* 309). The same cannot be said of Philip K. Dick's "A Little Something for Us Tempunauts," for example. Heinlein, through Bob, acknowledges that there is only one traveler, despite the fact that Bob encounters younger and older versions of himself. We know this because there is only one set of memories that keeps being added to as the world line of the traveler continues—as the traveler ages.

A second pitfall that Heinlein avoids involves the book itself. Again, Nahin points out that "when there is a physical artifact in the loop, there is an additional puzzle that nearly all writers seem to have missed," namely how an object that starts out shiny and new can remain so throughout the causal loop, from the past into the future and back into the past again (*Time Machines* 315). Heinlein does not fall into this trap, for he has Bob make a new copy of the then-old book. A third bit of master craftsmanship involves the causal loop itself. As Bob scoffs to his older self, "You would have me believe that causation can be completely circular. I went through because I came back from going through to persuade myself to go through. That's silly" (Heinlein, "Bootstraps" 75). Heinlein correctly understands that being "silly" does not negate its truthfulness. As philosopher Nicholas Smith argues, "it is only *because* you *will* make the trip—for whatever reason (forced or voluntary)—that your older self is there telling you about it in the first place. Your older self's tale is a report of what you will, as it happens, end up doing: the tale conforms to your future actions, rather than your actions having to conform to the tale" (386).

Sexual Paradoxes and "'All You Zombies—'"

As mind-boggling as the causal loops thus far considered may be, there is one extreme type of "bootstrapping" that is in a league of its own. Sexual paradoxes refer to a special class of causal loop, in which one does not only interact with him- or herself, but through a sexual act, one becomes his or her own ancestor, such as a mother or father (Nahin, *Time Machines* 553). Remember Wallace and his vacation in Paris in 1975? It turns out that while he is there, he engages in a brief, yet very intense love affair with a lovely young Parisian lady who gives birth to a baby boy nine months later. The baby is adopted by a young American serviceman and his French wife, and Wallace returns to the United States with his adoptive parents six months later. He is never told that he is adopted, but grows up hearing wonderful stories about Paris, where his parents met, thus motivating his vacation to 1975 Paris. According to Paul Nahin, Heinlein's "acclaimed classic 'All You Zombies—' [is] generally acknowledged as the best sexual paradox tale ever written" (*Time Machines* 321). Physicist J. Richard Gott III goes further, crowning the short story, first published in the March 1959 issue of *Fantasy and Science Fiction*, "one of the most remarkable time-travel stories ever written" (24).

The sexual paradox that is revealed near the tale's conclusion begins with a young man curiously referred to as "the Unmarried Mother." He explains to a bartender that he had been born a female and raised in an orphanage. During the cesarean delivery of a baby girl who had been conceived with a man who had not stood by the hence-unmarried mother, it had been discovered that the Unmarried Mother had a complete set of male sex organs, and a sex change operation had been performed without her—now his—consent. The baby soon after was stolen from the hospital, leaving the Unmarried

Mother in her current state of melancholy. The sympathetic bartender makes an offer to help the Unmarried Mother travel back in time in order to find the man who seemingly had set these events into motion, the baby's biological father. While in the past, the Unmarried Mother discovers not only that the father of the baby is the very same bartender who has made the time travel to the past possible, but that the bartender is, indeed, a future version of the Unmarried Mother himself. In this way, the Unmarried Mother, also named Jane, is his/her own mother *and* father!

Science and technical writer David Toomey notes that in "the hands of a less capable author such a premise might descend into mere gimmickry" (149), while Gott refers to it as "both bizarre and wonderful" and, importantly, "self-consistent" (25). As for Heinlein himself, in a 5 December 1958 letter to his literary agent, Lurton Blassingame, he offers, "I hope that I have written in that story the Farthest South in time paradoxes" (*Grumbles* 156). While the paradox is, indeed, extreme, physicist Michio Kaku's popular level science book *Hyperspace* includes a detailed diagram showing the various loops and personas that are central to "'All You Zombies—'" (241). It is, understandably, a complex mapping, but it *is* consistent.

The Circle Closes

When asked to explain why "'All You Zombies—'" was one of his favorite works, Heinlein offered that paradox stories "are fun to write. Some stories are chores, some are fun—this one I enjoyed writing" (*Grumbles* 112). Indeed, David Toomey contends that "most stories of pastward time travel provide the pleasure of a satisfying plot twist. But their real appeal, at least so it seems to me, is more enduring. They lead us to rather deeper inquiries, to questions of the reality of fate, and to the mystery of free will" (150). The apparent constraints on free will might prove inconvenient to some writers, who abandon science in the name of suspense. Indeed, astronomer and science writer Philip Plait laments that "most writers have no problem sacrificing accuracy to make a good plot" (245). In his influential philosophical examination of the paradoxes of time travel, David Lewis takes a more optimistic viewpoint: "Not all science fiction writers are clear-headed, to be sure, and inconsistent time travel stories have often been written. But some writers have thought the problems through with great care, and their stories are perfectly consistent." He explains in a footnote that when thinking about the latter, he has "particularly in mind" both "By His Bootstraps" and "'All You Zombies—'" (145).

It is due to Heinlein's attention to detail and willingness to work within the laws of physics that physicists themselves have embraced his works as examples *par excellence* of the physics itself—a causal loop of a different sort. For as physicist Kip Thorne reflects, "smart physicists seek insight everywhere, including from clever science fiction writers who long ago began probing seriously the logical consequences that would ensue if the laws of physics permitted time travel" (Nahin, *Time Machines* ix). An example Thorne offers is Igor Novikov's Principle of Self Consistency, explaining that physicists could "presumably have arrived at this principle on our own, without the aid of science fiction, but our familiarity with science fiction's grandfather paradox in fact was a powerful motivation for the principle" (Nahin, *Time Machines* x). Kip Thorne speaks from a position of authority here, for his own work on the possibility of a wormhole being used as a time machine itself owes much of its genesis to questions from his friend Carl Sagan about the physics of time machines while the latter was writing his own science fiction novel *Contact* in 1985 (Thorne 483–90). Thus it is as Jane/bartender/Unmarried Mother opines, "bartenders and psychiatrists learn that nothing is stranger than truth" (Heinlein, "'Zombies'" 403). To that list, I would certainly add physicists and some particularly gifted science fiction authors.

Works Cited

Booker, M. Keith & Anne-Marie Thomas. *The Science Fiction Handbook.* Chichester: Wiley-Blackwell, 2009.

Everett, Allen & Thomas Roman. *Time Travel and Warp Drives.* Chicago: U of Chicago P, 2012.

Franklin, H. Bruce. *Robert A Heinlein: America as Science Fiction.* Science-Fiction Writers Ser. Oxford: Oxford UP, 1980.

Freeman, Jan. "Bootstraps and Baron Munchausen." *The Word Blog*. Boston Globe Media Partners, LLC, 27 Jan. 2009. Web. 13 May 2007. <http://www.boston.com/bostonglobe/ideas/theword/2009/01/bootstraps_and.html>.

Hawking, S. W. "Chronology Protection Conjecture." *Physical Review D* 46 (1992): 603–11.

_____. & G. F. R. Ellis. *The Large Scale Structure of Space-Time*. Cambridge, UK: Cambridge UP, 1973.

Heinlein, Robert A. "'All You Zombies—',". *Science Fiction: A Historical Anthology*. Ed. Eric S. Rabkin. Oxford: Oxford UP, 1983. 402–14.

_____. "By His Bootstraps." *The Menace from Earth*. New York: Baen, 1987. 49–115.

_____. *Grumbles from the Grave*. Ed. Virginia Heinlein. New York: Ballantine, 1989.

Jensen, Jeff. "'Star Trek' vs. 'Lost': Competing Time-Travel Theories." *Entertainment Weekly* Entertainment Weekly, Inc, 15 Aug. 2009. Web. 1 May 2015. <http://www.ew.com/article/2009/08/15/star-trek-lost-time-travel-theories>.

Kaku, Michio. *Hyperspace*. Oxford, UK: Oxford UP, 1994.

Lewis, David. "The Paradoxes of Time Travel." *American Philosophical Quarterly* 13.2 (1976): 145–52.

Nahin, Paul J. *Time Machines*, 2nd ed. New York: Springer, 1999.

_____. *Time Travel: A Writer's Guide to the Real Science of Time Travel*. Baltimore: Johns Hopkins UP, 2011.

Novikov, I. D. *Evolution of the Universe*. Cambridge, UK: Cambridge UP, 1983.

Plait, Philip C. *Bad Astronomy*. New York: Wiley, 2002.

Smith, Nicholas J. J. "Bananas Enough for Time Travel?" *British Journal for the Philosophy of Science* 48 (1997): 363–89.

Thorne, Kip. *Black Holes and Time Warps*. New York: Norton, 1994.

Toomey, David. *The New Time Travelers*. New York: Norton, 2007.

"Trope Codifier." *TV Tropes*. TVTropes.org, n.d. Web. 7 May 2015. <http://tvtropes.org/pmwiki/pmwiki.php/Main/TropeCodifier>.

Wittenberg, David. *Time Travel: The Popular Philosophy of Narrative*. New York: Fordham UP, 2013.

What *Podkayne of Mars* Says about Humans of Earth, Or, Stranger in a Strange Reading Practice Land

Marleen S. Barr

Thomas Clareson and Joe Sanders note that "[i]n addition to other information it conveys, *Podkayne*'s opening demonstrates that things are not what they seem, that things are happening in and around Poddy that she doesn't quite grasp…. The trip aboard the spaceliner *Tricorn*…does give her more experience proving that appearances are deceptive" (141, 142). Readers share the standpoint Clareson and Sanders attribute to Podkayne Fries, called Poddy. The readers initially cannot grasp Heinlein's efforts to create a failed reading practice in relation to interpreting things in Podkayne's cultural milieu; these things are not what they seem. Their sense of logical order in relation to false front appearances is deceptive.

The obfuscated meaning in *Podkayne* leads Alexei Panshin to conclude that Poddy's younger brother Clark "is the novel's central character" (Clareson & Sanders 141; Panshin 105). Rampant destabilization reigns to the extent that *Podkayne* has two endings. In the original version, Poddy is killed by a nuclear explosion; in the published version, Poddy is in a coma and will recover (Clareson & Sanders 143–144). Heinlein purposefully estranges readers, stymying their attempts to see beyond the veneer of his Martian and Venerian civilizations. Interpretation at first fails; all readers of *Podkayne* are positioned as strangers in a strange reading practice land. I will explore how Heinlein uses a faux posthuman and a failed "resisting reader" lens, to use Judith Fetterley's term, to confront discrimination.

In addition to its two endings, *Podkayne* also contains two interludes. Reflecting the dizzying structure that characterizes *Podkayne*, this essay has several components. I begin with four introductory sections: "Unquantifiable Chronology and Undefinable Language" explains Heinlein's obfuscation penchant; "Resistance

Is Futile" brings Fetterley's "resisting reader" to bear upon the discussion; "Maori of Mars" links Podkayne to her fellow Maori connected to science fiction—Jemaine Clements and Taika Waititi, who created the humorous vampire movie *What We Do in the Shadows*; and "Faux Posthuman Podkayne," which situates Podkayne as a human Martian. My "Interlude," called "Podkayne of Female Heroism," defines Podkayne as the new feminist science fiction hero that feminist science fiction critics now want. "*Podkayne's* Readers Reading Racism" asserts that Heinlein purposefully prevents readers from resisting racism. The concluding "iPod Poddy" explains that Podkayne herself ultimately diffuses Heinlein's prankish reading-practice booby traps.

Unquantifiable Chronology and Undefinable Language

Podkayne's age exemplifies Heinlein's obfuscation penchant. She states that she is "eight years plus a few months" before announcing that "a female citizen of Mars may contract plenary marriage without a guardian's waiver on her ninth birthday" (Heinlein 2). Readers, who immediately think of child bride atrocities, do not consider that Martian years chronologically differ from Earth years. Podkayne states that "Praxiteles—would not have given me a second look" (Heinlein 4). Since a Martian year is over ten months longer than an Earth year, Podkayne is a teenager. Teenagers do not normally refer to Praxiteles, and "John Campbell thought Podkayne or Poddy too precocious to be real, citing his own teenage daughters as the norm" (Stover 46). Because Podkayne is ultimately unknowable, readers cannot make accurate social value judgments about her.

Readers' lack of the ability to interpret precisely also applies to the age of Poddy's Uncle Tom, a venerated senator: "I've never seen him look so old—fifty at least, or call it a hundred and fifty of the years they use here [on Venus]" (Heinlein 161). Readers are not told precisely how to measure Venerian years in relation to Earth years. No matter. Heinlein's Venus does not conform to reality. Yes, some like it hot. But Venus is just too hot to handle the Las Vegas counterpart Poddy encounters there. She inhabits a solar system which differs from our own.

So, too, for defining some examples of Poddy's language. She says that "I canalize most readily" (Heinlein 8). "Canalize" can only denote a prison house of language, which readers cannot access. Heinlein renders the culture and language operative on Mars as textual "things" that are not what they seem. Further underscoring the unknowable, "*Podkayne of Mars* is a novel about a voyage to Earth...yet the voyage never gets her [Poddy] there" (Franklin 146). Heinlein situates Earth as a forever unreadable and unknowable blank page. A failed reading practice characterizes Heinlein's Earth, Mars, and Venus.

Resistance Is Futile

This situation also applies to the "resisting reader." Fetterley explains that Washington Irving is less than fair to Dame Van Winkle:

> [A]n essential part of the Americanness of Irving's story is the creation of woman as villain.... While not identifying with Dame Van Winkle, she [the female reader] nevertheless cannot fully escape the sense of being implicated in the indictment of her sex that Dame Van Winkle represents. She cannot read the story without being assaulted by the negative images of women it presents. (Fetterley 3, 10)

Readers can resist Irving's text, which gives Rip Van Winkle's dog greater subjectivity than his wife: Rip's "dog Wolf was as much henpecked as his master.... [H]e was as courageous an animal as ever scoured the woods—but what courage can withstand the ever during and all besetting terrors of a woman's tongue?" (Irving 36). They can call Irving's story sexist. They can rail that Dame Van Winkle is a forever silenced subaltern. Conversely, a resisting reader response fails in relation to females marrying at age nine on Mars. This social practice is logical in relation to Mars, not sexist. Leon Stover refers to Heinlein's purposeful reading practice traps as "a prank": "The mischief done here is all in the rhetoric, a prank played on the reader's complacency with a limited world view" (Stover 11). It is impossible to be a resisting reader when closely encountering Heinlein's unknowable Mars culture prank. Resistance is futile.

Applying an early twenty-first century social sensibility to *Podkayne* is the most constructive way to read it. Readers should recognize that indigenous Martians and Venerians are positioned as extraterrestrial versions of Dame Van Winkle. Like her, they are marginalized and silenced. *Podkayne of Mars* says this about humans of Earth: some humans habitually define their fellow humans as subhuman. *Podkayne* is a text that deservedly erases Earth. Due to racism, sexism, and imperialism—to list only some isms—Earth, for some humans, is artificially constructed as being "[n]ot suited to human habitation" (Heinlein 1).

Maori of Mars

The humorous vampire film *What We Do in the Shadows* addresses interpreting *Podkayne* in light of Fetterley. This film, "a goofily amusing mockumentary from the New Zealand comedians and actors Jemaine Clement and Taika Waititi," which chronicles "the daily lives of four vampire housemates" (Catsoulis C16), can shed light on what I am claiming for *Podkayne*. Like Podkayne, who inhabits an outpost colony world, Clement and Waititi also come from an out-of-the-way place, and they share Podkayne's Maori background. Podkayne is a fictitious Scandinavian Maori; Waititi is a real Jewish Maori, who sometimes uses his mother's surname, Cohen. A Jewish Maori hits the racial diversity jackpot.

Both *Podkayne* and *Shadows* emphasize that change can fail to happen even within a highly fantastic premise. This lack of transformation addresses reality. In the film, amidst the tumult of four vampire roommates witnessing multitudinous humans becoming vampires and werewolves, an easygoing tech guy Everyman named Stu, played by Stuart Rutherford, adheres to his mundane demeanor. He remains calm even after becoming a werewolf. Waititi explains that Rutherford, an easygoing tech guy in real life, "is playing himself. The Stu you see in the film is the real life Stu. He is a boring IT guy both in the film and in real life" (Waititi). The Stu who lives with vampires and becomes a werewolf on screen does not lose his humanity. Nor do the vampires deviate from treating him in a compassionate and poignant manner. The vampire "group's determination to befriend a bewildered techie—without eating him—is strangely touching" (Catsoulis C16). Despite Stu's extremely fantastic circumstances, this protagonist remains as human as Rutherford; Stu is a human and humane werewolf.

Faux Posthuman Podkayne

So, too, for Podkayne. Although she inhabits an exceedingly technologically sophisticated Mars that is as unreal as Stu's vampire-sodden environment, she also remains human and humane. In fact, this purported Martian is even more biologically human than the alive-and-well-by-dint-of-becoming-a-werewolf Stu. Podkayne is not of Mars. She is *from* Mars. She is human and of Earth; her ancestors immigrated from Earth to Mars. Poddy, born of birth technology which is light years beyond real IVF, is a faux posthuman. She is not a native Martian.

Podkayne is a sophisticated commentary on constructed race and gender distinctions. Understanding Heinlein's purposefully failed resisting reader reading practice depends upon categorizing Poddy in terms of "faux posthumanism"—i.e., readers' false expectation of encountering a science fictional posthuman society on Mars. Poddy and her Mars-inhabiting family are as human as New Zealand-inhabiting Clement and Waititi. Clement and Waititi, Maori, are native to New Zealand. Podkayne, a descendant of Maori, is also native to New Zealand—not Mars.

Podkayne describes the societies that exist on Mars and Venus. They consist of humans who immigrated from Earth and Maori-like Martian and Venerian native people. These natives are not posthumans; they are a silenced extraterrestrial indigenous population—i.e., fantastic Maori. Podkayne, a member of a society that includes post-biological, cryogenically preserved fetuses, is not posthuman. She is a human Earthling who was born on Mars. Heinlein's mid-twentieth-century faux posthumanism allows him to grapple with racism and sexism in a manner pertinent to the present. Just as the fantastic Stu is the same as the real Stu, the Podkayne born on Mars is the same as humans born on Earth. *Podkayne* addresses very real race and gender constructions.

Heinlein's faux posthumanism and failed resisting reader reading practice lens play with readers' abilities to interpret with an eye attuned to racism and sexism; Heinlein purposefully blinds readers, obfuscates their reading. As I will explain, readers initially do not see that Uncle Tom is black and that Poddy's attention to nurturing babies is necessary rather than sexist. Because Poddy's Scandinavian blondness is emphasized—and her Maori ancestry is presented as an afterthought—Uncle Tom is the man whose blackness readers initially do not see. Statesman Uncle Tom's stateroom on the *Tricorn*—or, Uncle Tom's cabin—serves as a good vantage point to understand that Poddy's successful efforts to save babies on the spaceship is necessary. Heinlein's text, not sophisticated twenty-first century readers, metafictionally acts as a resisting reader in relation to Poddy and Uncle Tom.

Podkayne from Mars, no extraterrestrial biological Martian, is as human and as prone to being the target of real "isms" as readers. Readers who closely encounter her are forced to do so from a false perspective located within the textual traps Heinlein purposefully sets. Readers read from a standpoint of racism and sexism. Heinlein at once erases Earth, holds a mirror up to readers, and forces them to see their racist and sexist selves. The reflection is not complimentary. "As everybody knows, Terra is a wonderful place to visit but not to live. Not truly suited to human habitation" (Heinlein 1). These opening lines ring true. Earth is not suited to social humane human habitation. No human is immune to being adversely impacted upon by "isms." Heinlein spares Poddy from ever setting foot on Earth. *Podkayne* erases Earth with "good riddance" assurance.

"Interlude" (Heinlein 9–10, 49–50): Podkayne of Female Heroism

I follow this statement about Terran deletion with an Earth-shattering observation: Podkayne, created in 1963, is the newly needed feminist science fiction hero for the early twenty-first century. What do feminist science fiction critics now want? They want something new under the sun in relation to female heroes. Nicola Griffith addresses this need: "I am tired of token women being strong in a man's world by taking on male attributes.... Women are not inherently passive or dominant, maternal, or vicious.... We are people" (375–76). Silvia Moreno-Garcia echoes Griffith's call for a new definition of "strong" female science fiction protagonists: she advocates an alternative to defining a strong women as the "kind that must demonstrate her chops via feats of physical strength.... [M]y point is not to demand a particular type of character but to remark that we should not yearn for 'strong' women but for a wide variety of women" (Moreno-Garcia). What do Griffiths and Moreno-Garcia want? They want Podkayne. Podkayne is no bodysuit-wearing ass-kicker. Instead, she is a nurturer-in-chief who rescues babies about to be fried by radiation. She is also a hero who saves a baby indigenous Venerian named Ariel. *Podkayne*, which has received relatively little critical attention, provides the new female hero feminist science fiction critics presently want.

Writing in 1980, H. Bruce Franklin understandably does not concur with Griffiths' and Moreno-Garcia's assertions. He explains that Podkayne's

> ambition to be the captain of a spaceship is a self-delusion. Throughout the book, Poddy is inept at everything except taking care of babies and some social relations. When the spaceship passes through an emergency, Poddy discovers her true calling, as she and the stewardesses take care of the babies.... But this leads Podkayne to alter her aspirations, accepting a traditional woman's role personally and professionally. (142)

Close attention to the point that the narrators of the two sections Heinlein designates as "Interlude" (Heinlein 9–10, 49–50) logically differ, however, reveals that Poddy's ambition is no self-delusion. The narrator of the second "Interlude" mentions "hypothetical happy dust" (Heinlein 50). The narrator must be Clark, who—anticipating the post 9/11 verboten nature of joking about terrorism while taking public transportation—says, in a prankster-like voice, that he is sneaking "happy dust" (Heinlein 39) on to the *Tricorn*.

The narrator of the first "Interlude," who calls Poddy "Sister dear," says this: "A lot you know about me! Poddy—oh, excuse me

'Captain' Podkayne Fries, I mean the famous space Explorer and Master of men" (Heinlein 9). Since Poddy certainly knows Clark, this narrator differs from the narrator of the second "Interlude" and seems to be one of Poddy's three infant siblings speaking as an adult. This narrator's sarcasm indicates that Poddy did indeed become a spaceship Captain—and that Captain Fries did not take the time to "know" her sibling. A Captain who ignores her sibling is not acting in accordance with traditional women's roles. Further, traditional women's roles, which involve saving a plethora of choking babies, are beyond reproach. The point is that Poddy is a leader, who assumes power in terms of valorizing nurturing. She is an eventual spaceship captain who can save any baby in distress aboard her ship.

Rodney M. DeaVault's recent attention to *Podkayne* omits Griffith's and Moreno-Garcia's call for a new feminist science fiction hero. He explains that "[n]ear the close of her story, Podkayne nurtures a baby fairy and ends up comatose protecting it, becoming the very angel her looks suggest she is" (DeaVault 195). The "fairy" is not an "it." "Fairy" is a pejorative term. The "fairy," no Tinkerbell, is an indigenous Venerian. Further, Podkayne is no mere blond angel. As I have emphasized, she is a partly an indigenous person. Her Maori genes may have manifested themselves as brown skin; a combined Maori and Scandinavian person is not completely Caucasian. Podkayne is passing for white.

Podkayne finally recognizes Ariel's personhood when she decides that, like the endangered babies on the *Tricorn*, Ariel is worth saving. Poddy's racial catharsis is heroic, not angelic. The "tragic ending" certainly does not deprive Podkayne of a "moment of self-discovery"; she is not prevented "from making any mature life decisions." She is not "deliberately frozen in her adolescent state, as passive and beatific as Sleeping Beauty" (DeaVault 196–97). She aggressively thaws the "Sleeping Beauty" stereotype. Podkayne, a new alternatively strong woman, is a transcending Wonder Woman in relation to her culture's racist attitudes. DeaVault perceptively states that "Podkayne, who ponders the difficulties of having a career and motherhood, is a pioneer for being brave enough to seek both" (DeaVault 197). Although the narrator of the first "Interlude" implies that Podkayne becomes a spaceship captain, nowhere does Heinlein state that she becomes a mother. Podkayne is a female heroism pioneer who is brave enough to be a leader who ultimately values the lives of babies. She is Griffith's and Moreno-Garcia's wished-for new alternative female hero.

I turn to exploring how this new hero, who springs from the early 1960s, functions in terms of Heinlein's resisting-reader text and faux posthuman Mars residents. I closely read Heinlein's prank-filled novel—his toying with readers' inability to interpret in a manner completely devoid of prejudice. He situates inevitable racist reactions within an—in relation to readers—impregnable prison house of language.

Podkayne's Readers Reading Racism

Heinlein prevents readers from resisting racism. His most apparent "prank," his purposeful reading practice trap, functions most pronouncedly in terms of Uncle Tom. Podkayne's self-description manipulatively causes readers to elide the race of her family member. She describes herself as having "eyes of blue" (Heinlein 2) and states that her "hair is pale blond and wavy and I'm pretty" (Heinlein 4). She further announces that "I'm colonial mongrel in ancestry, but the Swedish part is dominant in my looks, with Polynesian and Asiatic fractions adding no more than a not-unpleasing exotic flavor" (Heinlein 3–4). Unfortunately, "pretty" most often denotes "Swedish" blondness, not "colonial mongrel" "exotic flavor." Most readers accentuate the "pretty" Western aspects of her appearance and minimalize the "exotic" difference. Hence, they view Uncle Tom as being Caucasian. It is shocking for readers to learn that "Uncle Tom is as dark as I am blond; his Maori blood and desert tan make him the color of beautiful old leather" (Heinlein 78). It is highly unusual for a blond to be a dark man's niece.

In the early 1960s, it also was highly unusual for a dark-skinned man to be a venerated statesman. Heinlein plays with readers racist conceptions. He traps them into thinking that Uncle Tom is white. Readers are blind to the fact that someone named, of all things, *Uncle Tom* is black. Tom's *Tricorn* stateroom is in fact Uncle Tom's cabin. "Aliens," that is to say indigenous people from Mars, are "the handful of aliens in the ship we never see; each remains in his specially conditioned stateroom" (Heinlein 64–65). If the native Martians are subhuman, why do they desire to travel in a spaceship? The discrimination directed at native Martians is illogical. The reaction of Mrs. Royer, a *Tricorn* passenger from Earth, also lacks sense: "[H]ave you noticed that little Martian girl [Podkayne]? The niece...of that big black savage [Uncle Tom]?" (Heinlein 78). It is shocking to know that *Senator* Fries—the Mars-based equivalent of Kofi Annan, Barack Obama, and Nelson Mandela—is called a "big black savage."

Even more shockingly, Podkayne initially manifests her society's racist attitudes. When describing indigenous Martians, she refers to them as "it": A "Martian doesn't select which of three sexes to be until just before it matures" (Heinlein 73). "It" is an inappropriate way to describe members of a complex multi-sexual society. Racism is what we see in the shadows—in the textual interstices of human Martian society.

Heinlein's textually dizzying commentary upon racism is further complicated when Poddy and Uncle Tom attribute a positive connotation to the "savage." They valorize the rude Maori gesture of teeth-picking. Poddy explains that "I won't even hint at what it is we are supposed to be picking out of our teeth.... 'You're the blondest blue-eyed savage I ever saw. But you're a savage all right. And me, too [says Uncle Tom].... Or have we brought too much Norse blood into the family?'" (Heinlein 165). Interpretation fails here; most non-Maori readers do not know the cultural significance of teeth-picking. Poddy at once feels superior to "savage" native Martians and exults in being a savage herself. Her complex racial background indicates that Heinlein is being as much of a prankster as Clark. Readers cannot resist racism in the face of encountering Maori/Norse protagonists.

Do Maori/Norse people exist? Even the exceedingly multiracial Obama family lacks Maori/Norse people. Science fiction criticism is just recently catching up with multicultural perspectives. No one is focusing on Maori science fiction. Clement and Waititi are probably the only Maori on planet Earth who generate science fiction. Yet Heinlein created Maori science fiction protagonists in 1963. Maori science fiction protagonists are strangers in a strange reading practice land. They pose a textual trap for readers who, via a kneejerk reaction, initially construe Poddy to be a posthuman Martian. No posthuman, Poddy is a racially complex human from Mars and of Earth. She is an indigenous person who initially discriminates against indigenous Martians. Reading *Podkayne of Mars* involves not being fully aware of her complexities. Reader response criticism fails.

Podkayne addresses this failure in terms of her genetic and cultural heritage: "[S]cratch my Nordic skin and a savage is just underneath, I wanted to pick my teeth at her [Mr. Cunha's secretary] only she wouldn't have understood it" (Heinlein 175). Most readers who are not Maori do not understand "it" either. This analysis blind spot is endemic to reading *Podkayne*.

Back to the garden variety racism Mrs. Royer spews. This spaceship passenger's racist attitudes ironically harken to the past. She says when Poddy arrives on Earth, it will be necessary for her to meet "the right People. 'Perhaps such things don't matter in an outpost like Mars, my dear child, but it is Terribly Important to get Started Right in New York'" (Heinlein 74–75). She sounds like an Edith Wharton protagonist. Mrs. Royer's attention to Poddy's potential future place in Earth society constitutes another reading practice trap. This Earthling considers all humans who live on Mars to be "[t]hose dreadful people.... After all, they're all criminals" (Heinlein 77). The fact that racism based on skin color, not individual people, is criminal is underscored when Mrs. Royer changes from "bright red instead of yellow" (Heinlein 104). This capricious action occurs because a spaceship passenger is a trickster: "[s]omebody in the ship...soaked two washcloths in the inactive dyes.... Then that somebody sneaked those two prepared washcloths into those two staterooms and substituted them for washcloths they found there on stateroom wash trays" (Heinlein 105). This subterfuge, probably perpetrated by Heinlein's fellow prankster Clark (Heinlein 106), indicates that racial bias is an artificial construction.

The purposefully changed skin color is "an appropriate reminder for the bigots of how subjective skin color can be in social situations" (Clareson & Sanders 142). Heinlein underscores this fact: he creates Earth humans who look down on Mars humans—even though all Mars humans hail from Earth. In addition, a part-Maori protagonist looks down on indigenous Martians. This discriminatory complexity is illogical; we are all human. Differences among humans are as artificially constructed as Mrs. Royer changing from red to yellow by dint of sabotaged washcloth. Heinlein uses science fiction tropes to indicate a real truth: racial difference is science fiction. Science defines individuals who are able to mate and reproduce as being members of the same species. Maori and Norse people—people who are glaringly culturally different—can reproduce, as Podkayne's existence illustrates.

Unlike racial difference, cultural difference is of course real. But many cultural differences between readers' Earth and Heinlein's Mars and Venus also do not exist. Mars has "Guggenheim grants" (Heinlein 5), "the hilton [sic]" (Heinlein 114), and "the Kiwanis Klub" (Heinlein 116). Venus has "Macy's" (Heinlein 173). Mars is culturally an Earth country, not an alien planet. "Mars is the Switzerland of the Solar Systems" (Heinlein 164). In Heinlein's solar system, Venus is Las Vegas—and Earth is news from nowhere. The indigenous people from Mars and Venus are treated as "less than"—as the Other—in relation to humans.

Real Earth racism is alive and well and living in Mars culture. There are Jews on Mars. Poddy converses with "Dr. Hymie Schoenstein" (Heinlein 26). Perhaps his family members are Holocaust survivors who immigrated to Mars. *Podkayne* alludes to the Holocaust. The radiation shelter space on the *Tricorn* affords Podkayne a billet which "is a shelf space…just a trifle longer than I am—with other females brushing my elbows on each side of me…. [A] a coffin would be roomier" (Heinlein 83). Her billet, which resembles Auschwitz barracks, describes the place of Jewish extermination, which did not afford Jews coffins. If this allusion is not dead-on enough, Heinlein mentions "I.G. Farbenindustrie"

(Heinlein 165). The corporation that manufactured the gas used at Auschwitz is still extant in Podkayne's social orbit.

At least the *Tricorn* improves upon the *Titanic*. During the radiation storm, everyone is welcome within the shelter; no one dies due to their class. Captain Darling says, "No one...is going to be hurt" (Heinlein 98). But the *Tricorn* is not devoid of class stratification: "[A]s for third class, I [Poddy] would rather be shipped as freight.... [T]he half-dozen aliens aboard...don't take shelter; they simply remained locked in their specially conditioned staterooms.... [T]hey aren't allowed to fry" (Heinlein 88). Aliens who are not be allowed to "fry" foreshadow Podkayne's penultimate decision not to allow Ariel to fry in an atomic bomb blast. This decision allows Podkayne Fries to free herself from the prison house of racism. The name "Captain Darling" alludes to human love relationships. "Podkayne embodies love" (Franklin 144). She deserves readers' love. Captain Podkayne Fries is Captain Darling, in fact.

"Fries" can be pronounced as either "fries" or "frees"—a fact which relates to *Podkayne*'s two endings. In the first ending, Podkayne is killed by an atomic bomb; she fries. In the second ending, she saves Ariel and survives; she frees herself from prejudice and becomes a hero. "Podkayne" more directly refers to discrimination's relation to caprice. "Podkayne" is the name of an indigenous Martian saint: "[M]any living Martians claim descent from Saint Podkayne.... [W]e know Martian history of millions of years ago.... [M]ost Martians include 'Podkayne' in their long lists of names...because of the tradition that anyone named for Saint Podkayne can call on him (or 'her'—or 'it') in time of trouble" (Heinlein 74). Indigenous Martians enjoy a rich and lengthy cultural history—and they are Christians. The name "Podkayne"—an aspect of native Martian culture—indicates that it is ludicrous to label indigenous Martians as a subspecies in relation to humans. Indigenous Martians—who have successfully eradicated the Sturm und Drang of gender categories—are culturally superior to humans.

The indigenous Venerians also are culturally sophisticated. Regardless, native Venerians are, as I have explained, called "fairies." Poddy initially equates Venerians with animals: "fairies have very sharp teeth and claws; they're carnivorous" (Heinlein 180). She refers to a native servant as "Pinhead," a name reminiscent of "Sambo." Her description of Pinhead is not a pretty picture: "but pictures don't give you the smell and that drooling loose mouth, nor the impression that this *thing* has been dead a long time" (Heinlein 180–181). Podkayne of Mars is a racist of Earth. Pinhead could appropriately say, "Call me Mr. Tibbs"—and call himself Kunta Kinte.

Conclusion: iPod Poddy

After the atomic bomb detonates and Poddy makes the bombshell, life-changing decision no longer to function as a racist, Clark describes her fate: she is found with "a live baby fairy in her arms— her body had protected it; it doesn't appear to have been hurt at all…. I think she decided to save the baby fairy all along" (Heinlein 211). In the spirit of Griffiths and Moreno-Garcia, Podkayne is no female incarnation of a typical male hero. She is a hero who valiantly rescues babies on the *Tricorn* and, in the end, extends her lifesaving hand to an indigenous baby Venerian. There is nothing science fictionally unreal about her decisions; they are merely necessary.

Uncle Tom, in response to the injured Podkayne, says this to her father: "tell your wife, sir, that building bridges and space stations and such gadgets is all very well…but that a woman has more important work to do" (Heinlein 213). Uncle Tom is correct, not sexist. Having and protecting babies is more important than building "such gadgets"; if babies did not exist, no one would make or use the gadgets. Poddy's mother is a very successful professional—and the mother of five children. This professional almost-Superwoman—a member of a society that enjoys ultra-fantastic birth technology— still interrupts her career to engage in childcare. She is doing necessary work. Readers, who are initially blind to Uncle Tom's race, should not be blind to this fact. Poddy the hero can nurture children—and be a spaceship captain. She is an appropriate positive exemplar of early twenty-first century women's roles.

Podkayne underscores that nurturing is important for men, too. Clark, a science prodigy, ultimately nurtures Ariel. *Podkayne* ends with Clark's words: "I guess it [Ariel] thinks I'm its mother. I don't mind, I don't have much to do. It seems to like me" (Heinlein 214). Clark-as-mother needs to progress further; he does have "much to do." He needs to stop referring to Ariel as "it." In relation to combatting discrimination, there is work to be done on Mars and Venus—and on our Earth.

Podkayne Fries ultimately frees herself from her culture's discriminatory practices. She accomplishes what Heinlein's readers cannot accomplish vis-à-vis their initial inability to see that Uncle Tom is black. She moves beyond racism to view Ariel as a person— or, as Jewish/Maori Taika Waititi might say, a *mensch*.

Even though Heinlein created a new twenty-first century female science fiction hero, his prescience does not include an appellation I reserve for Podkayne—although the "Interlude" greeting "Hi, Pod" (Heinlein 9) does come close. Poddy is a nurturing, female science fiction hero iPod—no *I, Robot*, business-as-usual, mechanistic, female-appropriation-of-male-roles hero. Vinnie Chieco coined the name "iPod" after being inspired by this line from *2001: A Space Odyssey*: "Open the pod bay door, Hal." Hal is told to open the door of the *Discovery One* spaceship's Extra Vehicular Activity Pod. Hal, of course, prefers not to. An EVA Pod can function as an escape mechanism. Perhaps it represents an escape from the prison house of "isms." Although Hal—and many humans—do not open this door, Poddy almost dies while doing so. Readers can love her effort—and love her.

I would like to think that Podkayne is a Maori descendant of vampire film creators Clements and Waititi. Her success at discharging the textual reading practice booby traps Heinlein purposefully sets results in readers clearly seeing that racism and sexism is what humans of Earth do in the shadows. Racism and sexism suck the lifeblood out of people. We are all humans of Earth.

Works Cited

Catsoulis, Jeannette. "What We Do in the Shadows" *New York Times* 13 Feb. 2015: C16.

Clareson, Thomas & Joe Sanders. *The Heritage of Heinlein: A Critical Reading of the Fiction*. Critical Explorations in Science Fiction and Fantasy 42. Jefferson, NC: McFarland, 2014.

DeaVault, Rodney M. "The Masks of Femininity: Perceptions of the Feminine in *The Hunger Games* and *Podkayne of Mars*." *Of Bread, Blood and "The Hunger Games": Critical Essays on the Suzanne Collins Trilogy*. Critical Explorations in Science Fiction and Fantasy 35. Ed. Mary F. Pharr & Leisa A. Clark. Jefferson, NC: McFarland, 2012. 190–198.

Fetterley, Judith. *The Resisting Reader: A Feminist Approach to American Fiction*. Bloomington: Indiana UP, 1978.

Franklin, H. Bruce. *Robert A. Heinlein: America as Science Fiction*. Science-Fiction Writers Ser. New York: Oxford UP, 1980.

Griffith, Nicola. "Nicola Griffith Talks about Writing *Ammonite*." *Ammonite*. 1992. New York: Del Rey, 2002. 375–76.

Heinlein, Robert A. *Podkayne of Mars*. 1963. New York: Berkley, 1970.

Irving, Washington. "Rip Van Winkle." *The Legend of Sleepy Hollow and Other Stories*. Introduction and Notes, Elizabeth L. Bradley. New York: Penguin, 2014. 32–49.

Moreno-Garcia, Sylvia. "Say No to Strong Female Characters." *Locus Magazine*. Locus Publications, 10 Feb. 2015. Web. 21 Aug. 2015. <http://www.locusmag.com/Roundtable/2015/02/silvia-moreno-garcia-guest-post-say-no-to-strong-female-characters>.

Panshin, Alexei. *Heinlein in Dimension*. Chicago: Advent, 1968.

Stover, Leon. *Robert A. Heinlein*. Twayne's United States Authors Ser. 522. Boston: Twayne, 1987.

*2001: A Space Odyssey.*1968. MGM. Dir. Stanley Kubrick. Written by Stanley Kubrick & Arthur C. Clarke. Perf. Keir Dullea, Gary Lockwood, and William Sylvester.

Waititi, Taika. "Interview." Center for Communication. *What We Do in the Shadows*. Screening. The School of Visual Arts Theater, New York City, 12 February 2015.

What We Do in the Shadows. 2014. Unison Films. Dir. Jemaine Clement and Taika Waititi. Written by Jemaine Clement & Taika Waititi. Perf. Jemaine Clement, Taika Waititi, Jonathan Brugh, and Stuart Rutherford.

"Locked in Somewhere Safe": Robert A. Heinlein and the Bomb Shelter_____

Rafeeq O. McGiveron

In *Time Enough for Love* (1973) Lazarus Long advises against removing one's sidearms unless "locked in somewhere safe" (292), and various incarnations of this "somewhere safe"—whether we term it *bomb shelter, emergency home, survival retreat*, or even *safe room*—recur in the writings of Robert A. Heinlein across five decades. In some respects, Heinlein can be an easy target for drollery or lofty sniping, and his apparent love of the bomb shelter in both nonfiction and fiction might seem, at best, very quaint indeed. Really, however, although the Cold War threat of full-scale nuclear attack has dwindled greatly, the utility of preparing for the unforeseen has not. While Heinlein of course usually plans against the potential attack of Soviet bombers and intercontinental ballistic missiles, his philosophy of preparing shelter, supplies, and means of defense,[1] along with—perhaps most importantly—acquiring survival skills, may work equally well against other, more prosaic threats that never quite seem to disappear.

Heinlein's first discussions of shelter preparation occur in his early postwar articles on the dangers of the nuclear age, in purposeful advocacy spelled out almost step by step. Although at the time no enemy of the United States yet even possessed fission weapons, international tensions were running high—in occupied Europe, in China, in Indochina, on the floor of the United Nations—and Frank H. Tucker is correct to note that within a few years "it is not an especially fanciful of pessimistic author" who postulates a coming Third World War (191). Despite the deadly earnestness of his intent, however, Heinlein is disarmingly breezy when assuring late-1940s readers that surviving the atomic bomb is "very simple": "Don't be there when it goes off!" (Heinlein, "How to Be" 165). Yet rather than jumping aimlessly from the atomic fire into the squalid frying pan of the first available cave, perhaps ending up "trying to roast a rabbit while scratching your lice-infested hide" (Heinlein, "Pie" 175), Heinlein instead suggests retreating to "an emergency home" within driving distance, where one might live off "fish, game, [and] garden plot" ("How to Be" 167).

The stocking of this "emergency home"—or "survival retreat," as more modern survival authors would term it now—depends on the lay of the land, the size and health of one's family, and distance from the target, but Heinlein naturally emphasizes basic yet irreplaceable tools like "pickax or burning glass," along with replacement pairs for any eyeglasses, a stock of lowly but necessary shoes, and a "liberal" supply of medicines, salt, and canned goods to supplement the aforementioned fish, game, and garden ("How to Be" 168–172). Heinlein cautions, though, that adequate means of defense should be on hand as well, for he predicts that survivors of nuclear attack "would in a few short days be reduced to a starving, thirst-crazed mob, ready for murder and cannibalism" ("Last Days" 157–58). "You will be on your own," we are reminded soberly, "with no one to tell you what to do and no policeman on the corner to turn to for protection. And you will be surrounded with dangerous carnivores, worse than the grizzlies Daniel Boone tackled—the two-legged kind" (Heinlein, "How to Be" 164). Thus, in addition to the weapons that he supposes ultimately will be needed to harry and drive out the occupying enemy, Heinlein also suggests "a rifle, high-powered and with telescopic sights…. A deer or a man should be about the limit of your targets…a deer when you need meat; a man when hiding or running is not enough" ("How to Be" 172–73).

Finally, Heinlein reminds us that in addition to "acquiring…a survival point of view, the spiritual orientation which will enable you to face hardship, danger, cold, and hunger without losing your zest and courage and sense of humor" ("How to Be" 168), the survivor also must learn primitive-living skills:

> Can you fell a tree? Can you trim a stone? Do you know where to dig a cesspool? Where and how to dig a well? Can you pull a tooth? Can you shoot a rifle accurately and economically? Can you spot tularemia…in cleaning a rabbit? Do you know the rudiments of farming? Given simple tools, could you build a log, or adobe,

or rammed-earth, or native-stone cabin from materials at hand and have it be weather-tight, varmint-proof, and reasonably comfortable? ("How to Be" 169–70)

These, according to Heinlein, writing even before the Soviet Union had tested its first nuclear weapon, are basic questions for the survivor of an imagined atomic attack circa 1950. Therefore, aside from studying in the *Boy Scout Manual*, we are advised to stock "handbooks of various trades you have not had time to master," along with color-illustrated references on wild edibles, medical texts, and books on guerrilla warfare as well ("How to Be" 169–74).

To modern readers of another century, Heinlein's insistence on planning for years of very basic pioneering, followed by armed resistance against an occupying army, seems quaint and unrealistic. Yet, of course, it must be remembered that he writes ten or fifteen years before the era of the overkill of "mutually assured destruction," back when a nuclear first strike might be imagined to entail perhaps one or two hundred fission bombs comparable to those used to end the Second World War, not thousands of thermonuclear weapons each a hundred or even a thousand times more powerful.[2] From the perspective of the late 1940s and early 1950s, such planning would be common-sense caution, not paranoid fantasy.

While in early postwar articles Heinlein lectures on the wisdom of maintaining a well-stocked cabin in the countryside, he returns to the concept, naturally and without the earlier didactic insistence, in fiction that follows. Sometimes these cabins are reached by careful planning, sometimes almost by happenstance. Some are primitive, while some are elaborate and technologically self-sustaining. Some are designed for fairly brief stays, others for nearly permanent residence. Whether built as a retreat from impending conflict or simply as a place of privacy and relaxation, such "getaway" cabins by their very nature—isolated, well stocked, well protected—are useful to survival-minded characters in risky situations, and they recur to nearly the end of Heinlein's career.

In *Rocket Ship Galileo* (1947), for example, Heinlein's first published novel, "Doc" Cargraves and his team of teenaged rocket experimenters develop their nuclear-powered Moon rocket on an ordnance-strewn abandoned military training ground in the Southwestern desert, behind a "strong fence" with barbed wire on top (43). The site's simple cabin, with its well, its stove, and its "tight roof overhead" (Heinlein, 47), is tucked away from the prying eyes of all but the most insistent—and hence dangerous. The team have shelter and privacy, they have supplies, and, led by a nuclear physicist who helped developed the atomic bomb, they certainly have intelligence and skills. As suspicious prowlers grow bolder, however, Cargraves, who first had considered firearms "a useless expense" on this endeavor, realizes that they may need more security than mere isolation, and a little "reluctant to explain," he purchases tools quite commonsensical indeed for people miles from the nearest help: two military-surplus semiautomatic rifles and a sturdy revolver (58, 60).

"The Year of the Jackpot" (1952) features another remote cabin, a hunting lodge used as shelter against an early 1950s imagining of World War III. Although protagonist Potiphar Breen apparently has not read any of Heinlein's helpful postwar articles on planning against nuclear war—for he has made no preparations until literally almost the last minute—the statistician realizes that various rising indices promise some unknown but deadly cosmic "jackpot." Breen knows of the cabin through some friends, and on the day he and his girlfriend realize "it's *time to jump*," they pack the car "on a 'Survival Kit' basis[3]—canned goods, all his warm clothing, a sporting rifle he ha[s] not fired in over two years, a first-aid kit and the contents of his medicine chest," plus "cans and books and coats" and "all the blankets of the house" (Heinlein, "Year" 27). Stopping at a gas station on their journey into the hills, Breen picks up extra tires and camping equipment, and he buys for his girlfriend "a .32 automatic, a lady's social-purposes gun," which he presents to her "somewhat sheepishly" (28).

Yet once Los Angeles is atom-bombed behind them, that little .32 gets the couple out of a carjacking attempt (Heinlein, "Year" 31), and Breen's final purchase of fuel and oil takes the two safely up to the cabin—whose pantry, fortunately, already happens to be stocked with enough canned goods to "pull through a hard winter" (32). A sturdy survival retreat in the Sierra Madres, canned food, endless cords of firewood chopped for heating, and the rifle for harvesting game and for killing stray "Russki paratroopers" (36) then keep the couple safe and even contented: with his "lean belly...stuffed with venison and corn fritters," Breen "lack[s] only tobacco to make him completely happy" (35). The "shortest big war in history," with "forty cities gone" (35), is not enough to stop these belatedly well-prepared survivors—only the explosion of the sun, the final "jackpot" at the story's sudden, melancholy conclusion, can do that.

"Sam," the secret-agent narrator of *The Puppet Masters* (1951), maintains an Adirondack cabin with a year's worth of food in the "deep freeze" (61). Like the protagonists of *Rocket Ship Galileo*, he may not necessarily have planned his cabin as a retreat against conflict or civil disturbance, but its remote location and self-sufficiency—along, of course, with the skilled Sam's tough-minded outlook—definitely make the place well suited to dangerous times. When invading parasitic slugs from Titan begin to possess more and more people while the public seems not to notice, Sam tells himself, "I would go up there...and the world could save itself, or go to hell, without me" (Heinlein, *Puppet Masters* 61).

The cabin, Sam apologizes to his wife during their honeymoon on the eve of the potential fall of humanity, is "really just a simple shack" (Heinlein, *Puppet Masters* 112). By the standards of a science-fictional 2007 imagined from 1951, this means "not even an indoor pool" (112): a "conventional steel-and-fiber-glass" structure sheathed inside and out in artificial log, a traditional log-cabin interior that includes a fireplace, and, crucially, the "Kompacto special" with "air-conditioner, power pack, cleansing system, sound equipment, plumbing, radiation alarm, [and] servos" safely hidden beneath the foundation (112–13). Thus in addition to being "about as near as a man could get to a real log cabin and still have inside plumbing" (113), Sam's Adirondack retreat is, more importantly from a survival point of view, very nearly self-sufficient. The well-armed agent believes that while he is "holed up on the mountain" (127), any enemy approaching "within a hundred yards" would easily "be burned down" (61). Although his wife ends up falling for a slug's Trojan Horse ploy, it seems likely had the threat been anything except their beloved tomcat controlled by a Titanian invader, Sam would have been right.

In *The Number of the Beast* (1980), the four intrepid explorers of the multitudinous dimensions of the "multiverse" begin their journey from "Snug Harbor," a "nowhere place" or "hideout" in the wilderness described at first glance by one character merely as a "cabin, fireproof, with underground parking" for "duos," the flying cars of the day (32–33). In an imagined future without our present Global Positioning System satellite network, Snug Harbor is situated somewhere north of the Grand Canyon, in an area remote enough that it is not covered by Air Traffic Control radar (32). With all purchases hidden through front companies, and with foreign laborers flown in blind to a homing beacon now removed, it was built not precisely in secrecy, but with, as the owner's daughter explains, habitual "jungle caution" (73–74). A "concealed" spring provides water, waste goes into an old mine shaft a thousand feet deep, and electricity comes from "power packs" brought in and removed by the homeowners themselves (44–45), while fireplaces with sophisticated heat recycling and hidden exhaust ducts, along with backup Franklin stoves needing no electricity, complete the energy package (59). Like Sam's cabin in *The Puppet Masters*, Snug Harbor is built less for protection from anticipated conflict than for simple privacy and self-sufficiency, but the latter qualities of course also bring the former.

With the combined talents of an experienced combat pilot, a feisty and imaginative scientist, a gifted young Ph.D. in computer science, and a wealthy university donor who is trained in biology and has taught herself to read and speak Russian, the four are as prepared as any could be for the dangers of exploring parallel universes. Wisely, however, weapons are not lacking either. The professor keeps a "rifle and a case of ammo" in the cabin (Heinlein, *Number* 98), along with "an oldstyle Army automatic" .45 caliber pistol[4] (156), while his daughter has a shotgun (194) and "a lady's purse gun" whose a magazine holds a whopping 90 rounds of

"Skoda fléchettes" that "either poison or…break up and expand" (98). The owner of the "duo" in which they mount the professor's dimension-traveling device also carries an "unlicensed"[5] rifle of the same caliber as his father-in-law's (98), and his aircraft even sports "a highly illegal laser cannon" (74). As the scientist and his son-in-law demonstrate by killing—with sabers—a malevolent alien masquerading as a Federal Ranger, when one's hiding place is disturbed by intruders, sometimes "guts and speed" with a weapon are needed (90).

In addition to the survival retreat originally advocated in his early postwar articles, Heinlein of course works the dedicated bomb shelter into his fiction as well. Whereas the well-stocked cabin in the wilderness might be merely a place to vacation rather than necessarily intended to save one's life in an emergency, the actual bomb shelter is planned very purposefully to protect against the dangers of nuclear war, be they blast and radiation and fire, suffocation and thirst and starvation, or intruder of one kind or another. Some of Heinlein's bomb shelters, matter-of-factly mentioned and then quickly passed over, are the expensive, almost inevitable artifacts of nuclear-age big business and the government. Corporate bunkers are seen in "The Man Who Sold the Moon" (1950), for example, and governmental ones in "If This Goes on—" (1940), "'All You Zombies—'" (1959), and *The Moon Is a Harsh Mistress* (1966).

More interesting than the multi-million-dollar excavation of corporations and major governments, however, is the outgrowth of the more humble "emergency home" or wilderness cabin: the bomb shelter of the private individual committed to survival. The true Cold War bomb shelter must be stocked even more carefully and thoroughly than the getaway cabin, yet whereas Heinlein's early "head for the hills" philosophy of avoiding World War III emphasizes getting "somewhere out in the country, away from the radioactive areas that were targets a short time before" ("How to Be" 167), and gives only a perfunctory nod to the dangers of fallout ("Jackpot" 34),[6] planning a nuclear shelter requires paying much more attention to radiological protection and to self-sufficiency. Of course, it is *Farnham's Freehold* (1964) that gives Heinlein's most thorough treatment of the mature Cold War bomb shelter.[7]

While Hugh Farnham admits to his skeptical adult son that life will "[p]robably not" be worth living after a thermonuclear war, he nevertheless feels duty-bound to try to protect his whining, alcoholic wife (Heinlein, *Farnham's* 12), and he has constructed an elaborate bomb shelter six feet below even his basement. Farnham knows that "no citizen can build anything strong enough to stop a direct hit," but he likens civil defense to automobile insurance, and he terms own shelter "[t]he best insurance I can afford" (11). As his second in command explains, it is not merely "a 'hole in the ground'" but "a machine—a survival machine" (53).

Living "a hundred miles" closer to a military base than makes purely tactical sense (Heinlein, *Farnham's* 11) means that Farnham must get his security not from distance but from engineering. A steel door in Farnham's basement gives access to stairs leading down to another two doors. The outer blast door of the shelter weighs "a ton or so" and is moved "by a rack and gear driven by a crank" (52), while the inner steel door is "secured with ten inch-thick bolts" (19). The occupants of this 250-ton "block" of concrete and steel "twenty feet square and twelve high" (71) have "thirty inches of concrete above [them], then two feet of dirt" (32). A periscope might permit post-attack visual inspection of the world above (105), and uncapping a narrow pipe in the ceiling allows a radio mast to be sledgehammered up through the rubble (37).

Space not taken up by bunks is filled with provisions (Heinlein, *Farnham's* 19), and yet even the escape tunnel—a "[t]hirty inch culvert pipe with concrete around it" that "[l]eads to a gully back of the garden" (38)—is "packed" with supplies as well (53). "Air intakes and exhausts, capped off,…plus a hand-or-power blower, and scavengers for carbon dioxide and water vapor" (28) allow for underground survival, but Farnham must hedge against not only airborne fallout but also possible chemical and biological warfare agents. Thus, in addition to food, water, and medicines—for the latter, "not just sleeping pills," but also hypodermics and "[s]everal drugs, some poisonous and some addictive and all irreplaceable"

(76)—the shelter also includes bottled oxygen for "thirty-six hours for four people, so...nominally twenty-four hours for six...." (28).

Prudently, though, within his marvel of passive defense, Farnham also has packed efficient means of active defense as well: a small armory of firearms, plus the means for making explosives. In case "a stranger had popped up" when the attack occurred and "somebody...g[o]t out of hand," Farnham and his second-in-command have a Thompson submachine gun, along with .45 caliber pistols (Heinlein, *Farnham's* 24–25). For hunting small game, they have "two lovely ladies' guns, .22 magnum rimfires with telescopic sights" (103), while for heavier targets like dear and bear—and, if necessary, humans—Farnham apparently has higher caliber hunting rifles as well. He also has stored ammonia and iodine, for while "[o]ccupying troops take a sour view of native troops having explosives,...there is nothing suspicious about ammonia or iodine" (103)—except, of course, that these ingredients can make nitrogen triiodide, a powerful though dangerously impact-sensitive explosive.

Just as important as any material supplies, however, are Hugh Farnham's fundamental stubbornness and determination to survive, in his own way and on his own terms. In deciding whether to move or to keep living only ten miles from a prime military target, Farnham admits that he "couldn't relish running away" from Soviet Premier Khrushchev, "that pig-faced peasant with the manners of a pig," and he "felt relieved" at his wife's desire to stay (Heinlein, *Farnham's* 13). "America is the best thing in history, *I* think," asserts the stubborn patriot,[8] "and if those scoundrels kill our country, I want to kill a few of them. Eight sideboys. Not less" (13). The broadly trained and fiercely dogged ex-Seabee is, to use Joseph F. Brown's description of Heinlein's Cold War ideal, "[s]trong, brave, responsible, rational..." (120).

Farnham is correct to realize, though, that no individual can be an expert in all the skills that might be required after the collapse of civilization. Harking back to Heinlein's early postwar articles, the man has made sure to stock "sound books of the brown and useful sort," such as the *Encyclopaedia Britannica, Boy Scout Handbook*, military manuals, and "how-to" references on all aspects of primitive living (*Farnham's* 84). Yet Farnham's survival library includes more than the immediately practical:

> *The Oxford Book of English Verse, A Treasury of American Poetry, Hoyle's Book of Games*, Burton's *Anatomy of Melancholy*, another Burton's *Thousand Nights and a Night*, the good old *Odyssey* with the Wyeth illustrations, Kipling's *Collected Verse*, and his *Just So Stories*, a one-volume Shakespeare, the Book of Common Prayer, The Bible, *Mathematical Recreations and Essays, Thus Spake Zarathustra*, T.S. Eliot's *The Old Possum's Book of Practical Cats*, Robert Frost's *Verse, Men Against the Sea*—
> He wished that he had found time to stock the list of fiction he had started. He wished that he had fetched down his works of Mark Twain, regardless of space. He wished—
> Too late, too late. This was it. All that was left of a mighty civilization. *"The cloud-capped towers—"* (84)

Thus in Heinlein's conception, the truly thoughtful survivor plans to take care not only of body, but also of mind and spirit as well. The "books which contain information you could look up in an emergency" (Heinlein, "How to Be" 170–71) first emphasized in his early postwar articles of course are present, yet at the pinnacle of his Cold War musings, a more somber, almost elegiac Heinlein also begins the attempt at building something of a cultural and literary Noah's Ark as well.

Finally, though, writing in the last full decade of the Cold War, Heinlein in *Friday* (1982) hypothesizes a future of political decentralization and ideological depolarization, wherein the United States has been Balkanized, most of the "four hundred-odd 'nations' in the UN" are merely "ciphers" (164), and "anyone who can count above ten with his shoes on knows where the real power is": "the corporate states," or "multinationals" (113). Such a future is even more unstable than the superpower joustings of previous decades, with "[a]ssassinations, fires, explosions, all sorts of sabotage, riots, terrorism of all kinds—but no pattern. It's not East against West, or Marxists against fascists, or blacks against whites" (86). A woman living on "a country estate designed to hold off anything short of professional military attack" (80) explains that her survival shelter—which we now might term a *safe room*—is built not against nuclear threats but against the more common dangers of the modern world: "No, I would never have bothered to build this were it just a bomb shelter. If we get H-bombed, I am not especially eager to live through it. I designed primarily to protect us from what is quaintly called 'civil disorder'" (109).

Because any human threats still prowling the hydrogen-bombed wastelands after World War III would be either very few or very radiation-sick, the classic Cold War bomb shelter need not necessarily be especially hidden, but the postmodern "hidey-hole" where one can "lie doggo" (Heinlein, *Friday* 106) must remain undetected by intruders,[9] be they looters or governmental tyrants. This particular shelter is accessed through a short underwater tunnel whose entrance is concealed within an indoor hot-tub, and then the retreat itself, sealed off with an "overpressure door," is stout enough to withstand a "near" hit (107–108) and is self-sufficient enough to outlast any casual intruders encamped overhead. With sealed power units lasting "forever, practically," and with "food supplies, freezer, reserve air, hand pump for water if pressure fails, clothing, medicines, etc.," the shelter can support "three people for three months" (110). Some of the design notions from the height of Cold War thus are used against more prosaic, yet equally deadly, threats.

It would be fairly easy, I suppose, to sniff at Heinlein's philosophy of shelter preparation. After all, as Robert Sholes and Eric S. Rabkin have observed, many of Heinlein's notions "are unpalatable to most critics" (56), particularly his Darwinistic strain. Certainly the hypothesis that nuclear war, "where it makes any distinction," might "improve the breed" by "kill[ing] the stupid rather than the bright and able" (Heinlein, *Farnham's* 35) is, at best, a severe underestimation of both the immediate and the long-term effects of thermonuclear weaponry. In *Have Space Suit—Will Travel* (1958), Heinlein is a bit less sanguinary in discussing preparation for the unknown, yet although he still speaks rather over-broadly in asserting that "[t]here is no such thing as luck; there is only adequate or inadequate preparation to cope with a statistical universe" (16), there nevertheless is a core of truth in his idea that "'good luck' follows careful preparation; 'bad luck' comes from sloppiness" (250). Fire extinguishers, Band-Aids, and automobile seat belts are difficult to sneer at, for example.

In addition, although David N. Samuelson is correct to note Heinlein's "positive attitude toward the frontier" (147), it is hard to argue, despite the occasional breeziness of the early postwar articles, that Heinlein overly romanticizes the admittedly "grim business" ("Pie" 178) of primitive post-catastrophe survival. "Coventry" (1940), for example, archly deflates the type of self-styled "rugged individualists" who imagine that modern tools and technology could be replicated with mere brains and bare hands (589–91), and the lesson is similar in the post-nuclear *Farnham's Freehold* (1964), wherein even "a scrap of paper, a dirty rag, a pin, all must be hoarded" (72). *Beyond This Horizon* (1948) debunks "the brave simple life" with wry gusto: "[Y]ou just ought to try tackling a two-holer on a frosty morning" (73), suggests a man originally from 1926, but now released from a stasis field into the deep future: [T]he noble primitive, simple and self-sufficient," he reminds his modern listener, of course has not even an ax or a rifle, and "[h]e'd be an ignorant savage, with dirt on his skin and lice in his hair. He would work sixteen hours a day to stay alive at all. He'd sleep in a filthy hut on a dirt floor. And his point of view and his mental processes would be just two jumps above an animal" (Heinlein, *Beyond* 73–74).

Yes, Heinlein loves the idea of pioneering—in *Farmer in the Sky* (1950), in "The Year of the Jackpot" (1952), in *Starman Jones* (1953), in *Tunnel in the Sky* (1955), in *Farnham's Freehold* (1964), in *Time Enough for Love* (1973), in *Friday* (1982)—but he never suggests it as a lark.

In advocating "careful preparation" against "a statistical universe," therefore, Robert A. Heinlein neither inhabits a paranoid fantasy nor spins a romantic one, and despite clinging for two decades to the notion of preparing to survive World War III, near the end of his career, he finally comes around to the more modern threat of "what is quaintly called 'civil disorder.'" The elaborate Cold War bomb shelter stocked for nuclear-war survival and post-apocalyptic pioneering may be something of a dinosaur, but events such as the 1992 Los Angeles riots, the 2001 terrorist attacks, and the 2005 Hurricane Katrina remind us that there still exists a place for some sort of emergency planning, whether it is keeping a car packed "on a 'Survival Kit' basis," having access to a modest country retreat, or even simply stocking common-sense supplies in the basement— purified drinking water in case of a temporary utility breakdown,[10] for example. As Heinlein shows us, adequately supplied shelter, chosen with skill and defended as appropriate, may indeed be a wise precaution against the various unpredictable events that, though unlikely, nevertheless never truly stop occurring.

Notes

1. For a slightly fuller account of Heinlein's notion of arming against possible civil disturbance, see McGiveron, especially pages 391–92.

2. Although the U.S. nuclear stockpile may increase to perhaps 18,000 weapons by the end of 1959 (Rosenberg 23), the October 1949 US war plan still only "called for attacks on 104 urban targets with 220 atomic bombs, plus a re-attack reserve of 72 weapons" (Rosenberg 16).

3. Such packing also can been seen in *Farnham's Freehold* (1964), wherein a father has equipped each car in his family with a "survival kit" that includes not only food and water and medicines, a sleeping bag, and extra clothing, but also extra gasoline, shovel, ax, and firearm (6–7). Near the end of the novel, after time travel allows the protagonist and his wife and young twins to ride out World War III in an old mine in the mountains rather than in his shelter almost on Ground Zero, the couple on the night of the attack pulls into a hastily abandoned gas station and emulates Breen's emergency packing, filling the car's tank with gasoline and its interior with groceries, including "all the canned milk" and "all the toilet paper or Kleenex" in sight (313–14).

4. The venerable Colt .45 pistol—or Browning 1911, from the name of its prolific designer and the year the U.S. Army adopted it for service—may not quite "blast a hole in a man big enough to throw a dog through" (*Beyond* 10), but it is a sidearm whose effectiveness is

difficult to argue. For Heinlein's use of the .45, see McGiveron 402, note 1.

5. For Heinlein's dislike of gun control laws, see *Grumbles* 54–57.

6. Actually, the assertion that Breen "picked their spot to keep them west of the fallout" ("Jackpot" 34) does not fit with the suddenness of the couple's departure—unless, of course, Breen has many friends' remote hunting lodges from which to choose.

7. For similarities between Farnham's fictional shelter and Heinlein's own, including double steel doors, bottled atmosphere, and periscope hole, see Crais, plus Patterson 217.

8. To term Farnham "a hard-line cold warrior" as David N. Samuelson does, is of course correct, but to add that he is "an unconscious stereotype of *white* male superiority" (141; emphasis added) to me seems incorrect. Even as harsh a critic as H. Bruce Franklin, after all, notes that Heinlein "excoriates the overt racists in the book," "exposes the unconscious racists," and has a black character "make a fierce denunciation of the racism of contemporary America" (156–157).

9. Snug Harbor in *The Number of the Beast* sports a slightly less hermetically sealed hidey-hole, with "a bookcase concealing a priest's hole" (44) that is unlocked only by faucets and lights operated in a certain order (48).

10. Even the U.S. government recommends "having your own food, water and other supplies in sufficie [sic] quantity to last for at least 72 hours" (FEMA par. 2).

Works Cited

Brown, Joseph F. "Heinlein and the Cold War: Epistemology and Politics in *The Puppet Masters* and *Double Star*." *Extrapolation* 49 (Spring 2008): 109–21.

Crais, Robert. "In Heinlein's Bomb Shelter." *Robert's World*. Robert Crais, n.d. Web. 22 Mar. 2015. <http://teq.org/heinlein/robertcrais/worldheinlein.htm>.

Federal Emergency Management Administration. "Build a Kit." *Ready.gov*. FEMA, 2 Sept. 2014. Web. 22 Mar. 2015. <http://www.ready.gov/build-a-kit.>

Heinlein, Robert A. "'All You Zombies—'" *Magazine of Fantasy and Science Fiction* (Mar. 1959). *The Unpleasant Profession of Jonathan Hoag*. New York: Berkley, 1980. 138–51.

_____. *Beyond This Horizon*. *Astounding Science-Fiction* (Apr.– May 1942). Revised version 1948. New York: Signet, 1975.

_____. "Coventry." *Astounding Science-Fiction* Jul. 1940. *Past* 585–632.

_____. *Expanded Universe*. 1980. New York: Ace, 1982.

_____. *Farmer in the Sky*. 1950. New York: Del Rey, 1975.

_____. *Farnham's Freehold*. 1964. New York: Berkley, 1981.

_____. *Friday*. 1982. New York: Del Rey, 1983.

_____. *Have Space Suit—Will Travel*. 1958. New York: Del Rey, 1978.

_____. "How to Be a Survivor: The Art of Staying Alive in the Atomic Age." *Expanded Universe*. 1980. New York: Ace, 1982. 163–74.

_____. "If This Goes On—" *Astounding Science-Fiction* Feb.– Mar. 1940. *The Past Through Tomorrow*. 1967. New York: Berkley, 1975. 449–584.

_____. "The Last Days of the United States." *Expanded Universe*. 1980. New York: Ace, 1982. 148–62.

_____. "The Man Who Sold the Moon." 1950. *The Past Through Tomorrow*. 1967. New York: Berkley, 1975. 121–212.

_____. *The Moon Is a Harsh Mistress*. 1966. New York: Berkley, 1980.

_____. *The Number of the Beast*. 1980. New York: Fawcett, 1982.

_____. *The Past Through Tomorrow*. 1967. New York: Berkley, 1975.

_____. "Pie from the Sky." *Expanded Universe*. 1980. New York: Ace, 1982. 175–180.

_____. *The Puppet Masters*. 1951. New York: Signet, n.d.

_____. *Rocket Ship Galileo*. 1947. New York: Del Rey, 1981.

_____. *Starman Jones*. 1953. New York: Del Rey, 1982.

_____. *Time Enough for Love*. 1973. New York: Berkley, 1974.

_____. *Tunnel in the Sky*. 1955. New York: Del Rey, 1983.

_____. "The Year of the Jackpot." *Galaxy* Mar. 1952. *The Menace from Earth*. 1959. New York: Signet, 1964. 7–38.

McGiveron, Rafeeq O. "He 'Just Plain Liked Guns': Robert A. Heinlein and the 'Older Orthodoxy' of an Armed Citizenry." *Extrapolation* 45 (Winter 2004): 388–407.

Patterson, William H., Jr. *Robert A. Heinlein: In Dialogue with His Century, Vol. 2: The Man Who Learned Better, 1948–1988.* New York: Tor, 2014.

Rosenberg, David Allen. "The Origins of Overkill: Nuclear Weapons and American Strategy, 1945–1960." *International Security* 7 (Spring 1983): 3–71.

Samuelson, David N. "The Frontier Worlds of Robert A. Heinlein." Ed. Thomas D. Clareson. *Voices for the Future*. Vol. 1. Bowling Green: Bowling Green U Popular P, 1976. 104–52.

Scholes, Robert & Eric S. Rabkin. *Science Fiction: History, Science, Vision*. New York: Oxford UP, 1977.

"There Ain't No Such Thing as a Free Lunch": Supply-Side Economics in *The Moon Is a Harsh Mistress*

Wolf Forrest

On 12 August 1980, the *New York Times* Arts and Leisure section published a photo depicting the inclusion of Groucho Marx and Sylvester Stallone among the Allied leaders of World War II, to demonstrate the fallibility of formerly incontrovertible evidence in a new age of computerized tools—specifically, the dawn of Photoshop. Another photograph, however, also taken in 1945 and yet undoctored, is perhaps even more well-known to science fiction fans. Like the Yalta Conference picture of FDR, Stalin, and Churchill, this snapshot, taken for the magazine *Wind Scoops* at the Naval Air Material Center in Philadelphia, depicts arguably the "Big Three"[1] of fantastic literature at the time: L. Sprague de Camp, Isaac Asimov, and Robert A. Heinlein.

How do doctored photos and supply-side economics relate? Advertising—carefully crafted images and words designed to put a product in the best possible light and drive consumer interest—in a political context becomes brainwashing. Beyond content, a study of the Yalta photo imagines the most powerful men in the world carving up the conquered Axis countries, while a study of the Navy photo conjures up the three most influential speculative fiction writers carving a path writers would follow for generations to come.

Economics is the science of dull for the lay consumer, but economics drives people to do both heroic and stupid things. When Heinlein was growing up in Kansas City, Missouri, the prevailing economic theorist was John Maynard Keynes, whose view of aggregate demand and short-term solutions to recession, where government intervention can stabilize the economy, strongly influenced Heinlein's approach to writing; Heinlein moved from youthful FDR New Dealer and acolyte of Upton Sinclair, dabbling in politics himself, to a more seasoned style of libertarianism.

Heinlein's Navy experience exposed him to both the good and bad aspects of bureaucracy. When he was discharged due to tuberculosis, he moved to California in 1934 and enrolled at UCLA. His later involvement with the Los Angeles Science Fiction Society, a collection of writers and artists, led to solid friendships, and some relationships that were bound to clash. Of that group that included Forrest J. Ackerman, Ray Bradbury, Ray Harryhausen, Leigh Brackett, E. E. "Doc" Smith, Edmond Hamilton, and Jack Williamson, he mentored Bradbury, and his tutelage of other writers may have been made easier by their willingness to learn from him (Weller 102). He found in Ackerkman another devotee of Esperanto,[2] the language of the future (Patterson I: 238), and a social engineering path from which would develop his Future History series, a springboard to most of his other fiction.

When Heinlein's first story, "Life-Line," appeared in the August 1939 issue of *Astounding Science-Fiction*, he had worked as a real estate agent and invested in mining. In the tale, a machine predicting how long a person will live sends ripples across the insurance industry, sowing the seeds of recurring themes in his work, like personal freedom, "the resistance of the public to change, and the bad effect of government regulation on business" (Cox). The story also deals squarely with the conundrum of perpetual intellectual property rights (McClure 801). Whatever Heinlein's critics thought of his early contributions to the pulps, his work on the film *Destination Moon*—based loosely on his juvenile novel *Rocket Ship Galileo*—put him squarely in the bull's-eye of those who saw him going toe-to-toe with the Russians. After the U.S. nuclear monopoly was dismantled in 1949, the next arena of competition was space. Stalin's death and a new U.S. regime change in 1953 coincided with a shift in Heinlein's career, as he knew that communism would fail because political ideologies could control neither the weather nor natural disasters, which affect crop production. Stalin's five-year plans were implemented to offset these natural swings, yet they disintegrated partly because of them. Capitalism is no bellwether either when it comes to the whims of nature, but a least it does not discriminate beyond consumers' ability to pay whatever is required for what they want. Additionally, it sowed the seeds for Heinlein's tale of a lunar penal colony.

Heinlein once mused at an informal gathering that the hardest part about writing good science fiction was accurately predicting the social consequences of technological change. Brainwashing was revealed to have been more a media event than an actuality during the Korean War only much later, but the connection between manipulation and free-market economics can be made using the self-doctored algorithm of heuristics, those psychological shortcuts employed by humans to facilitate the decision-making process by ignoring extraneous details—now understood to be cognitive biases.

Brainwashing was the *sine qua non* for many SF novels and stories, including *Fahrenheit 451*, *1984*, and *Brave New World*. These dystopias exhibit manipulation by media or by direct intervention, modifying personal behavior to serve the needs of the State. John Frankenheimer directed two film masterpieces: *The Manchurian Candidate* in 1962, a case study of brainwashing during the Korean War, and then *Seconds*, dealing with the loss of identity, a type of brainwashing: in 1966, the year that *The Moon Is a Harsh Mistress* was published. In a system where the black market predominates, opportunists arise. Arthur Hamilton/Tony Wilson in *Seconds* is an operative who would fit right in at Novaya Luna because of his desire to reinvigorate his life with a new start through a physical reconfiguration—a sort of brainwashing. But does brainwashing occur in *Moon*? Demagoguery and propaganda are techniques of collective brainwashing, to be sure, and they strike at the very core of what it means to be human. Irresponsible science is often blamed as the cause, whether governments interfere or not.

As Dave Netsam pointed out in "The State is a Harsh Mistress,"

> If there's one libertarian position that is exceedingly difficult to argue, it is the notion that scientific research should not be the concern of the state. .... Moreover, the standard libertarian remark continues by showing that the addition of the state into such areas overrides the price mechanism, because the government is not bound by profit-and-loss constraints.... A philosophical explanation of the concept

of "barrier to entry" provides the key to understanding scientific progress in a free society.

These dynamics are evident in the relationship between the Moon and Earth in Heinlein's novel and are driven by an information machine. Commercial propaganda to increase capital for the informer, or to manipulate the messagee to an inferior bargaining position, is an important component of supply-side, or free-market, economics—terms used interchangeably—and is dependent on aggressive methods.

Heinlein had employed dramatic conflicts with utopias ever since "By His Bootstraps" was published, and it encompasses his own philosophy—the general becomes the warrior. In 1966, the 100th anniversary of H. G. Wells' birth, and the year the world would end according to the 1960 filmed version of his book *The Time Machine*,[3] *The Moon Is a Harsh Mistress* was born. Heinlein had visited the Moon before, in *Rocket Ship Galileo*, "The Man Who Sold the Moon," and "The Black Pits of Luna"—three pre-Sputnik attempts to capitalize on America's early postwar success with captured German rocket technology. The world was a different place as this book was being published, however, with the Sino-Soviet paradigm in full force, particularly the Cultural Revolution of the People's Republic of China.

Moon began life with a preposterous title, *The Brass Cannon: Being the Personal Memoir of Manuel Garcia O'Kelly Davis, Freeman, Concerning the Lunar Rebellion: A True History* (Patterson II: 266), and some of it a reworking of Philip K. Dick's *Time Out of Joint*, divided into three books. The first, *That Dinkum Thinkum*—from the Australian slang *fair dinkum*—opens sixty years from now, or 109 years after its first publication, in May of 2075. We are introduced to the computer Mike, Mycroft Holmes, via the lunar narrator, Manuel O'Kelly, a one-armed engineer who speaks in a patois of Russian and pidgin English à la Alex in *A Clockwork Orange*. "Wyoh" Knott, a Julie Newmar-esque activist, goes with Mannie to see his old professor, Bernardo de la Paz, who is concerned about the Moon's imbalance of trade with Earth. During a conversation with the Professor, Wyoh says, "Mike agreed to keep our secrets," to which he responds, "He's safer than we are: he can't be brainwashed. Can you be, Mike dear?" (*Moon* 77) Heinlein's analysis is of the human being as a superior tool or mechanism, if one accepts Mike as a living character who proves finally that "the purpose of life is fun and games" (Garr 79).

Mike says that he could paralyze any government assault of voltage smashing or subjection to solvents or positive energy, and emphasizes that he would never be compelled to surrender their secrets. Did Mike the computer influence Stanley Kubrick and Arthur C. Clarke while assembling pieces for *2001: A Space Odyssey* in 1965? *Moon*, after all, was serialized in *Worlds of If* at that time. That a society puts its trust in, and turns over critical functions of commerce to, an all-powerful computer was not new in science fiction, of course, but a computer mimicking human foibles like fear, jealously, suspicion, and impishness was. Indeed, considering his penchant for practical jokes, which involves bureaucratic snafus by spitting out statistical, actuarial, and bookkeeping data that wreak havoc in the colony, Mike is more alive and engaged than the HAL 9000 computer from *2001: A Space Odyssey*, appearing in 1968.

Book Two, *A Rabble In Arms*, chronicles the lunar revolt, followed by *TANSTAAFL!*, the cornerstone of Heinleinian economic philosophy, and the shortest of the lot. Jerry Pournelle provided Heinlein with the acronym, explaining that he grew up in the deep South hearing the phrase "There ain't no such thing as a free lunch" (Patterson II: 264). Rooted in the early 1800s, it hammered home the philosophy that you don't get something for nothing—here, Earth's quota of hydroponic wheat in exchange for more prisoners.

As with much of Heinlein's work, the novel is driven by dialogue and point-of-view observation by its main character rather than by descriptive passages. That Heinlein can keep this method from becoming tedious, even in discussing political philosophy, is a tribute to his campfire skills. As Lazarus Long says elsewhere, "Political tags—such as loyalist, communist, democrat, populist, fascist, liberal, conservative, and so forth—are never basic criteria. The human race divides politically into those who want people to be controlled and those who have no such desire" (*Time Enough* 351). Heinlein, therefore, points out that the revolutionary

> [o]rganization must be no larger than necessary—*never* recruit anyone merely because he wants to join. Nor seek to persuade for the pleasure of having another share your views. He'll share them when the time comes....or, you've misjudged the moment in history. Oh, there will be an educational organization but it must be separate; agitprop is no part of basic structure. (*Moon* 59–60)

Propaganda is brainwashing on a massive scale and can also be effected through character assassination of a prominent and influential figure—as in the poison-pen letters sent about the doctor in Henri-Georges Clouzot's film *Le Corbeau*, for example. Driving the masses to hysteria makes it easier to manipulate them with further lies—conspicuously, Earth authorities let the Loonies believe they actually have autonomy. Robert P. Rogers notes that

> Emerging continually from Heinlein's work is that contradiction between his belief in a market-centered society and his ideal of the omnipotent all-knowing individual. On the one hand, he believes that the market-centered libertarian society is the best economic and social environment for most humans. On the other hand, he seems to believe that ultimate personal fulfillment only comes from engaging in enterprises that would not occur in a smoothly running market society. (291)

Yet black market economies are subject to the same entropic pulses as collectives. The Bank of Hong Kong Luna dollar, for example, guides both white and black markets, applying here a severe form of economic principles including depreciation. Wealth cannot grow indefinitely and spread uniformly—someone has to draw the short straw, leading to the revolt.

That a barren outpost should become the breadbasket for a dysfunctional Earth is an amusing and ironic trope. The two-to-one ratio of men to women demonstrates supply-side economics at its most basic. Mannie claims that Luna feeds "one hundred million

Hindus" back on Earth (*Moon* 185), another trope that is revisited throughout the book. When Mannie speaks to the growing revolt— "Comrades, I beg of you—do *not* resort to compulsory taxation. There is no worse tyranny than to force a man to pay for what he does not want merely because *you* think it would be good for him" (242)—he does so knowing that ultimately he will abandon the cause. *Kaizen*, the business philosophy that stresses continual improvement in the workplace, and its companion PDCA (Plan-Do-Check-Act), which helped Japan rises from the ashes of World War II, does not seem to have made a difference on Earth in 2075. The home planet's bureaucratic incompetence invites the Loonies to make something happen. As Brian Domitrovic notes, "Supply-side economics was never meant to be a sustained policy requiring annual recalibration and reapplication" (19), yet the economies of Earth, dependent on a rag-tag heterogeneous band of inmates for their nourishment, seem precariously fragile when considering Mike's prediction of cannibalism in nine years on Luna, which would cause the whole tandem system to collapse.

The revolution is heavily financed by Mike's creative bookkeeping; he also has control of the phone system and is able to allow the revolutionaries relative freedom to do as they will and contact each other without interference. By posing as Adam Selene—a masquerade like Tony Wilson's in *Seconds*—he takes on a persona to jump-start the revolution. Finally the Luna Declaration of Independence is issued on the TriCentennial, July 4, 2076, and the issue of citizens' rights comes to the forefront, although Heinlein never delineates how these constructs will evolve. H. Bruce Franklin points out that

> the true model for this revolution…is the American Revolution of the eighteenth century (which itself had roots in economics issues, like the Sugar Act of 1764, the Stamp and Townshend Acts, and finally the Tea Act of 1773, which sowed the seeds for war). It is not precisely a revolution attempting to accelerate the historical forces repeating in the 20th century. Rather, it is a revolution that attempts to reverse history to overthrow the industrial monopolies. (165)

Mannie's reiteration near the end of the novel that there "seems to be a deep instinct in human beings for making everything compulsory that isn't forbidden" (*Moon* 301) is a warning. His choice to venture out to the asteroids is just another reaction to the weary status quo—any fresh start has the potential of being an improvement over the system already in place. In *Moon* the central government is so weak, lacking in social programs or laws to protect the disenfranchised, that currency is the only driving force. The death rate among those new to the colony is staggering, but they are just scrip that can, and will, be replaced. In the words of Wilhelm Ropke, "Economic policy will tend to be irrational, that is, determined by what is 'politically feasible' rather than by what is economically rational and just" (146).

During an uprising, we read this exchange between Mannie and the Professor: "This planet isn't crowded, it is just mismanaged... and the unkindest thing you can do for a hungry man is to give him food. 'Give.' Read Malthus. It is never safe to laugh at Dr. Malthus; he always has the last laugh" (*Moon* 206). It would not be the only time this philosopher's worldview crept into Heinlein's writings, along with those of Keynes and Marx. Malthus' theory—that food supply will not keep up with population growth—had some evolutionary biologists applying his principles, and his doomsday scenarios have been moderately accurate.[4] This "Chicken Little" approach is a recurring theme in Heinlein's work.[5] There is a section of the book that deals with hurling rocks from the Moon toward Earth, as captive primates in zoos might fling their waste at curious observers from behind steel bars. While this may seem juvenile and atavistic, the twenty-first century version certainly exhibits the same kind of contempt for their respective "captors." This is Mike's idea—"Throw rocks at 'em...literally" (*Moon* 78)—another example of his impish nature and a base response to a complex problem. Heinlein was a supporter of Reagan's proposed Strategic Defense Initiative—more rocks hurled at Earth—and in a letter to research scientist Joseph Martino states that his "political position was rested entirely on an unsentimental pragmatism and was not based on our 'Bill of Rights' or 'Libertarian theory'" (McCray).

Conservatives generally embrace the book and its approach to revolt, but they balk at the inclusion of communal living and widespread polygamy/polyamory. The revolution of the penal colony of Luna is spearheaded by a small group supporting "rational anarchism" or "anarcho-capitalism." Each such individual

> believes that concepts such as "state" and "society" and "government" have no existence save as physically exemplified in the acts of self-responsible individuals.[6] The essence of rational anarchism is the understanding that personal responsibility for one's actions are neither increased or lessened by hiding an action behind the curtain of governmental sovereignty. (Schulman 190)

The acronym TANSTAAFL reappeared aggressively and was applied to the growing environmental movement during the first Earth Day in April of 1970—that is, "no free lunch," we reap what we sow, and no change occurs without consequences....turning up on buttons at NoreasCon, as science fiction conventions were attracting fans in record numbers, and as Heinlein's popularity was renewed with the publication of *I Will Fear No Evil*. The notion is rooted in historical works as well—Edward Bellamy's *Looking Backward*[7] and "The Parable of the Water Tank" promote socialist forms of economic organization and cooperation, as does Percy Bysshe Shelly's "Song to the Men of England," to cite only a few examples. On the other hand, Aldous Huxley's *Brave New World* and Ayn Rand's *The Fountainhead* and *Atlas Shrugged* offer eloquent defenses of conservative ideas on individual freedom, growth, and economic efficiency. Moreover, both these authors warn of abuses when economic and political power are concentrated and held by different kinds of public agencies (Watt 299).

The *New Oxford American Dictionary* defines *opportunity cost* as "the loss of potential gain from other alternatives when one alternative is chosen," that is, the cost incurred by not enjoying "the benefit that would be had by taking the second best choice available." Creating an environment in the penal colony of Luna that will forestall continued shipments of hydroponic wheat to Earth becomes market speculation without tangible goods, leading to disaster—consider the dot-com bubble collapse in 2001. What if Heinlein had lived long enough to incorporate Martin Odersky's Scala programming language in a new edition of *Moon*? Or the cookbook by Alvin Alexander that spins useful application and anticipates a biomimetric, organic system that grows with the sophistication of the user? Mike singlehandedly could have stopped the revolution and generated a sophisticated and programmable autocracy, perhaps leading to the sustainability and stability of Novaya Luna. The penal colony produces grain for a malnourished Earth and, other than a steady stream of new convicts, receives very little else in the way of compensation.

Heinlein's libertarian/utilitarianism makeup is straight out of C. H. Douglas' "social credit theory"—a cross-pollination of economics, political science, and history, designed to give economic power to the individual. More than one analyst has suggested that Heinlein's politics were influenced by whomever he was married to at the time. Heinlein's *For Us The Living: A Comedy of Customs*—a Randian pun written in 1938 but not published until 2003—is an interesting summation of plots then covered in his late novels, and in *Moon*, Heinlein reiterates issues of personal responsibility and what it means to be human. Serendipity, applied to economics, becomes the opportunity cost.

Atlas Shrugged created a society that operated on a premise of non-aggression. Does Rand's theory of objectivism hold any value for the economics in *Moon*? Moral purpose disguised as rational self-interest guides much of the characters' choices. Although Heinlein had rejected Rand's style of libertarianism, references appear in *Moon*—Mike the computer is referred to as a John Galt, a character in *Atlas Shrugged*, and when Wyoh and the Professor discuss politics, he says he is a rational anarchist, and she asks him if he means *randite* (*Moon* 64).

The voodoo economics that George H. W. Bush during the 1980 election accused Reagan of promulgating—"supply-side economics," meaning that increasing supply also increases demand, another type of brainwashing—probably appealed to the solipsistic Heinlein, who embraced the notion that nothing exists but the self.

The entire text of *Moon*, given that it is Mannie's point of view, could be his own creation, the product of a delusional, institutionalized individual for whom the revolution is just a fevered dream.

A common thread in much of Heinlein's earlier work is the indistinguishability of magic from engineering, given the separation of technological sophistication. As an economic parameter, magic also can be part of brainwashing. Two diverse tales were paired by a prescient agent—*Waldo* and *Magic, Inc.*—causing Heinlein to remark that they went "together as well as mustard and watermelon" (Patterson II, 22). A "waldo" now is a term for a robotic extension of human arms and hands first described in Heinlein's 1942 work, often used to handle radioactive isotopes behind barriers, or even to perform microsurgeries from miles away while watching a television monitor. Inspired by Tesla's theory of wireless transmission of power, Heinlein introduces the reader to Waldo F. Jones, hauntingly like real-life Stephen Hawking and fictional Dr. Strangelove—brilliant and tethered to his zero-gravity home mockingly called "Wheelchair." When the de Kalb receptors on Earth need technical intervention, he is confronted by the possibility of the "Other World," whose physical laws may be different from our own. By interfacing with a magician, the new commercial applications work beautifully—another demonstration of opportunity cost.

Magic, Inc., is an agency complete with bargain rates and guaranteed services, squeezing out independent competition and extending its sphere of influence to a stranglehold on Congress. Whether we agree that this is the essence of capitalism, unfettered by the reins of ethics, "Here the unseen energy is present both as an applied commercial resource and as a future potential" (Garr 66). In *Magic, Inc.*, building contractor Archie Fraser uses "cold iron"—a term from a Kipling poem—to repel the magic used by his competitors and others in different professions. As he is strong-armed by someone in the "protection business," his efforts to let economics choose the victor are circumvented and shunted. The stunning Mrs. Jennings, a redhead who reads tea leaves and uses familiars and other creatures we would consider mythical in her conjuring, helps Archie. A bill to regulate magicians gives Ditworth, the head of Magic, Inc., a monopoly. Archie and his friend Jedson use Jennings' "powers" to expose the reality that a demon from the underworld is behind it and more corrupt than the politicians who hide behind jargon and appropriation committees. Whereas *Waldo* has the inference of profit—though as far as Waldo is concerned, he is immune to such tactics—in *Magic, Inc.* folks are just trying to do business.

Podkayne of Mars and *Starship Troopers* signaled a transition from Heinlein's juvenile novels to more adult themes.[8] *Podkayne*, narrated by a fifteen-year old girl, gives the reader a glimpse of the capitalistic, luck-driven society on Venus—another example of free-market economics and a satire of the advertising industry. "Lurid displays overwhelm the senses, everything is for sale, and the opulent casinos are the highest form of culture on the planet. The commercialism is so oppressive that even Poddy, with her deep faith in 'free enterprise,' has a few doubts" (Franklin 145). The taxi driver taking them to the casino must navigate through huge advertising screens while Poddy and company react:

> Venusberg assaults the eye and ear even from inside a taxi. I believe in free enterprise; all Marsmen do, it's an article of faith and the main reason we won't federate with Earth (and be outvoted five hundred to one). But free enterprise is not enough excuse to blare in your ears and glare in your eyes every time you leave your own roof. (*Podkayne* 115)

As in Frederik Pohl and C. M. Kornbluth's *The Space Merchants*, advertising drives commerce, which has almost replaced government. When Poddy and her younger brother Clark are going through customs, an agent asks, "Anything to declare?" and Clark responds, "Two kilos of happy dust!" (*Podkayne* 42), revealing the impish behavior that will reappear in Mike the Computer. Clark drives a major portion of the story; in this passage, with the cynicism that even a child can demonstrate, "Clark just looked bored and contemptuous and said nothing, because Clark would not bother to interfere with Armageddon unless there was ten per cent in it for him" (70). Another companion, "Uncle Tom" Fries, not the martyr of Harriet Beecher Stowe's novel, but someone of great power and perception nonetheless and a Senator on Mars, remarks,

> "Homo sapiens is the most deadly of all the animals in the solar system. Yet he invented politics. Politics is the human race's most magnificent achievement. When politics is good, it's wonderful... and when politics is bad—well, it's still pretty good....politics is just a name for how we get things done...without fighting." (39)

Heinlein's story "'—We Also Walk Dogs,'" first published in 1941 in *Astounding Science-Fiction*, points out that opportunity exists for anyone who is observant and aggressive. The great General Services (GS) corporation will do an astounding array of tasks for a price—except murder—with specialization and longevity being key to its success. An interplanetary conference is to take place on Earth, whose gravity makes this difficult. Dr. Krathwohl, a free-floating scientist on the staff of GS, is allowed to tinker with any scientific theory that pleases him so long as he turns a profit for the company, but for an unheard-of breakthrough in gravity manipulation, he needs the help of a leading physicist who is interested only in his own research...and Ming china. By promising the self-centered theoretician "The Flower of Forgetfulness," a Chinese porcelain bowl that humanizes participants—and which they must steal from the British Museum and replace with a copy—"they cynically manipulate a rich dowager, opportunistically rig contractual rights to the gravity neutralizer, and treat the whole operation as a matter of course" (Samuelson 113). And both entities succumb to the power of the bowl—Heinlein superimposed the you-don't-get-something-for-nothing equation with a lasting impact.

Heinlein's opinions on economics, influencing politics, human colonization on other worlds, and technological breakthroughs once thought impossible are everywhere. His stories are populated by opportunistic businessmen and greedy yet inept bureaucrats, and his sensibilities flow easily through these shadowy realms that break into adamantine steel and super-polymers. His military background, his liberal-turned-libertarian outlook, and even his interest in nudism all have percolating power once transformed into the printed word—and his unique perspective and polarizing influence makes Heinlein impossible to toss aside. When he writes of the Moon as a penal colony or Venus as one big gambling house, we are reminded that the darkest side of any dystopia is the inability to measure its long-term effects.

Robert A. Heinlein died on 8 May 1988,[9] closing a chapter in the golden age of American science fiction. Like Asimov,[10] who would die in 1992, Heinlein added sticks to the bundle of a literary fasces that has grown in appreciation. His predictions of a return to the Moon to set up a lunar base may well yet have social ramifications, if prison reform does not include new ways of dealing with and transforming those incorrigibles of society—and may include our nearest neighbor becoming not just a scientific laboratory but also a raw material cash cow. The darkness of Heinlein's pen surrounded the luminescence of his idealism. Still, as writer Tom Clancy noted, "What makes Mr. Heinlein part of the American literary tradition is that his characters do prevail" (qtd. in Powell).

Notes

1. Arthur C. Clarke's first appearance in a science fiction magazine would not come until 1946.

2. Heinlein often clashed with members of LASFS like Ackerman, whose world-view and embrace of the future was not as cynical and cautionary.

3. The Morlocks who supply the Eloi with material goods for their survival and the lunar inmates of Heinlein's novel have a good deal in common.

4. See, for example, Alvin Toffler's 1970 *Future Shock*.

5. Contraceptive known as "Malthusian lozenges" appear in *Stranger in A Strange Land*.

6. Strangely, though, nobody questions the authority of machines that is central to much conflict in science fiction stories.

7. Bellamy's book was a favorite of Heinlein's growing up.

8. John C. Wright, however, sees Heinlein's "juvenile" *Tunnel in the Sky* as an answer to William Golding's *Lord of the Flies*, refuting the inevitability of young people to revert to savagery if abandoned in

the wilderness, particularly if their upbringing included an interest in saving civilization.

9. Coincidentally, on the birthday of another Missourian, Harry S. Truman. The two were born only fifty-seven miles apart.

10. Asimov's original surname was spelled Ozimov—which some sources claim is a word for a type of winter wheat—so Heinlein missed an opportunity to use the name of his friend and colleague as the main commodity in *The Moon Is a Harsh Mistress*.

Works Cited

Cox, Patrick. "Robert A. Heinlein: A Conservative View of the Future." *The Wall Street Journal* (10 Dec. 1985). The Heinlein Society, 2 Jul. 2001. Web. May 2015. <http://www.heinleinsociety.org/rah/conservativeview.html>.

Domitrovic, Brian. *Econoclasts: The Rebels Who Sparked the Supply-Side Revolution and Restored American Prosperity*. Wilmington, DE: ISI, 2009.

Franklin, H. Bruce. *Robert A. Heinlein: America as Science Fiction*. New York, Oxford: Oxford UP, 1980. Science-Fiction Writers Ser.

Garr, Alice Carol. "The Human as Machine Analog: The Big Daddy of Interchangeable Parts in the Fiction of Robert A. Heinlein." *Robert A. Heinlein*. Eds. Joseph D. Olander & Martin Harry Greenberg. Writers of the 21st Century Ser. New York: Taplinger, 1978. 64–84.

Heinlein, Robert A. *The Moon Is a Harsh Mistress*. New York: Tor, 1997.

_____. *Podkayne of Mars*. New York: G.P. Putnam's Sons, 1963.

_____. *Time Enough for Love*. 1973. New York: Berkley, 1974.

_____. *Waldo & Magic, Inc*. New York: New American Library, 1970.

_____. "'—We Also Walk Dogs.'" *The Green Hills of Earth*. Chicago: Shasta, 1951. 129–59.

McClure, Ian. "Be Careful What You Wish For: Copyright's Campaign for Property Rights and an Eminent Consequence of Intellectual Monopoly." *Chapman Law Review* 10.3 (Spring 2007): 2–32.

McCray, Patrick. "Robert Heinlein and the Harsh Politics of Science Fictin." *Patrick McCray: Leaping Robot Blog*. W. Patrick McCray, 12 Sep. 2013. Web. May 2015. <http://www.patrickmccray.com/2013/09/12/robert-heinlein-and-the-harsh-politics-of-science-fiction/>.

Netsam, Dave. "The State Is a Harsh Mistress." *Mises Daily*. Mises Institute, 5 Mar. 2012. Web. May 2015. <https://mises.org/library/state-harsh-mistress>.

Patterson, William H., Jr. *Robert A. Heinlein: In Dialogue with His Century, Vol. 1: Learning Curve, 1907–1948*. New York: Tor, 2010.

_____. *Robert A. Heinlein: In Dialogue with His Century, Vol. 2: The Man Who Learned Better, 1948–1988*. New York: Tor, 2014.

Powell, Jim. "Robert Heinlein's Soaring Spirit of Liberty." *The Freeman* 1 July 1997. Web. May 2015. <http://fee.org/freeman/detail/robert-a-heinleins-soaring-spirit-of-liberty>.

Rogers, Robert P. "The Economic Mind in America." *Robert A. Heinlein and Issues in American Economics*. Ed. Malcolm Rutherford. London: Routledge, 1998. 272–95.

Ropke, Wilhelm. *A Humane Economy: The Social Framework of the Free Market*. Chicago: Regnery, 1960.

Samuelson, David N. "The Frontier Worlds of Robert A. Heinlein." *Voices for The Future: Essays on Major Science Fiction Writers*. Vol. 1. Ed. Thomas D. Clareson. Bowling Green, OH: Bowling Green U Popular P, 1976. 104–52.

Schulman, J. Neil & Brad Linaweaver. *The Robert Heinlein Interview and Other Heinleiniana*. Mill Valley, CA: Pulpless, 1999.

Watt, Michael & Robert F. Smith. "Economics in Literature and Drama." *The Journal of Economic Education* 20.3 (Summer 1989): 294–99.

Weller, Sam. *The Bradbury Chronicles*. New York: Harper, 2006.

Wright, John C. "Heinlein's Answer to *Lord of the Flies*." *John C. Wright Author*. John C. Wright's Journal, 22 May 2006. Web. May 2015. <http://www.scifiwright.com/2006/05/heinleins-answer-to-lord-of-the-flies/>.

Robert A. Heinlein: Building and Defending the Empire[1]

C. W. Sullivan III

The majority of critics who write about Robert A. Heinlein, however correct their observations are, tend to be glib in one of two ways, especially about the juvenile novels. On one hand, some critics, from Marleen S. Barr to Brian Aldiss, focus on one element of Heinlein's writing and perhaps one element in one novel, and addressing themselves to "women in Heinlein's fiction" or "war in *Starship Troopers*," respectively, they fail to see the larger picture, the way or ways that the examples on which they focus fit into the larger framework of Heinlein's writing. On the other hand, critics who try to evaluate the sweep of Heinlein's literary career, as do Alexei Panshin, in *Heinlein in Dimension*, and H. Bruce Franklin, in *Robert A. Heinlein: America as Science Fiction*, are forced, by reason of the length and breadth of Heinlein's career, to give short shrift to some important elements; in Franklin's case, Heinlein's juvenile novels do not receive the consideration they deserve.

Heinlein, himself, did have larger frameworks in mind and knew where many of his works fit into those frameworks. In 1941, he began to create the first of his large frameworks, the Future History chart. On this chart, he created a timeline and an event line, on which he proposed the dates of scientific advances, world wars, specific space trips, and the like. He later placed many of his short stories, their characters, and some of his own notes on that chart as well (Patterson, I: 276). All of the short stories and the chart itself were collected in *The Past Through Tomorrow* (1967). The other large framework he created was the structure and progression of the building and defending of the empire in the juvenile novels, up through and including *Starship Troopers*. For further evidence that Heinlein saw all of his fiction as of one piece, one need only look at his final novel, *To Sail Beyond the Sunset* (1987), and some of the works that prefigured it, especially *Time Enough for Love* (1973) and *The Cat Who Walks Through Walls* (1985). These are works that reinvigorated Heinlein's writing in the same way that travel into the past reinvigorated Lazarus Long in *Time Enough for Love*; that is, in these latter novels, Heinlein is mining his own past, both literary and biographical, to create a new kind of science fiction and a science fiction that he could be excited about writing.

It is in the juveniles, however, and in some of his other fiction and his non-fiction published at the same time, that we see the clearest statement of his attitude toward the Empire. The first twelve juvenile novels, from *Rocket Ship Galileo* to *Have Space Suit—Will Travel,* chronicle nothing less than the expansion of the human race out of the solar system, throughout the galaxy, and beyond. From *Rocket Ship Galileo* (1947) through *Space Cadet* (1948), *Red Planet* (1949), and *Farmer in the Sky* (1950) to *Between Planets* (1951), Heinlein explores the possibilities of the moons and planets near Earth: our Moon, the Asteroid Belt and Venus, Mars, Ganymede (a moon of Jupiter), and Venus again, respectively. *The Rolling Stones* (1952) begins as a family vacation leaving from the Moon to visit Mars and the Asteroid Belt; but at the end, the Stone family, instead of going back to the Moon, continues outward as humanity goes "rolling on out to the stars…outward bound to the ends of the Universe" (253). *Starman Jones* (1953) follows up on the lead from *The Rolling Stones* and finds the *Asgard* lost in unknown space when a "jump" from one planetary system to another is miscalculated; the ship is able to return to the known universe, of course, thanks to the talents of the book's young protagonist. *The Star Beast* (1954), *Tunnel in the Sky* (1955), *Time for the Stars* (1956), *Citizen of the Galaxy* (1957) and *Have Space Suit—Will Travel* (1958) describe travel to increasingly distant planetary systems and, finally, galaxies.

In addition to depicting humanity moving farther and farther out into our galaxy and other galaxies from Earth, Heinlein consciously constructs this expansion to parallel the European discovery, exploration, and settlement of the North American continent. For example, *Farmer in the Sky* illustrates the difficulties of traveling to and settling in inhospitable territories, comparing the settlers on Ganymede to those of the first New England colonies.

Red Planet and *Between Planets* contain consistent references to the American Revolution as Mars and Venus attempt to break free from the absentee rulers back on Earth. *Tunnel in the Sky* describes the equipment settlers will take with them to new planets in terms appropriate to the settlement of the American West in the nineteenth century and explores the way in which a government might be established on a planet that has none. *Time for the Stars* looks at the dangers explorers might face in unexplored territories and depicts what happens when advanced technology makes earlier technology obsolete. *Citizen of the Galaxy* shows that the civilized center of the empire can be as corrupt as the lawless frontier outposts. And *The Star Beast* and *Have Space Suit—Will Travel* introduce their characters and the reader to beings and empires that may be more powerful than the reader's own.

In the first eleven novels of the series, there are no aliens that threaten humans—except the ones into whose territories humans blunder, as they do in *Time for the Stars*, the ones, like Willis in *Red Planet*, whom humans mistreat, or the ones like Lummox in *The Star Beast*, whose integrity humans have violated. In the last juvenile proper, *Have Space Suit—Will Travel*, Kip travels out to the Lesser Magellanic Cloud and returns by a circular route, metaphorically encompassing known space. In that novel, the Wormfaces have established a large base on Pluto and a smaller scouting base on the Moon as they prepare to invade Earth. Heinlein describes them as the stereotypically hideous and amoral aliens of 1950s popular culture, but they are not the real threat and are taken care of quite handily by the Court of the Three Galaxies. Heinlein's real point, like that of the film *The Day the Earth Stood Still* (1951), as revealed by the Court of the Three Galaxies, is that humans are a danger to the rest of the civilized planets and are, in fact, their own worst enemies as well—a possibility at which he had hinted, in the juveniles at least, as early as *Space Cadet*.

In the 1940s and early 1950s, at the same time as he was beginning to chronicle the building of the Empire and humankind's expansion throughout the Solar System, Heinlein was also writing nine nonfiction essays (*Expanded Universe* 145) and various short stories fueled by his concern for the survival of the United States of America in the face of the looming threat posed by the USSR; some of that material was published for the first time and other previously published short stories and essays were republished in *Expanded Universe* in 1980, along with various forewords and afterwords in which Heinlein comments on his purposes for writing what he wrote then. "The Last Days of the United States" begins, after citing a fictitious gravestone inscription for the USA, "The next war can destroy us, utterly, as a nation—and World War III is staring us right in the face. So far, we have done little to avert it and less to prepare for it" (148). In that essay, he discusses the short-sightedness of the American people and their government as well as his desire for a "planetary organization so strong that it can enforce peace, forbid national armaments, atomic or otherwise, and generally police the globe so that a decent man can raise his kids and his dog and smoke his pipe free from the worry of sudden death" (153)—the kind of planetary organization he presents in *Space Cadet*. Another essay, "How to be a Survivor: The Art of Staying Alive in the Atomic Age," details the measures one should take and the skills one should develop to survive after the first attack of World War III destroys some forty million people and those who remain are left "to build a new life" (163). In "Pie from the Sky," he details some of the benefits, real and ironic, for the survivors of an atomic war, "No more alarm clocks. … No more 'Hate Roosevelt' clubs" (176), and concludes with the demand that the reader "telegraph your congressman to get off the dime and get on with the difficult business of forming an honest-to-goodness world union…to get on with it promptly, while there is still time, before Washington, D.C., is reduced to radioactive dust—and he with it, poor devil" (180). In addition, he wrote a stunning short story, "On the Slopes of Vesuvius," in which a bartender chatting with a couple of scientist customers becomes so worried about the possibility of an atomic attack that he leaves Manhattan on a train and, feeling a bit foolish for his haste, looks back an hour or so later from Princeton Junction, New Jersey, to see a mushroom cloud rising over New York City (268–75). These and others seem not to have found a publisher when Heinlein first wrote them.

Later, after the Heinleins' first world tour in the middle 1950s, a trip that included countries in Africa and Asia as well as Australia and New Zealand, Heinlein gave up on the idea that there could be an effective world union—even though he continued to speculate about a World Union or Galactic Empire in his fiction. In October and November of 1961, he built a fallout shelter, and in 1962, he spent much of October "glued to the radio tuned to COLENRAD" as the Cuban Missile Crisis unfolded (Patterson II: 113, 216, 230). In 1964, he published *Farnham's Freehold*, a novel about surviving an atomic blast that contained many of the elements from "How to be a Survivor" as well as a time-travel paradox and some interesting socio-cultural speculations about race relations. But in April of 1958, the Heinleins did begin a campaign that drew public attention. In response to a full-page ad in the local paper from a "Committee for a SANE Nuclear Policy" urging people to petition the White House to unilaterally halt nuclear testing, the Heinleins created "Who Are the Heirs of Patrick Henry?," an essentially grassroots movement aimed at stopping Congress and President Eisenhower from such unilateral action. Robert wrote a point-by-point refutation of the SANE proposal, and he and Ginny paid for an ad in the local paper, complete with a ready-to-send petition for representatives, senators, and the President. They sent materials to friends and other publications, ran ads in various places, sent letters to editors, and spent a lot of time on the project; in the end, they figured that over five-hundred signed and registered letters had reached the President's desk (although none, even "return receipt requested" letters, was acknowledged), and the effort, after donations, had cost them about $1,000 out of pocket as well as quite a few of their friends (Patterson II: 151–157). Eisenhower signed an executive order canceling all nuclear testing without requiring mutual inspection, and Heinlein returned to his writing—*Starship Troopers*. In his 1980 "Afterword" to "Who Are the Heirs of Patrick Henry?," Heinlein noted, "The 'Patrick Henry' ad shocked 'em; *Starship Troopers* outraged 'em" (*Expanded Universe* 396).

In 1959, Heinlein's proposed thirteenth novel in the juvenile series, *Starship Troopers*, was rejected by Scribner's, publisher of the first twelve, as too violent, and when it was published by Putnam (after which it won the Hugo Award), the initial reviews suggested that Scribner's had been correct. A *Kirkus* review said that the novel depicted "a virtual reign of terror by force" and was "a dogmatic airing of very personal attitudes" (5 October 1959, 27), while the *San Francisco Chronicle* called Heinlein "a peddler of dangerous ideologies" and someone who thinks that "violence is the answer to every problem" (8 November 1959, 8).[2] I would argue that the reviewers seriously misread the novel. Moreover, looking at *Starship Troopers* in the light of the previous twelve novels, I would argue that Heinlein had come to the point of having built an empire and now felt that the inhabitants of that empire needed to be ready to defend it against beings from another empire that might want to move in and conquer (or even exterminate) humanity; and so, he wrote a novel discussing various elements of that concept.

An overview of *Starship Troopers* provides a hint that the comments of the reviewers—above, and others—are perhaps overstated. Only three of the fourteen chapters—Chapters 1, 10, and 13—depict battle scenes between the expanding empires of the Humans and the "Bugs," and while not all of those chapters describe actual combat, much of the rest being about strategy, most of the description might seem, to a modern reader, relatively mild. In fact, the battle scenes in *Starship Troopers* are much less graphic than the battle scenes in 1940s and 1950s World War II movies and novels. Chapters 2 through 9 are about Johnnie Rico's decision to enlist and his experiences in basic training; interspersed throughout those chapters are scenes from his high school class, history and moral philosophy. Chapter 11 explains that humans may well be losing the war and presents Rico with the possibility of going to Officer's Candidate School, and chapter 12 depicts the OCS curriculum and instruction, including an advanced class in history and moral philosophy. What the reviewers actually may have focused on were the scenes of "violence" and the "personal attitudes," to use their words, that appear in the non-battle chapters, scenes from the classes in history and moral philosophy, and scenes in which Rico contemplates and struggles to understand his own attitudes and beliefs.

In the high school history and moral philosophy class, the teacher, Mr. DuBois, responds to a student who says, "My mother says that violence never settles anything" by suggesting "the city fathers of Carthage would be glad to know that," since "violence... settled their destinies rather thoroughly" (*Starship Troopers* 25), the expanding Roman Empire wiping out its North African rival. Elsewhere in that chapter, we get the first hint that public flogging was a standard punishment for civil crimes (21). Flogging is also a military punishment. Later in the book, a recruit is sentenced to "ten lashes and Bad Conduct Discharge" for striking a superior officer (75). And one of the officers comments later that this might actually encourage another dissatisfied recruit to strike an officer, as ten lashes is "not even the number of lashes for drunken driving" (83). Rico also receives military punishment, five lashes, for "gross negligence which would in action have caused the death of a teammate" (107) and implies that he was paddled in school (87). Other incidents of flogging, both civil and military, are referred to at various places in the novel, but not described. Perhaps the reviewers found the idea of public flogging abhorrent.

Mr. DuBois' most explicit defense of such physical punishments as flogging appears in his analysis of the problems that destroyed the North American republic in the latter half of the twentieth century. DuBois uses juvenile delinquency as the prime example of what was wrong with American society at that time (*Starship Troopers* 112–20); the argument should be quoted in its entirety to do it justice, but I will make do with a précis. DuBois argues that juvenile delinquents had only a survival instinct and a shaky loyalty to a gang; the beatings, robberies, and killings—of other gang members and of private citizens—and the violence in schools, parks, and other public places occurred because the young people had no morality and because the authorities tried to appeal to a basic human moral instinct that does not exist. "Man has no moral instinct," argues DuBois. "We acquire moral sense, when we do, through training, experience, and hard sweat of the mind" (117–18). There was no punishment, DuBois continues, because spanking at home "did a child permanent psychic damage," "Corporal punishment in schools was forbidden by law," juvenile sentences were extremely mild, and juvenile criminal records were not released to the public (115, 116). Young people who behaved badly at home, in school, or in public received no severe punishment; punishment, DuBois argues, must in fact be cruel and unusual, or at least unusual, "so unusual as to be significant, to deter, to instruct" (115). Hardly a "reign of terror by force," as the *Kirkus* reviewer called it, but it is certainly the opposite of the 1950s ideas promulgated by what DuBois calls "a pre-scientific pseudo-professional class who called themselves 'social workers' or sometimes 'child psychologists'" (117).

This emphasis on acting responsibly, or morally, or being punished for acting irresponsibly, or criminally, and the concept of a developed moral sense, rather than an instinctual one, is the basis on which the novel, in both history and moral philosophy courses and through the comments of individual members of the military, builds the philosophical case for military service as the only way to become a voting member of society. Very early in the novel, Rico is asked by DuBois if he knows the difference between a soldier and a civilian. Rico gives the textbook answer: "The difference…lies in the field of civic virtue. A soldier accepts personal responsibility for the safety of the body politic of which he is a member, defending it, if need be, with his life. The civilian does not" (*Starship Troopers* 26). Dubois asks if he understands it and believes it. Rico answers honestly that he does not know. The bulk of the novel is an explanation for and justification of both the war against the Bugs, i.e., the defense of the empire, and the requirement of military service for voting rights; the first is not completely explained, but the second one is.

The Terran Federation enters a state of war with "The Bugs" while Rico is in Basic Training. The enemy is called Bugs because they resemble arachnids, but more important, they have a "hive mentality," a mental and physical culture much like Earth ants. There are strict castes, and members of each caste, and all castes, follow orders that come down from leaders, who, in turn, follow orders from the Queen; moreover, warriors only fight and workers can only work. The Bugs, therefore, are a direct contrast to the individuality of humans. But why the war? Each group wants to expand into the same territory. As Rico asserts, "All wars arise from population pressure" (*Starship Troopers* 185). But does humankind have a "right" to spread its empire outward into the universe? Heinlein does not have Rico or any of his teachers answer that question; instead, Rico says that the universe will answer that question later and that he and the rest of the mobile infantry will be there, "on the bounce and swinging, on the side of our own race" until that happens (186).

The other problem, and the one that may have upset the critics the most, is the requirement that one must be a military veteran before one can vote or hold elected office. This certainly could be seen as an "airing of personal attitudes" and could be the "dangerous ideology" that the critics felt they saw in the novel. Heinlein had, at age five, heard this idea from his father (Patterson II: 161), and as an Annapolis graduate and a military veteran himself, he might well have had a personal stake in the political system he proposes in *Starship Troopers*. But the critics miss his actual rationale. In the OCS history and moral philosophy class, Major Reid asks how "the present political organization evolved out of the Disorders" (*Starship Troopers* 179). After dismissing such answers as that the veterans are "picked men" and that "service men are disciplined," Reid admits that he asked a trick question. The real answer, he says, is that "The practical reason for continuing our system is the same as the practical reason for continuing anything: It works satisfactorily" (181). In other words, Reid presents no philosophical or moral justification for his proposed system; he explains that the previous system collapsed, some veterans stepped in to restore order, and the present system evolved therefrom and continues to "work satisfactorily." But, echoing Rico's comment from the first chapter, above, Reid also says,

> "Since sovereign franchise is the ultimate in human authority, we insure that all who wield it accept the ultimate in social responsibility—we require each person who wishes to exert control over the state to wager his own life—and lose it, if need be—to save the life of the state. The maximum responsibility a human can accept

is thus equated to the ultimate authority a human can exert." (*Starship Troopers* 183–84)

Ironically, the requirement for military service came after the establishment of a government by veterans, a government that continues to exist, as Major Reid says, because "it works satisfactorily." In actuality, moral behavior is the philosophical point of *Starship Troopers*; this is what the book is about.

Again, Heinlein's own words are the key here. After mentioning that, in 1980, *Starship Troopers* was continuing to receive "lots of 'nasty' fan mail and not much favorable fan mail," he goes on to say that such "criticisms are usually based on a failure to understand simple indicative English sentences, couched in simple words." Heinlein then refers to the text of *Starship Troopers* to explain the terms "veteran" and "militaristic" as well as delineate the kinds of service (including what we would now call "civil service") that would qualify one for voting rights, and he concludes by asserting that the most "dismaying idea [in the book may be] that a voice in governing the land should be earned instead of being handed to anyone who is eighteen years old and has a body temperature near 73°C" (*Expanded Universe* 396–99).

But Heinlein has an even deeper philosophical point in the novel. In a letter to Theodore Sturgeon, Heinlein insisted that *Starship Troopers* was "an inquiry into why men fight [i.e., why humans will defend the empire], investigated as a moral problem.... [sic] being a novelist, I tried to analyze as it a novelist" (qtd. in Patterson II: 162). Heinlein articulated this philosophy more directly in his essays and, especially, in his 1973 James Forrestal Memorial Lecture at the U.S. Naval Academy, the relevant section of which is included in *Expanded Universe*. Therein, Heinlein defines moral behavior as "behavior that tends toward survival" and delineates five levels of moral behavior. The first, he says, is when an individual, "man or animal fights for his own survival." The second is to "work, fight, and sometimes die for your own immediate family." The third is to "work, fight, and sometimes die for a group larger than the unit family—an extended family, a herd, a tribe." The fourth level "is that in which duty and loyalty are shown toward a group of your own kind too large for an individual to know all of them." This loyalty, Heinlein says, is called "patriotism" or as Rico says, above, being "on the ounce and swinging, *on the side of our own race*" (my italics). Finally, on an even higher level, there are those like "the astronauts who went to the Moon, for their actions tend toward the survival of the entire race of mankind." His conclusion: "Patriotism—Moral behavior at the national level.... It means you place the welfare of your nation ahead of your own even if it costs you your life" (*Expanded Universe* 464–467). This distinction between a civilian and a soldier that Johnny Rico does not fully understand on page 26 of *Starship Troopers* is what he grows to understand through the physical battles in which he participates as a soldier, through the classes in history and moral philosophy he takes in high school and in Officers' Candidate School, and through the "growing up" he does in the course of the story.

Heinlein's defense of the empire and his belief that patriotism is "moral behavior on a national level" was not a totally new idea in *Starship Troopers*. It is certainly there in *Space Cadet*, as Matt Dodson discovers that he is now a citizen of the Federation and the Patrol and, as he realizes, no longer a citizen of Des Moines or even the United States (113–24). Heinlein was exploring these ideas in his adult novels and short stories as well. As early as 1951, in *The Puppet Masters*, a novel with many similarities to *Starship Troopers*, he posited a war between humankind and a species from another part of the solar system. The "slugs" arrive and initially begin attaching themselves to the backs of whatever humans they find available; soon, they move to people in positions of power as well. The humans that have been taken over can only do as the parasites command, and it turns out that the parasites communicate in such a way that all the slugs know whatever one discovers. The slugs also reproduce as do amoebas; they divide, and one of the pair moves to a new host. All of this makes them difficult to battle, and the slugs fight as ferociously as do the Bugs. The ending of *The Puppet Masters* is as inconclusive as the ending of *Starship*

Troopers. Most of the slugs on Earth have been killed, but one can never be sure; and an attack vessel has been dispatched to the Slugs' home world, Titan, Saturn's moon, just as attack vessels are headed for Klendathu, a major Bug planet, at the end of *Starship Troopers*. In neither novel do negotiations work, and in *The Puppet Masters*, those who go to negotiate with the slugs are never heard from again. Sam, the main character in *The Puppet Masters*, echoes Johnnie Rico when he says, "Well, if Man wants to be top dog—or even a respected neighbor—he'll have to fight for it. Beat the plowshares back into swords; the other was a maiden aunt's fancy" (174). Thus, *Starship Troopers* is less about what kind of government would be best, although Heinlein certainly had ideas in that direction, than it is about the moral imperative to fight to protect the collective (state/country/world/empire)—including the government that is running it "satisfactorily."

Notes

1. A much shorter version of this paper was presented at the International Conference on the Fantastic in the Arts, Orlando, FL, March 2014.
2. All quotations from book reviews of Heinlein's juveniles were taken from *Book Review Digest*. The parenthetical page numbers refer to the actual review.

Works Cited

Aldiss, Brian. "Heinlein's Starship Troopers." *Vector* 13, *The Journal of the British Science Fiction Society* (1961). Alexei Panshin, 28 Oct. 2012. Web. 20 Aug. 2015. <www.panshin.com/critics/PITFCS/141aldiss. html>.

Barr, Marleen S. *Feminist Fabulation: Space/Postmodern Fiction*. Iowa City: U of Iowa P, 1992.

Franklin, H. Bruce. *Robert A. Heinlein: America as Science Fiction*. Science-Fiction Writers Ser. New York: Oxford UP, 1980.

Heinlein, Robert A. *Expanded Universe*. 1980. New York: Ace, 1982.

_____. *The Puppet Masters*. New York: Signet, 1951.

_____. *The Rolling Stones*. New York: Ace, 1952.

_____. *Space Cadet*. 1948. New York: Ballantine, 1978.

_____. *Starship Troopers*. 1959. New York: Ace, 1987.

Panshin, Alexei. *Heinlein in Dimension: A Critical Analysis.* Chicago: Advent, 1968.

Patterson, William H., Jr. *Robert A. Heinlein: In Dialogue with His Century, Vol. 1: Learning Curve, 1907–1948.* New York: Tor, 2010.

_____. *Robert A. Heinlein: In Dialogue with His Century, Vol. 2: The Man Who Learned Better, 1948–1988.* New York: Tor, 2014.

Finding Answers in *Stranger in a Strange Land*

Ira Halpern

"Well, what was I trying to *say* in it?" Robert Heinlein wrote in 1972 in a letter to a reader on the topic of *Stranger in a Strange Land* (1961).

> I was asking questions.
> I was *not* giving answers. I was trying to shake the reader loose from some preconceptions and induce him to think for himself, along new and fresh lines. In consequence, each reader gets something different out of that book *because he himself supplies the answers.* (*Grumbles* 245–46)

Contrary to Heinlein's interpretation of his own work, *Stranger in a Strange Land* does indeed supply answers to the questions that it poses. It positions the sexual cult of Michael Valentine Smith as the solution to the problems posed by monotheism and monogamy. Heinlein's notion that *Stranger in a Strange Land* does not provide answers stems from his interpretation of the novel as a satire, since he considered *Stranger in a Strange Land* a "Cabellesque satire on religion and sex" (*Grumbles* 228). Heinlein's intentions may have been satirical, but then *Stranger in a Stranger Land* took on a life of its own during the writing process.

The novel is not primarily a satire. Though Heinlein attempts to assert satirical control, another voice breaks through the cracks of this control: a utopian voice. Darko Suvin suggests that "[u]topia explicates what satire implicates, and vice versa" (54). In other words, whereas satire points toward foibles in society and asks questions, utopia presents an alternative that provides answers. Whereas satire suggests what should not be, utopia presents a model of what should be. *Stranger in a Strange Land* presents three major manifestations of utopian principles. The most prominent utopian community presented in *Stranger in a Strange Land* is the Church of All Worlds, the polyamorous cult founded by Mike Smith. The ritual "water-sharing" of this community is inspired by the water-sharing that takes place on Mars, the utopian planet where Smith is raised. Even Heinlein's invented Fosterite church—a religious institution featuring drinking, gambling, and strippers—contains utopian elements. *Stranger in a Strange Land,* in presenting radical utopian possibilities for human behavior, is more prescriptive than Heinlein himself was willing to accept. It is also more prescriptive than some of his critics have accepted. Some scholars have read the novel as one whose primary function is to test our standards (Patterson & Thornton 57). However, such a reading dilutes the groundbreaking, shocking, and controversial work done by *Stranger in a Strange Land*. The purpose of the novel goes further than testing our standards. It proposes radical solutions. By idealizing a polyamorous sexual cult and the radical theology of "Thou Art God," *Stranger in a Strange Land* broke the taboos of 1950s America with full force.

Perhaps part of the reason that Heinlein was so uncomfortable with the ideological work being done by his novel and part of the reason that critics have had trouble coming to terms with it, is that not only does *Stranger in a Strange Land* present a utopia, but it presents a religious utopia—a religious utopia of sexuality. In fact, it is almost impossible to discuss the utopian possibilities posed by the novel without framing them in religious terms. It is not difficult to imagine why Heinlein, who raged so vehemently against the institution of organized religion, would have been uncomfortable with the notion that he himself created one. Heinlein believed that *Stranger in a Strange Land* was "an invitation to think—not to believe" (*Grumbles* 246). However, belief is precisely what the novel espouses. When the Fosterite Patty Paiwonski is levitated by Smith in a hotel room, she feels "overpowering religious ecstasy like heat lightning in her loins" (*Stranger* 283). Excitement in the loins refers to sexual excitement, but Patty's ecstasy is described, without any irony, as religious. There is evidence to suggest that Christianity helped positively shape, to use the subtitle of Peter Gardella's book, America's "ethic of sexual pleasure." While evangelical Christianity provided staunch conservative opposition throughout the first half of the twentieth century to the liberal sexual ethics of the 1920s, American evangelism often harked back to a longstanding tradition of transcending sin in a moment of bodily ecstasy (Gardella 94). For instance, the evangelical radio personality Aimee Semple McPherson, active in the 1920s and 1930s, described moments of religious ecstasy in very bodily terms (Gardella 82). The link between bodily and religious ecstasy is, in fact, rooted in American tradition. Heinlein pushes this link one step further by comparing religious ecstasy to the sexual drive itself. Heinlein could have chosen the phrase "spiritual ecstasy" to describe Patty's experience, but he chose "religious ecstasy." In *Stranger in a Strange Land*, the sexual drive is not merely a substitute for the religious impulse. It is presented as a religious drive in and of itself.

Jubal Harshaw's suggestion that Smith's utopian sexual cult has analogs in early Christianity elevates the cult in terms that are at least somewhat familiar to the reader. Harshaw, often considered to be a stand-in for Heinlein, suggests that "group marriage" and the "kiss of brotherhood" are common to Smith's cult and the early Christians (364–65). Even if the reader is not familiar with the concept of the "kiss of brotherhood," he or she is likely familiar, on some level, with the Christian tradition. By framing the Church of All Worlds as similar to early Christianity, Heinlein suggests that Smith's cult is not a radical departure from the Christian tradition in the broadest sense of the term. The suggestion that early Christianity was sexualized, however, is likely shocking to the reader. This is because Harshaw paints a portrait of the Christian religion that is very different from the one to which most readers likely are accustomed. Heinlein suggests that religions can be utopian at their inception even if their utopianism is lost when they expand—when they morph from cults into institutions. However, the same sexual energy that animates early Christianity, Heinlein suggests, animates Smith's sexual cult. In Heinlein's scheme, religion and utopianism are not mutually exclusive. In fact, they often go hand in hand.

Smith and his cult actually are portrayed in a very conventionally Christian manner—despite Smith's unconventional attitudes toward sex. Smith is a savior because of his sexual power and sexual ethics, and yet he founds a church and is represented as Jesus, an angel, and the Messiah. Indeed, it is with ironic playfulness that Heinlein refers to Smith's "maculate origin" (*Stranger* 1). However, Heinlein's ironic playfulness does not undermine the fact that Smith, by this very analogy, is elevated to the status of Jesus. There is not even a trace of irony to undermine Harshaw's suggestion that Smith "might be the Messiah" (368). The statement is, though, delivered with the skeptical word "might." Harshaw presents Smith's Messianism as only a possibility. Heinlein thus constantly mutes the religious force of his novel. By framing Smith's Messianism as only a possibility, as opposed to a verifiable reality, Harshaw's statement is made consistent with his agnosticism. Yet by evoking Messianic possibilities, rather than not evoking such possibilities at all, Harshaw makes a religious suggestion, one that is affirmed by the ending of the novel. Indeed, it is with ironic playfulness that Heinlein represents angels in heaven as cogs in the machine of a corporate hierarchy: Smith operates in a "studio" with an "assistant," and he pushes back his halo in order to complete his next task (437–38). This ironic playfulness, however, does not undermine the fact that Heinlein elevates Smith, along with Reverend Foster and Bishop Digby, to the status of angels, nor does it make his heaven any less real.

The Church of All Worlds possesses the entire apparatus of an organized religion. It has rituals, and it has a temple. It also has a creed. Smith's mantra, "Thou Art God," is more than what Heinlein refers to in his correspondence as "an existentialist assumption of personal responsibility, devoid of all godding" (*Grumbles* 229). In his correspondence, Heinlein positions "Thou Art God" as an assertion of "comradeship with comrades no more divine (or just as divine) as you are" (*Grumbles* 229). Heinlein's parenthetical qualifier—"or just as divine"—reveals the truth that he tries to dance around. "Thou Art God" suggests, syntactically, that everyone is divine, not that nobody is divine. There is no irony applied to this mantra in the novel that would suggest any alternative reading. Heinlein's uneasy attitude toward religion is evident in his correspondence, and it is evident in *Stranger in a Strange Land* itself—evident, for instance, in the distancing ironic tone with which Heinlein often treats religious content. However, the religious nature of the project of *Stranger in a Strange Land* is an unavoidable reality. Though a religious interpretation of the text does not sit well with Heinlein's own statements on the novel, it is a truth inherent in the novel itself.

While satire operates on an intellectual level, utopia in *Stranger in a Strange Land* makes an instinctual, almost subliminal appeal. It is Harshaw who delivers much of the satire in the novel. He pokes holes in the institution of organized religion, for instance, by comparing the multiple, conflicting truth claims of various religions to lies about the number of hands that he possesses (*Stranger* 141). Harshaw has thought about religion deeply and then rejected it. He has considered faith in light of the principles of William of Ockham, the English scholastic philosopher to whom the concept of "Occam's Razor" is attributed (139). Harshaw often speaks in lengthy paragraphs. He seems to possess an encyclopedic knowledge of the Bible, from which he quotes readily, in order to point out religious hypocrisy (258). He uses his vast knowledge and logical prowess to weaken religious authority. He also uses the power of his intellect and his skillful rhetoric to celebrate Smith's Church of All Worlds and convince others of its integrity. It is through knowledge of history, logical capacity, and rhetorical flourish that Harshaw challenges widely held assumptions. His satire and his celebration of the Church of All Worlds both are intellectual exercises.

While Harshaw is skilled at undermining religious authority, he has trouble embracing solutions to the problems created by the absences that his position leaves gapingly open. Harshaw initially resists subscribing to Smith's model of living, due to instinctual repulsions that he cannot overcome. He is aware of the limitations of his cerebral nature. Referring to Digby and the rituals at the Fosterite church, he says, "I should have punched him. Instead he made me like it" (*Stranger* 256). Harshaw is seduced by the Fosterite church on an emotional level, even as he resists it on an intellectual level. It is only after leaving the Fosterite church that he is able to express how he should have responded. Conversely, on an intellectual level, Harshaw is able to celebrate Smith's sexual cult.

However, he admits that his conditioned instincts prevent him from becoming part of the group himself (361). We very well might be swayed by Harshaw's theoretical arguments against religion and in favor of Smith's cult, but like Harshaw himself, we might not accept Smith's cult on an instinctual level based on his opinions alone. In fact, we very well still might be repulsed by it. This is because Harshaw does not provide any satisfying answers to the problems posed by his position. He gives no alternatives to fill the void left by the prospect of a world without religion—at least not for those who, like Harshaw, are limited by their instincts. Perhaps this is the reason that, until Harshaw has sex with the stripper Dawn Ardent, he "had been getting through that black period between waking and the first cup of coffee by telling himself that tomorrow might be a little easier" (408). All that Harshaw's initial position seems to leave room for is nihilism and depression.

Smith helps fill the absences left by Harshaw's position by reorienting our instincts toward utopian possibilities. Heinlein deploys Smith, as he deploys Harshaw, to challenge assumptions. However, unlike Harshaw's questions, which leave little room for optimism, Smith's questions are predicated upon the existence of utopian answers, if only we are able to access them. Smith's challenging of assumptions often operates by means of defamiliarization. The Russian Formalist critic Viktor Shklovsky was the first to identify defamiliarization as a literary device. Shklovsky describes how "habitualization" causes the individual to lose his critical faculties in perceiving the objects that he encounters. For Shklovsky, "[t]he purpose of art is to impart the sensation of things as they are perceived and not as they are known. The technique of art is to make objects 'unfamiliar,' to make forms difficult, to increase the difficulty and length of perception..." (12).

Smith's defamiliarization often carries a utopian charge. A standard example of the device can be found in the episode where Harshaw attempts to explain truth and human religion to Smith. Smith cannot comprehend the idea of falsehood. He cannot "grok" the lie that Harshaw has seven hands. The use of the word "grok," because it is unfamiliar, forces us to slow our perception down, even if only by a fraction of a second. We are put in the headspace in which defamiliarization thrives. When Jubal explains that multiple religions all claim to speak truth, Smith responds, "All speak rightly? Jubal, I do not grok" (*Stranger* 141). While Smith is not a Martian, he has been raised as one. Though not a child, his newness to Earth makes him just as naive about our society. Smith defamiliarizes religion, a process which might unsettle our attitudes toward convention on an even deeper level than Harshaw's questions do because the process operates on the level of intuition and instinct rather than mere logic. However, unlike Harshaw, who offers no solutions, Smith has the Old Ones as moral guides. His questioning of multiple truths is predicated on the knowledge that there is indeed one singular truth. It is only a matter of tapping into it. Smith's piercing questions are informed by knowledge of a unified conception of the universe. The Old Ones of Mars represent the type of alien father figures that Norman J. King refers to as "a higher life transcending [humankind's] present ambiguity" (257). Mars, the model for Smith's Church of All Worlds, serves as the utopian core from whose vantage our world is made strange.

In addition to Smith's piercing questions, the defamiliarization created by his vocabulary for sex—including phrases such as "water-sharing," "water of life," and "water brothers"—helps create a religious, utopian solution to the problems left unresolved by Harshaw's worldview. Sexuality is defamiliarized by Smith's terminology to make it less bodily, more transcendent, and even religious. Water, scarce on Mars, is essential for survival. The phrase "water-sharing" thereby makes sex a fundamental condition of life. Furthermore, the phrase gives sex a transcendent quality, for water has archetypal associations with cleansing. Heinlein also evokes the baptismal associations of water when Harshaw refers to his inability to be "cleansed" in the "water of life" of Smith's cult (*Stranger* 364). The terminology of the "water of life" is drawn directly from Genesis and the Book of Revelation, with the phrase thus turning sex into something that is grounded in religious ritual and biblical text. Mike's notion of sex as occurring between "water brothers" defamiliarizes sexuality in another way. By calling the pairing

---

of male and female a relationship between "water brothers," the sexual binary is made strange. Heinlein's purpose is not to suggest a homosexual alternative, since the sex that occurs in the cult is always between men and women. Rather, his purpose is to give the male-female sex that takes place in the cult associations with Platonic love between men, which has cultural connotations of being the highest form of love. The use of the word "brothers" also evokes the spirit of utopian communism. Smith's defamiliarization of sex turns the experience into a religious, ideological, and utopian act. This is particularly important work on Heinlein's part, considering science fiction precedents such as *Brave New World* by Aldous Huxley, in which promiscuity and the lack of matrimony are features of a dystopia rather than a utopia. Heinlein thus uses defamiliarization with a utopian agenda to help undo prejudices that are manifest even within the genre of science fiction itself.

Even when Smith's defamiliarization unsettles rather than idealizes, it is always accompanied by salvation. The combination of Smith's unsettling defamiliarization and the salvation that he offers is demonstrated on a very distilled level in the episode of Gillian Boardman's showgirl performance in Las Vegas. Smith enables Jill literally to perceive her world through different eyes: "She had been letting herself receive the stranger's emotions, teasing him with eyes and body, and relaying what she felt to Mike—when suddenly she was seeing herself through strange eyes and feeling all the primitive need with which that stranger saw her" (*Stranger* 306). By seeing herself through strange eyes, Jill experiences defamiliarization in its most extreme form: the self is defamiliarized. This defamiliarization induces a heightened state of sexual experience in which Jill taps into a primitive human need. When she sees herself through various strangers' eyes at the club, her body is defamiliarized by the isolation of her different body parts: "one noticed her legs, another was fascinated by undulations of her torso, a third saw her proud bosom" (306). Seeing other girls through Smith's eyes excites her, nor is she repulsed by her own sexual objectification. Instead, she enters into a heightened state of eroticism.

The context of the showgirl performance usually is one where the heterosexual gaze is so pervasive that it becomes exhaustingly familiar. By displacing this voyeuristic gaze of the heterosexual male onto a female showgirl, however, the gaze is made strange and new. As a result, if Heinlein's strategy works for the reader, this voyeuristic gaze becomes more exciting. However, the new sexual power that Jill taps into is initially too overwhelming for her to handle. She stumbles and "would have fallen had not Mike caught her, lifted her, steadied her until she could walk unassisted..." (*Stranger* 306). The individual who unsettles Jill and overwhelms her with possibility, causing her to fall, is the same individual who is there to pick her up.

Similarly, in the larger structure of the novel, Smith delivers a shock to our systems and perhaps overwhelms us—but he also attempts to save us. The ultimate thrust of the text is toward conversion. The skeptical Ben Caxton, for example, joins the Church of All Worlds, and despite his initial resistance, Harshaw surrenders to having sex with Ardent, overcoming his conditioned sexual prudery (*Stranger* 408). At the conclusion of the novel, Harshaw tastes Smith without a second thought, in the form of a soup broth, demonstrating that he has conquered his instinctual repulsion toward cannibalism (434). If Harshaw represents Heinlein, then Smith represents the force that compels the author to come to terms with a new truth. The author, in embodying himself as Harshaw, puts himself into a position that is not authoritative. Harshaw is not the character who has the final word. Like Jill and Caxton, he is a flawed, incomplete human being, who requires a strange and estranging savior to show him the light.

The novel's intention—whether Heinlein was comfortable with it or not—is to continue the chain of conversion that takes place within the pages of the novel by converting the reader. There is reference in the novel to the "snowball" effect that hopefully will be spurred by the Church of All Worlds (*Stranger* 347). Heinlein thus positions the cult as something to be replicated. It is true that Smith's telepathic powers, which he shares with the members of the Church of All Worlds, cannot be copied by anyone. However, these telepathic powers speak to the connectivity created by open sexual arrangements. Even if telepathy cannot be replicated, this sense of connectivity presumably can be. Similarly, Smith's ability to "discorporate" clothing speaks to the inhibitions that can be removed if we free ourselves from taboos of prudery. We may not be able to imitate Smith's miracles, but the principles behind these miracles are intended to inspire action in our own world. For Alexei Panshin, "Mike's ability to do almost anything and the similar abilities of the followers of his religion make his religion right by definition… and hence trivial" (101). However, the word *utopia* comes from the Greek "no place." The purpose of a utopia is to reorient our perception toward that which is desirable, not necessarily to suggest an exact model of human behavior. Smith unsettles convention, but he also provides a rough blueprint for action, even if it is not precise. *Stranger in a Strange Land* is not only deconstructive. It is also constructive.

The utopianism of *Stranger in a Strange Land* even extends to Heinlein's Fosterite church. The Fosterite church cannot be classified as an object of satire, though it initially might appear to be one. Heinlein depicts gambling, drinking, and strippers at the Fosterite church—entertainments traditionally considered vices by mainstream Christianity. In the world of *Stranger in a Strange Land,* these entertainments have particularly sexual connotations. Ardent, the stripper, is sexual for obvious reasons. Drinking and gambling also accrue associations with sex and the sexual drive. Drinking is associated with the tearing off of clothes of the saved in Foster's Inner Circle (*Stranger* 293), and gambling is grokked by Smith as "a drive that felt intensely sexual" (302). Though Smith is uncomfortable with gambling, it is possible that this discomfort stems from the notion that gambling is not the appropriate outlet for the human desire for a heightened state of experience. Gambling is not wrong in Heinlein's scheme because of any religious or moral dogma, but because it is not the ideal outlet for the human craving for ecstasy—sex should fulfill that craving.

Nevertheless, Heinlein does not satirize the strippers, gambling, and drinking of the Fosterite church, but portrays these elements as steps in the right direction. All the Fosterite church has to do to become a utopian community is to eliminate some of the extraneous pleasures that it offers, such as gambling—and revise its theology. The theological claim of the Fosterite church, its "claim to gnosis through a direct line to Heaven," is indeed criticized by Harshaw, and by extension, Heinlein (*Stranger* 138). Smith's sexual cult does not posit a "direct line" to heaven above, but positions God as a being who is present within each of its members. It offers the theological solution to the Fosterites' theological problem. However, while the Fosterites' theology is criticized, the spiritual core of the Fosterite church, centered around the fulfillment of pleasure, is in fact privileged. Ardent's striptease is referred to by Senator Boone as "[h]ighly spiritual" (248). There is no irony applied to this statement to undermine this claim. For Heinlein, the bodily and the spiritual are in fact inextricably linked.

The spiritual core of the Fosterite church shares much in common with the Church of All Worlds. The parallels between the organizations are clearly represented by the twin kisses on Patty's body—one from Foster and one from Smith. Patty serves as a bridge from the Fosterite religion to behavior governed by Smith's sexual ethics. She traverses from the Fosterites to Smith's cult very readily, as though the Fosterite church has helped lay the foundation for Smith's sexual revolution. All it takes is the arrival of the appropriate Messiah. The similarity between the Fosterite church and Smith's cult is also rendered in the cooperation of Foster, Digby, and Smith in heaven in the final chapter of the novel. William H. Patterson and Andrew Thornton have gone so far as to suggest that the Fosterite church and the Church of All Worlds are "mirror-complements, not polar opposites" (101). On the one hand, the theology of the Fosterite church, which claims a "direct line to Heaven" (*Stranger* 138), could not be more different than the theology articulated by Smith's mantra, "Thou Art God." Still, Heinlein does not apply any satire to Fosterite spirituality or to the pleasures that the Fosterites support. He suggests that the Fosterite church is on the right track, despite the institution's imperfections. The Fosterite church is a step in the direction of the Church of All Worlds.

While Heinlein often attempts to maintain satirical control in his writing, at certain points the novel slips out of this control and enters into another realm entirely. It slips into a realm that is both utopian and religious. The satirical voice of the novel undermines the notion of a "personal god" and monogamy, which Heinlein referred to in his correspondence as the "two biggest, fattest, sacred cows of all, the two that every writer is supposed to give at least lip service to" (*Grumbles* 228). The utopian voice that cracks through Heinlein's satirical control posits a legitimately sacred alternative to these "sacred cows." In the world of the novel, open sexual arrangements are sacred, and the embodied, mass rituals that take place at the Fosterite church share in this sacredness. Smith first groks the Snake Dance that takes place at the Fosterite church as "a growing-closer as real as water ceremony" (*Stranger* 249). It is only later, with distance from the event, that he realizes that he had grokked the Fosterite church "incompletely" (264). For a moment, though, as the alcohol flows in the church, Heinlein actually idealizes the ritual dancing that takes place there. This is because there is something in the embodied ritual of the group that Heinlein finds appealing, even holy. It is only one step away from the ritualized sex that Heinlein so greatly privileges. Instead, Heinlein satirizes the absurdity of the Fosterites' claim to a direct line to Heaven, and it is likely because of this absurdity that Smith later realizes that the church was something that he had "incompletely grokked" (264). By suggesting incomplete grokking, Heinlein attempts to bring the text back under the realm of satire—back under the control of the voice that only goes so far as undermining monotheistic organized religion. However, another voice has already entered the text. This is the voice that espouses the mass religious ritual, and the pleasure value offered by the Fosterite church. This is the voice that transcends asking questions. It is the voice that provides utopian answers. And these utopian answers are inherently religious. James Blish positions *Stranger in a Strange Land* as a religious novel: "its dominant subject is religion, and its intellectual offerings and innovations are primarily religious too" (70). Indeed, a religious, utopian voice constantly breaks through Heinlein's satirical control.

Heinlein's treatment of sexuality perhaps was informed by the sexual liberty of the 1920s, the decade in which Heinlein grew up. But *Stranger in a Strange Land* goes much further than the legacy of the flapper generation, for Heinlein anticipates the sexual counterculture of the 1960s, the decade in which *Stranger in a Strange Land* became popular (Franklin 127). Though Heinlein claimed that his novel suggests that sex is "a hell of a lot of fun, not shameful in any aspect, and not a bit sacred" (*Grumbles* 229), *Stranger in a Strange Land* positions sex as something that is indeed sacred—when carried out in the appropriate, organized, and ritualized manner. It is for this reason that cults in the 1960s could feasibly use *Stranger in a Strange Land* as a Bible to govern their sexual behavior (*Grumbles* 236). Eventually, a real-life Church of All Worlds was created (Cusack 72–73, 86–91). Critics have accused fans of *Stranger in a Strange Land* of misinterpreting the message of the novel (Stover 57). Some critics have followed in Heinlein's footsteps by emphasizing the satirical elements of the text, without realizing the extent of the novel's utopianism—without acknowledging the answers that the text itself provides. On the other hand, by creating their own Church of All Worlds, the real-life disciples of Mike Smith were engaged in precisely the type of behavior that the novel prescribes.

Works Cited

Blish, James. Introduction. *The Issue at Hand: Studies in Contemporary Magazine Science Fiction.* By William Atheling, Jr. Chicago: Advent, 1973.

Cusack, Carole M. "Science Fiction as Scripture: Robert A. Heinlein's *Stranger in a Strange Land* and the Church of All Worlds." *Literature & Aesthetics* 19.2 (2009): 72–91.

Franklin, H. Bruce. *Robert A. Heinlein: America as Science Fiction.* Science-Fiction Writers Ser. Oxford: Oxford UP, 1980.

Gardella, Peter. *Innocent Ecstasy: How Christianity Gave America an Ethic of Sexual Pleasure.* Oxford: Oxford UP, 1985.

Heinlein, Robert A. *Stranger in a Strange Land.* 1961. New York: Ace, 1987.

Heinlein, Virginia, ed. *Grumbles from the Grave*. New York: Ballantine, 1989.

King, Norman J. "Theology, Science Fiction, and Man's Future Orientation." *Many Futures, Many Worlds*. Ed. Thomas D. Clareson. Kent, OH: Kent State UP, 1977. 237–59.

Panshin, Alexei. *Heinlein in Dimension*. Chicago: Advent, 1968.

Patterson, William H., Jr. & Andrew Thornton. *The Martian Named Smith: Critical Perspectives on Robert A. Heinlein's Stranger in a Strange Land*. Sacramento: Nitrosyncretic, 2001.

Shklovsky, Victor. "Art as Technique." *Russian Formalist Criticism: Four Essays*. Ed. Paul A. Olson. Lincoln: U of Nebraska P, 1965. 3–24.

Stover, Leon. *Robert A. Heinlein*. Boston: Hall, 1987.

Suvin, Darko. *Metamorphoses of Science Fiction: On the Poetics and History of a Literary Genre*. New Haven: Yale UP, 1979.

RESOURCES

Chronology of Robert A. Heinlein's Life_____

1907	Robert Anson Heinlein is born on July 7 in Butler, Missouri.
1908	Heinlein family moves to Kansas City, Missouri.
1925	Heinlein is accepted by the U.S. Naval Academy at Annapolis.
1929	Heinlein graduates from Annapolis as an ensign.
1929-1930	Heinlein's first marriage, with Elinor Curry.
1929-1933	Active duty aboard aircraft carrier *USS Lexington*, then destroyer *USS Roper*.
1932-1947	Heinlein's second marriage, with Leslyn MacDonald.
1934	Heinlein is given medical discharge due to tuberculosis, retiring as lieutenant, junior grade.
1934-1938	Heinlein invests in silver mining, attends classes at UCLA, and then works in Democratic politics in California.
1938	*For Us, The Living* written—rejected several times, but published posthumously in 2003.
1939	"Life-Line," Heinlein's first story, is published in *Astounding Science-Fiction* in August.
1939-1942	Twenty-eight more stories—including "Requiem," "They," "Solution Unsatisfactory," and "By His Bootstraps"—are published in various pulp science

fiction magazines under Heinlein byline, "Anson MacDonald," and other pseudonyms.

1941	Heinlein's "Future History" chart appears in *Astounding Science-Fiction* in May.
1941	Heinlein gives Guest of Honor Speech at the third World Science Fiction Convention in Denver.
1942-1945	Robert and Leslyn work at the Naval Air Experimental Station in Philadelphia with Isaac Asimov and L. Sprague de Camp, where they meet Lt. Virginia "Ginny" Gerstenfeld.
1947	*Rocket Ship Galileo* is published by Scribner.
1947	Leslyn's divorce is granted on August 28.
1947-1948	Seven stories are published in prestigious "slick" magazines: *Saturday Evening Post*, *Town and Country*, and *Argosy*.
1948	*Space Cadet* is published by Scribner.
1948	*Beyond This Horizon* is published by Fantasy Press.
1948	Robert and Ginny are married on October 21.
1949	*Red Planet* is published by Scribner.
1949-1950	Heinlein co-writes script for *Destination Moon* and serves as consultant during filming.
1950	Heinlein designs and builds house at 1776 Mesa Avenue in Colorado Springs.
1950	*Farmer in the Sky* is published by Scribner.

1950	*Waldo & Magic, Inc.* is published by Doubleday.
1951	*Between Planets* is published by Scribner.
1951	*The Puppet Masters* is published by Doubleday.
1952	*The Rolling Stones* is published by Scribner.
1953	*Starman Jones* is published by Scribner.
1953-1954	Robert and Ginny travel around the world, resulting in *Tramp Royale* travelogue, published posthumously in 1992.
1954	*The Star Beast* is published by Scribner.
1955	*Tunnel in the Sky* is published by Scribner.
1956	*Double Star* is published by Doubleday.
1956	*Time for the Stars* is published by Scribner.
1957	*Double Star* receives Hugo Award from the World Science Fiction Society for best novel of 1956.
1957	*The Door into Summer* is published by Doubleday.
1957	*Citizen of the Galaxy* is published by Scribner.
1958	*Methuselah's Children* is published by Gnome Press.
1958	Robert and Ginny run "Who Are the Heirs of Patrick Henry?" campaign against unilateral halt to nuclear testing.
1958	*Have Space Suit—Will Travel* is published by Scribner.

1959	*Starship Troopers* is published by Putnam.
1960	Robert and Ginny visit the Soviet Union.
1960	*Starship Troopers* receives Hugo Award from the World Science Fiction Society for best novel of 1959.
1961	*Stranger in a Strange Land* published by Putnam.
1961	Heinlein gives Guest of Honor Speech at the nineteenth World Science Fiction Convention in Seattle.
1961	Heinlein installs bomb shelter beneath his Colorado Springs home.
1962	*Stranger in a Strange Land* receives Hugo Award from the World Science Fiction Society for best novel of 1961.
1963	*Orphans of the Sky* is published by Gollancz.
1963	*Podkayne of Mars* is published by Putnam.
1963	*Glory Road* is published by Putnam.
1963-1964	Robert and Ginny raise funds for Barry Goldwater's presidential campaign.
1964	*Farnham's Freehold* is published by Putnam.
1966	Due to Ginny's altitude sickness, Robert and Ginny move from Colorado Springs to Santa Cruz, California, designing and building a house on Bonny Doon Road.
1966	*The Moon Is a Harsh Mistress* is published by Putnam.

1967	*The Moon Is a Harsh Mistress* receives Hugo Award from the World Science Fiction Society for best novel of 1966.
1969	Heinlein gives Guest of Honor Speech at the Rio de Janeiro Movie Festival.
1970	*I Will Fear No Evil* is published by Putnam.
1973	Heinlein gives Forrestal lecture at Annapolis on April 5.
1973	*Time Enough for Love* is published by Putnam.
1974	Heinlein receives Grand Master Nebula Award from the Science Fiction and Fantasy Writers of America.
1976	Heinlein gives Guest of Honor Speech at the thirty-fourth World Science Fiction Convention in Kansas City.
1978	Heinlein undergoes carotid bypass surgery on April 28.
1980	*The Number of the Beast* is published by Fawcett.
1982	*Friday* is published by Holt.
1983	Robert and Ginny visit Antarctica.
1984	*Job: A Comedy of Justice* is published by Del Rey.
1985	Robert diagnosed with emphysema in March.
1985	*The Cat Who Walks Through Walls* is published by Putnam.
1987	Robert and Ginny move to Carmel, California.

1987	*To Sail Beyond the Sunset* is published by Putnam.
1988	Heinlein dies on May 8 in Carmel, California.
1989	Ginny releases *Grumbles from the Grave*.
2001	*Farmer in the Sky* receives 1951 Retro Hugo Award from the World Science Fiction Society for best novel of 1950.
2003	*For Us, The Living* is published by Scribner.
2006	*Variable Star*, written by Spider Robinson based on seven existing pages of Heinlein's original eight-page outline, is published by Tor.

Works by Robert A. Heinlein

Novels

Rocket Ship Galileo (1947)

Beyond This Horizon (serialized 1942; revised 1948)

Space Cadet (1948)

Sixth Column / The Day After Tomorrow (as Anson MacDonald, serialized 1941; book version 1949)

Red Planet (1949)

Farmer in the Sky (1950)

Waldo & Magic, Inc. (1950)

Between Planets (1951)

The Puppet Masters (1951)

The Rolling Stones (1952)

Starman Jones (1953)

The Star Beast (1954)

Tunnel in the Sky (1955)

Double Star (1956)

Time for the Stars (1956)

The Door into Summer (1957)

Citizen of the Galaxy (1957)

Methuselah's Children (serialized 1941; book version 1958)

Have Space Suit—Will Travel (1958)

Starship Troopers (1959)

Stranger in a Strange Land (1961)

Orphans of the Sky (in *Astounding* 1941; book version 1963)

Podkayne of Mars (1963)

Glory Road (1963)

Farnham's Freehold (1964)

The Moon Is a Harsh Mistress (1966)

I Will Fear No Evil (1970)

Time Enough for Love (1973)

The Number of the Beast (1980)

Friday (1982)

Job: A Comedy of Justice (1984)

The Cat Who Walks through Walls (1985)

To Sail Beyond the Sunset (1987)

For Us, The Living: A Comedy of Customs (2003; written 1938)

Variable Star (with Spider Robinson, 2006)

Stories and Novellas

"Life-Line" (1939)

"Misfit" (1939"

"Requiem" (1940)

"'If This Goes On—'" (1940)

"'Let There Be Light'" (as Lyle Monroe, 1940)

"The Roads Must Roll" (1940)

"Coventry" (1940)

"Heil!" / "Successful Operation" (as Lyle Monroe, 1940)

"Blowups Happen" (1940)

"The Devil Makes the Law"/"Magic, Inc." (1940)

"Sixth Colum" (as Anson MacDonald, 1940)

"'—And He Built a Crooked House—'" (1941)

"Logic of Empire" (1941)

"Beyond Doubt" (as Lyle Monroe, with Elma Wentz, 1941)

"They" (1941)

"Universe" (1941)

"Solution Unsatisfactory" (1941)

"'—We Also Walk Dogs'" (1941)

"Elsewhere" / "Elsewhen" (as Caleb Saunders, 1941)

"By His Bootstraps" (as Anson MacDonald, 1941)

"Commonsense" (1941)

"Lost Legion" / "Lost Legacy" (as Lyle Monroe, 1941)

"'My Object All Sublime'" (1942)

"Goldfish Bowl" (as Anson MacDonald, 1942)

"Pied Piper" (as Lyle Monroe, 1942)

"Waldo" (as Anson MacDonald, 1942)

"The Unpleasant Profession of Jonathan Hoag" (as John Riverside, 1942)

"The Green Hills of Earth" (1947)

"Space Jockey" (1947)

"Columbus Was a Dope" (as Lyle Monroe, 1947)

"They Do It with Mirrors" (as Simon York, 1947)

"'It's Great To Be Back!'" (1947)

"Jerry Is a Man" / "Jerry Was a Man" (1947)

"Water Is for Washing" (1947)

"The Black Pits of Luna" (1948)

"Gentleman, Be Seated!" (1948)

"Ordeal in Space" (1948)

"Our Fair City" (1949)

"Nothing Ever Happens on the Moon" (1949)

"Poor Daddy" (1949)

"Gulf" (1949)

"Delilah and the Space Rigger" (1949)

"The Long Watch" (1949)

"Cliff and the Calories" (1950)

"Destination Moon" (1950)

"The Man Who Sold the Moon" (1950)

"The Year of the Jackpot" (1952)

"Project Nightmare" (1953)

"Skylift" (1953)

"The Menace from Earth" (1957)

"The Elephant Circuit" / "The Man Who Traveled in Elephants" (1957)

"Tenderfoot in Space" (1958)

"'—All You Zombies—'" (1959)

"Searchlight" (1962)

"Free Men" (1966)

"No Bands Playing, No Flags Flying—" (1973)

"The Last Days of the United States" (1980; written 1946)

"How to Be a Survivor" (1980; written 1946)

"Pie from the Sky" (1980; written 1946)

"A Bathroom of Her Own" (1980; written 1946)

"On the Slopes of Vesuvius" (1980; written 1947)

"The Bulletin Board" (1992; written 1951)

Collections

The Man Who Sold the Moon (1950)

The Green Hills of Earth (1951)

Tomorrow, The Stars (editor) (1952)

Assignment in Eternity (1953)

Revolt in 2100 (1953)

The Menace from Earth (1959)

The Unpleasant Profession of Jonathan Hoag / *6xH* (1959)

The Worlds of Robert A. Heinlein (1966)

Expanded Universe (1980)

The Past Through Tomorrow (1967)

Grumbles from the Grave, ed. Virginia Heinlein (1989)

Essays, Articles, and Speeches

"Back of the Moon" (1947)

"Flight into the Future" (1947)

"On the Writing of Speculative Fiction" (1947)

"Baedecker of the Solar System" (1949)

"The Historical Novel of the Future" (1950)

"Shooting *Destination Moon*" (1950)

"Where To?" (1952)

"This I Believe" (1952)

"Ray Guns and Rocket Ships" (1952)

"The Third Millennium Opens" (1956)

"Science Fiction: Its Nature, Faults and Virtues" (1959)

"Who Are the Heirs of Patrick Henry?" (1958)

"'PRAVDA' Means 'TRUTH'" (1960)

"Appointment in Space" / "All Aboard the *Gemini*" (1963)

"The Happy Road to Science Fiction" (1964)

"Science Fiction: The World of 'What If?'" (1964)

"Channel Markers" (1973)

"A United States Citizen Thinks about Canada" (1975)

"Paul Dirac, Antimatter and You" (1975; revised 1980).

"Are You a Rare Blood?" (1976)

"Inside Intourist" (1980; written 1960)

"Spinoff" (1980)

"Larger Than Life" (1980)

"Agape and Eros: The Art of Theodore Sturgeon" (1985)

"The Discovery of the Future" (1992; delivered 1941)

"The Future Revisited" (1992; delivered 1961)

Guest of Honor Speech, Rio de Janeiro Movie Festival (1992; delivered 1969)

Guest of Honor Speech, 34th World Science Fiction Convention (1992; delivered 1976)

Tramp Royale (1992; written 1954)

How To Be a Politician / *Take Back Your Government* (1992; written 1946)

Editor's note: The entirety of the works of Robert A. Heinlein—including even minor works previously not reprinted, plus four-hundred-fifty thousand words of correspondence—are available in the forty-six-volume Virginia Edition; the production run of this authoritative set, however, which is leather-bound, printed on acid-free paper, and hand-numbered, was only two thousand, and it thus is correspondingly expensive, and rare.

Still, all of Heinlein's novels also remain in print in individual paperbacks and hardcovers from various publishers, as do the collections containing the great majority of his short fiction.

The 1989 *Grumbles from the Grave* provides not only an interesting and entertaining selection of Heinlein's letters but also a chronological listing of his works, and is a fine place for the student of Heinlein to begin. The 2014 second volume of William H. Pattersion's *Robert A. Heinlein* biography gives an even more detailed list, including specifying which stories appeared in various collections. The most comprehensive and useful categorizing of Heinlein's nearly fifty-year output, however, is the 2000 *Robert A. Heinlein: A Reader's Companion* by James Gifford, which also includes unpublished pieces and even works only planned, with all helpfully discussed, and cross-referenced by title, type, and even chronology.

Bibliography

Blackmore, Tim. "Talking with *Strangers*: Interrogating the Many Texts That Became *Stranger in a Strange Land*." *Extrapolation* 36 (Summer 1995): 136–50.

Brown, Joseph F. "Heinlein and the Cold War: Epistemology and Politics in *The Puppet Masters* and *Double Star*." *Extrapolation* 49 (Spring 2008): 109–21.

Cansler, Ronald Lee. "*Stranger in a Strange Land*: Science Fiction as Literature of Creative Imagination, Social Criticism, and Entertainment." *Journal of Popular Culture* 5 (Spring 1972): 944–54.

Clareson, Thomas D. & Joe Sanders. *The Heritage of Heinlein: A Critical Reading of the Fiction*. Critical Explorations in Science Fiction and Fantasy 42. Jefferson, NC: McFarland, 2014.

Colebach, Hal. "Starship Stormtroopers." *Quadrant* Jan.–Feb. 1999: 62–63.

Crais, Robert. "In Heinlein's Bomb Shelter." *Robert's World*. Teq.org, n.d. Web. <http://teq.org/heinlein/robertcrais/worldheinlein.htm>.

Cusack, Carole M. "Science Fiction as Scripture: Robert A. Heinlein's *Stranger in a Strange Land* and the Church of All Worlds." *Literature & Aesthetics* 19 (December 2009): 72–91.

Davit, Jane. "*Red Planet*—Blue Pencil." *The Heinlein Journal* no. 8 (Jan. 2001). The Heinlein Society, 2003. Web. <http://www.heinleinsociety.org/2003/10/red-planet-blue-pencil/>.

Elhefnawy, Nader. "Robert Heinlein's *Starship Troopers*." *The Explicator* 68 (2010): 62–63.

Erisman, Fred. "Robert A. Heinlein's Primers of Politics." *Extrapolation* 38 (Summer 1997): 94–101.

_____. "Robert Heinlein, the Scribner Juveniles, and Cultural Literacy." *Extrapolation* (Spring 1991): 45–53.

_____. "Robert Heinlein's Case for Racial Tolerance, 1954–1956." *Extrapolation* 29 (Fall 1988): 216–26.

Feofanov, Dimitry N. "Luna Law: The Libertarian Vision in Heinlein's *The Moon Is a Harsh Mistress*." *Tennessee Law Review* 63 (Fall 1995): 71–141.

Frank, Marietta. "Women in Heinlein's Juveniles." *Young Adult Science Fiction*. Ed. C.W. Sullivan III. Contributions to the Study of Science Fiction and Fantasy 79. Westport, CN: Greenwood, 1999. 119–30.

Franklin, H. Bruce. *Robert A. Heinlein: America as Science Fiction*. Science-Fiction Writers Ser. Oxford: Oxford UP, 1980.

Gaar, Alice Carol. "The Human as Machine Analog: The Big Daddy of Interchangeable Parts in the Fiction of Robert A. Heinlein." *Robert A. Heinlein*. Ed. Joseph D. Olander & Martin Harry Greenberg. Writers of the 21st Century Ser. New York: Taplinger, 1978. 64–82.

Gifford, James. *Robert A. Heinlein: A Reader's Companion*. Tolland, CT: Nitrosyncretic, 2000.

Golden, Kenneth L. "*Stranger in a Strange Land* as Modern Myth: Robert A. Heinlein and Carl Jung." *Extrapolation* 27 (Winter 1986): 295–303.

Heinlein, Robert A. "Science Fictions: Its Nature, Faults and Virtues." 1957. *The Science Fiction Novel*. Ed. Basil Davenport. Chicago: Advent, 1969. 14–48.

Heinlein, Virginia, ed. *Grumbles from the Grave*. New York: Del Rey, 1989.

Higgins, David M. "Psychic Decolonization in 1960s Science Fiction." *Science Fiction Studies* 40 (July 2013): 228–45.

Kennedy, Robert G. III. "Robert A. Heinlein's Influence on Spaceflight." *Remembering the Space Age: Proceedings of the 50th Anniversary Conference*. Ed. Steven J. Dick. Washington, DC: NASA, 2008. 341–52.

Knight, Damon. *In Search of Wonder: Essays on Modern Science Fiction*. 2nd ed. 1967. Chicago: Advent, 1971.

Le Guin, Ursula K. "American SF and the Other." *Science-Fiction Studies* 2 (Nov. 1975): 208–10.

Letson, Russell. "The Returns of Lazarus Long." *Robert A. Heinlein*. Ed. Joseph D. Olander & Martin Harry Greenberg. Writers of the 21st Century Ser. New York: Taplinger, 1978. 194–221.

Lockett, Christopher. "Domesticity as Redemption in *The Puppet Masters*: Robert A. Heinlein's Model for Consensus." *Science Fiction Studies* 34 (Mar. 2007): 42–58.

McGiveron, Rafeeq O. "From Free Love to the Free-Fire Zone: Heinlein's Mars, 1939–1987." *Extrapolation* 42 (Summer 2001): 137–49.

_____. "From Selenite Suicide to Bonestell Backdrops: Robert A. Heinlein on the Course to *Destination Moon*." *Text to Screen: Spinning Words into Film in the Science-Fiction and Fantasy Genres.* Ed. Matthew Wilhelm Kapell & Ace G. Pilkington. Jefferson, NC: McFarland, 2015. 28–42.

_____. "Heinlein's *Have Space Suit—Will Travel*." *The Explicator* 59 (Spring 2001): 144–47.

_____. "Heinlein's Inhabited Solar System, 1940–1952." *Science-Fiction Studies* 23 (July 1996): 245–52.

_____. "He 'Just Plain Liked Guns': Robert A. Heinlein and the 'Older Orthodoxy' of an Armed Citizenry." *Extrapolation* 45 (Winter 2004): 388–407.

_____. "'Maybe the Hardest Job of All—Particularly When You Have No Talen For It': Heinlein's Fictional Parents, 1939–1987." *Extrapolation* 44 (Summer 2003): 169–200.

_____. "'Starry-Eyed Internationalists' *Versus* the Social Darwinists: Heinlein's Transnational Governments." *Extrapolation* 40 (Spring 1999): 53–70.

Nicholls, Peter. "Heinlein—A Lazarus Too Long?" Rev. of *Time Enough for Love. Foundation: The Review of Science Fiction* 7/8 [double issue] (Mar. 1975): 73–80.

_____. "Robert A. Heinlein." *Science Fiction Writers: Critical Studies of the Major Authors from the Early Nineteenth Century to the Present Day.* Ed. E.F. Breiler. New York: Scribner's, 1982. 185–96.

Olander, Joseph D. & Martin Harry Greenberg, eds. *Robert A. Heinlein.* Writers of the 21st Century Ser. New York: Taplinger, 1978.

Owenby, Phillip H. "Silent Partner: The Power Behind the Throne." *The Power and Potential of Collaborative Learning.* Ed. Iris M. Saltiel, Angela Sgroi, & Ralph C. Brockett. New Directions for Adult and Continuing Education 79. San Francisco: Jossey-Bass, 1998. 33–41.

Panshin, Alexei. *Heinlein in Dimension: A Critical Analysis.* Chicago: Advent, 1968.

Parkin-Speer, Diane. "Almost a Feminist: Robert A. Heinlein." *Extrapolation* 36 (Summer 1995): 112–25.

Patterson, William H., Jr. *Robert A. Heinlein: In Dialogue with His Century, Vol. 1: Learning Curve, 1907–1948.* New York: Tor, 2010.

_____. *Robert A. Heinlein: In Dialogue with His Century, Vol. 2: The Man Who Learned Better, 1948–1988*. New York: Tor, 2014.

Pielke, Robert G. "Grokking the Stranger." *Philosophers Look at Science Fiction*. Ed. Nicholas D. Smith. Chicago: Nelson-Hall, 1982. 153–63.

Plank, Robert. "Omnipotent Cannibals: Thoughts on Reading Robert A. Heinlein's *Stranger in a Strange Land*." *Robert A. Heinlein*. Ed. Joseph D. Olander & Martin Harry Greenberg. Writers of the 21st Century Ser. New York: Taplinger, 1978. 83–106.

Reno, Shaun. "The Zuni Indian Tribe: A Model for *Stranger in a Strange Land*'s Martian Culture." *Extrapolation* 36 (Summer 1995): 151–58.

Rogers, Ivor A. "Robert Heinlein: Folklorist of Outer Space." *Robert A. Heinlein*. Ed. Joseph D. Olander & Martin Harry Greenberg. Writers of the 21st Century Ser. New York: Taplinger, 1978. 222–239.

Rule, Deb Houdek. "Heinlein's Women: Strong Women Characters in the Heinlein Juveniles." *The Heinlein Society*. The Heinlein Society, 2003. Web. <Available at http://www.heinleinsociety.org/2004/02/heinleins-women/>.

Rule, G. E. "Strong Women Characters in Early Heinlein." *The Heinlein Society*. The Heinlein Society, 2003. Web. <http://www.heinleinsociety.org/2004/02/strong-women/>.

Samuelson, David N. "Frontiers of the Future: Heinlein's Future History Stories." *Robert A. Heinlein*. Ed. Joseph D. Olander & Martin Harry Greenberg. Writers of the 21st Century Ser. New York: Taplinger, 1978. 32–63.

Sarti, Ronald. "Variations on a Theme: Human Sexuality in the Work of Robert A. Heinlein." *Robert A. Heinlein*. Ed. Joseph D. Olander & Martin Harry Greenberg. Writers of the 21st Century Ser. New York: Taplinger, 1978. 107–36.

Scholes, Robert & Eric S. Rabkin. *Science Fiction: History, Science, Vision*. New York: Oxford UP, 1977.

Showalter, Dennis E. "Heinlein's *Starship Troopers*: An Exercise in Rehabilitation." *Extrapolation* 16 (1975): 113–24.

Slusser, George Edgar. *The Classic Years of Robert A. Heinlein*. Milford Series, Popular Writers of Today 11. San Bernadino: Borgo, 1977.

_____. "Heinlein's Fallen Futures." *Extrapolation* 36 (Summer 1995): 96–112.

_____. *Robert A. Heinlein: Stranger in His Own Land.* 2nd ed. San Bernadino: Borgo, 1977.

Smith, Philip E., II. "The Evolution of Politics and the Politics of Evolution: Social Darwinism in Heinlein's Fiction." *Robert A. Heinlein.* Ed. Joseph D. Olander & Martin Harry Greenberg. Writers of the 21st Century Ser. New York: Taplinger, 1978. 137–71.

Stover, Leon. *Robert A. Heinlein.* Twayne's United States Authors Series 522. Boston: Twayne, 1987.

Sullivan, C. W., III. *Heinlein's Juvenile Novels: A Cultural Dictionary.* Critical Explorations in Science Fiction and Fantasy 32. Jefferson, NC: McFarland, 2011.

_____. "Heinlein's Juveniles: Growing Up in Outer Space." *Science Fiction for Young Readers.* Ed. C. W. Sullivan, III. Contributions to the Study of Science Fiction and Fantasy 56. Westport, CT: Greenwood, 1993. 21–35.

_____. "Heinlein's Juveniles: Still Contemporary After All These Years." *ChLA Quarterly* 10 (1985): 64–66.

_____. "Robert A. Heinlein: Reinventing Series SF in the 1950s." *Extrapolation* 47 (Spring 2006): 66–76.

Telotte, J.P. "Heinlein, Verhoeven, and the Problem of the Real: *Starship Troopers.*" *Literature/Film Quarterly* 29 (2001): 196–202.

Tucker, Frank H. "Major Political and Social Elements in Heinlein's Fiction." *Robert A. Heinlein.* Ed. Joseph D. Olander & Martin Harry Greenberg. Writers of the 21st Century Ser. New York: Taplinger, 1978. 172–193.

Westfahl, Gary. "The Dark Side of the Moon: Robert A. Heinlein's *Project Moonbase.*" *Extrapolation* 36 (Summer 1995): 126–135.

Williams, Donna Glee. "The Moons of Le Guin and Heinlein." *Science-Fiction Studies* 21 (July 1994): 164–75.

Williamson, Jack. "Youth Against Space: Heinlein's Juveniles Revisited." *Robert A. Heinlein.* Ed. Joseph D. Olander & Martin Harry Greenberg. Writers of the 21st Century Ser. New York: Taplinger, 1978. 15–31.

About the Editor

Rafeeq O. McGiveron holds a B.A. with Honors in English and history from Michigan State University, an M.A. in English and history from MSU, and an M.A. in English from Western Michigan University. Having taught literature and composition for many years at a number of schools, including MSU, WMU, and Lansing Community College, in positions that have allowed his scholarship to be driven by personal interest and the serendipity of the classroom rather than by necessity, he has published some three-dozen articles of literary criticism on the works of authors ranging from Robert A. Heinlein and Ray Bradbury, to Willa Cather, to Shakespeare, and most recently editing *Critical Insights: Fahrenheit 451* for Salem Press in 2013. Currently he works in student services at Lansing Community College, where he has served since 1992. He also dabbles in fiction, occasionally poetry, and mobile art. His novel *Student Body*—the sensual, allusive, and introspective tale of a glib yet secretly troubled young professor-to-be and the women who love him—was released in 2014. More on McGiveron's interests and expertise is available on his web site, www.rafeeqmcgiveron.com.

Contributors _____

Marleen S. Barr is known for her pioneering work in feminist science fiction and teaches English at the City University of New York. She has won the Science Fiction Research Association Pilgrim Award for lifetime achievement in science fiction criticism. Barr is the author of *Alien to Femininity: Speculative Fiction and Feminist Theory*, *Lost in Space: Probing Feminist Science Fiction and Beyond*, *Feminist Fabulation: Space/Postmodern Fiction,* and *Genre Fission: A New Discourse Practice for Cultural Studies*. Barr has edited many anthologies and coedited the science fiction issue of *PMLA*, the journal of the Modern Language Association. She is the author of the novels *Oy Pioneer!* and *Oy Feminist Planets: A Fake Memoir.*

Wolf Forrest graduated with a degree in biology from St. Mary's College of Maryland and studied architecture at the University of Arizona. He has been a freelance artist and writer for over thirty years. He sold his first cartoon to *Boy's Life* at seventeen, and his articles and illustrations have appeared in such publications as *Cinefantastique*, *Midnight Marquee*, *The Asheville Citizen*, *Backyard Bugwatching*, and *Orbiting Ray Bradbury's Mars*. He has also contributed to Sky Harbor Airport's continuing art exhibitions like "Baseball Hits" and "Arizona Valentine," and is preparing a volume of short biographical sketches of major league baseball players. He lives in Tucson.

Ira Halpern is a student at the University of Toronto. He has particular interests in modern American literature, including the role of religion in American fiction. His essay entitled "Secret Love, Private Space, and Inner Sanctuary: The Concealed in *The Age of Innocence*" was published in the June 2015 issue of the journal *The Explicator*. Outside of academia, he has done work in documentary film for the company YAP Films. He would like to thank Professor Christine Bolus-Reichert of the University of Toronto for her guidance in developing his book chapter included here.

Donald M. Hassler served nearly twenty years as the prime editor of the journal *Extrapolation* immediately after Thomas D. Clareson, who had founded the journal, stepped down. Hassler taught English at Kent State University from 1965 until his retirement in the spring of 2014. He has published a number of books on writers such as Erasmus Darwin, Isaac Asimov, Hal Clement, and Arthur Machen, and he has edited, with Clyde Wilcox, two collections that deal with politics and science fiction, both published by the University of South Carolina Press. Most recently, he has seen one of his poems published in the June 2015 issue of the pulp magazine *Analog*. He is a great fan of the work of Heinlein.

Zahra Jannessari Ladani is an assistant professor of English Literature at the University of Isfahan. She is the Persian translator of Kristina Nelson's *The Art of Reciting the Qur'an* and English editor of *Qur'an Recitation Skills*. She has also translated a number of Stanley G. Weinbaum's SF stories to Persian for the first time. Her major contributions to the science fiction domain consist of her lecture "The Rise of the Pulps, 1900s–1930s," given to Lars Schmeink's online teaching resource, *The Virtual Introduction to Science Fiction*, and her chapter "John W. Campbell and his Writers" was published in Leigh Grossman's 2011 anthology, *Sense of Wonder: A Century of Science Fiction*.

Kristine Larsen is professor of astronomy at Central Connecticut State University. Her scholarship and teaching focus on the intersections between science and society, including science and gender, science and popular culture (especially as depicted in the works of J. R. R. Tolkien), and the history of science. She is the author of *Stephen Hawking: A Biography* and *Cosmology 101*, and she is coeditor of *The Mythological Dimensions of Doctor Who* and *The Mythological Dimensions of Neil Gaiman*.

Anna R. McHugh taught at the universities of Sydney, Bristol, and Oxford. She has published studies of medieval anchoritism, memory culture, and medieval Scottish history. She contributed to Salem's Critical Insights volume on *Fahrenheit 451*, also edited by Rafeeq O. McGiveron. She now lives in Sydney, Australia, where she writes children's literature and English textbooks, and is working on a monograph about Boethius' *Consolation of Philosophy*.

John J. Pierce (born 1941) has read science fiction since childhood and really did grow up on Heinlein. He was later editor of *Galaxy* magazine (1977–78) and edited SF collections of the best of Murray Leinster, Raymond Z. Gallun, and Cordwainer Smith; he has written introductions to other books by Smith. He has contributed essays and reviews to academic and fan publications, including *Science Fiction Studies* and *Science Fiction Review*, and is currently working on a revised, expanded, and updated version of his SF history, *Imagination and Evolution*, originally published as *Foundations of Science Fiction* (1987), *Great Themes of Science Fiction* (1987), *When World Views Collide* (1989), and *Odd Genre* (1994).

Robin Anne Reid is a professor in the Department of Literature and Languages at Texas A&M University–Commerce. Her teaching areas are creative writing, critical theory, and marginalized literatures. Her research interests include queer theory, intersectionality, digital literary studies, fan studies, and Tolkien studies. She edited the first encyclopedia on *Women in Science Fiction and Fantasy* (Greenwood 2008). Her recent publications include an intersectional analysis of Nicola Griffith's *Hild* and an analysis of critical race and intersectional work being done in online science fiction fandom communities by people of color.

Garyn G. Roberts is the author and editor of a range of books, essays, encyclopedia entries, and other publications. Science fiction, detective fiction, and popular fiction are the subjects of many of these writings. He has been awarded The Ray and Pat Browne National Book Award for *The Prentice Hall Anthology of Science Fiction and Fantasy* and The Munsey Award for contributions to pulp magazine scholarship and has been a finalist for the Mystery Writers of America Edgar Award for *Dick Tracy and American Culture*. An award-winning college and university professor, Roberts lives and works in the greater Midwest.

C. W. Sullivan III is Emeritus Distinguished Professor of Arts and Sciences, retired from East Carolina University, and a Full Member of the Welsh Academy for his contributions to the study of medieval Welsh Celtic myth and legend. He is the author of *Welsh Celtic Myth in Modern Fantasy* and editor of *The Mabinogi: A Book of Essays*, as well as several other books of essays. Former editor of the online journal, *Celtic Cultural*

Studies, Sullivan is a past president of the International Association for the Fantastic in the Arts, and his articles on mythology, folklore, fantasy, and science fiction have appeared in a variety of anthologies and journals. He currently teaches in the Summer Graduate Program in Children's Literature at Hollins University.

Gary Westfahl, currently an adjunct professor at the University of La Verne, is the author, editor, or coeditor of twenty-four books about science fiction and fantasy, including the Hugo Award-nominated *Science Fiction Quotations: From the Inner Mind to the Outer Limits* (2005) and the three-volume *Greenwood Encyclopedia of Science Fiction and Fantasy* (2005); he has also published hundreds of articles, reviews, and reference book entries. His most recent works are *The Spacesuit Film: A History, 1918–1969* (2012), *A Sense-of-Wonderful Century: Explorations of Science Fiction and Fantasy Films* (2012), *William Gibson* (2013), and the three-volume *A Day in a Working Life: 300 Trades and Professions through History* (2015), his first book not focused on science fiction. In 2003, he received the Science Fiction Research Association's Pilgrim Award for his lifetime contributions to science fiction and fantasy scholarship.

Index
